Fencing, Form and Cognition on the Early Modern Stage

Fencing, Form and Cognition on the Early Modern Stage

Artful Devices

Dori Coblentz

EDINBURGH
University Press

Edinburgh University Press is one of the leading university presses in the UK. We publish academic books and journals in our selected subject areas across the humanities and social sciences, combining cutting-edge scholarship with high editorial and production values to produce academic works of lasting importance. For more information visit our website: edinburghuniversitypress.com

Edinburgh University Press Ltd
The Tun – Holyrood Road
12(2f) Jackson's Entry
Edinburgh EH8 8PJ

First published in hardback by Edinburgh University Press 2022

Typeset in 11/13 Adobe Sabon by
IDSUK (DataConnection) Ltd, and
printed and bound by CPI Group (UK) Ltd,
Croydon, CR0 4YY

A CIP record for this book is available from the British Library

ISBN 978 1 4744 8226 4 (hardback)
ISBN 978 1 4744 8227 1 (paperback)
ISBN 978 1 4744 8228 8 (webready PDF)
ISBN 978 1 4744 8229 5 (epub)

Contents

List of Figures

Acknowledgements

This research for this book was conducted over the course of ten years, three universities and three fencing communities. I am grateful to the many people who made its writing possible. Special thanks are due to Kathy Harris and Adrienne Eastwood, who helped the early stages of this project take coherent form. Ross Knecht, Sharon Strocchia, Dalia Judovitz and Paul Kelleher provided feedback through many points of my project's life cycle. I am also grateful for the support I received from fellow graduate students: among them, James Howard, who first encouraged me to think about fencing in temporal term; McKenna Rose, who challenged me in many phone calls and walks to think carefully about language; and Karma DeGruy, whose insights on the history of the body were immensely illuminating.

I am especially thankful to my doctoral advisor, Patricia Cahill, who has guided me throughout this project with challenging critique and encouraging words. My masters advisor, Deanna Shemek, encouraged me through early explorations of the intersection of Renaissance Italian fencing manuals and literature. Evelyn Tribble, Allison Hobgood, Barbara Ravelhofer and Bill Engel provided important feedback at later stages in this project. The participants at the Shakespeare Association of America's 'New Histories of Embodiment' seminar in 2015 did much to shape this work through their stimulating discussions. Gaia Castagnoli at InClasse, an Italian language school in Verona, proved an invaluable aid as I learned to translate Italian fencing manuals. Cecily Boles and Eli Smedley provided me with acute feedback and editorial advice at several critical junctures.

Thanks to a Dissertation Completion Fellowship at the Bill and Carol Fox Center for Humanistic Inquiry, I was able to dedicate an academic year to revising my dissertation research. I was fortunate to be a part of the 2016 cohort and benefited from the support of my colleagues. The Laney Graduate School Arts and Sciences

Fellowship provided me with summer funding so that I could dedicate those months to research and writing during my time as a graduate student at Emory. Support from the Director and Associate Director of the Writing and Communication Program at Georgia Tech, Rebecca Burnett and Andy Frazee, enabled me to complete the manuscript during my tenure as a Marion L. Brittain Postdoctoral Fellow. Students in my 'Defending Society' class of 2018 yielded several formative insights into Ben Jonson's *Bartholomew Fair*.

I would like to thank the University of Pennsylvania Press for permission to reprint a section of Chapter 1, which originally appeared as 'Killing Time in *Titus Andronicus*: Timing, Rhetoric, and the Art of Defense' in the *Journal for Early Modern Cultural Studies* 15.4 (2015): 52–80. Thanks are also due to Taylor & Francis for the permission to reuse portions of '"Maister of al artificiall force and sleight": Tempo and Dissimulation in Castiglione's Book of the Courtier', *Italian Studies* 71.1 (2018): 53–65. I thank the readers, editors and editorial assistants at *Italian Studies* and *JEMCS*, as their feedback immensely improved these chapters. I am also grateful to Devon Boorman and Academie Duello, whose digital scans of Capoferro's *Gran simulacro* illustrate several chapters in this book; to Guy Windsor, who allowed the use of Fabris's Plate 73; and to Michael Chidester, whose collection on the Wiktenauer provided an illustration from Saviolo's fencing manual.

I am grateful for insights from members of the San Jose Fencing Masters Program, especially Ralph Sahm and Tony Barajas. My thanks also to those at the Sonoma State Fencing Certificate Program who provided feedback, especially John Sullins. My own focus group has provided an audience and the encouragement I needed to finish this project. They include Greg Smedley, Kevin Murakoshi, Tom Smedley, Sydney Thomson, Monica Gaudio and Laura Smedley.

David Coblentz, my husband and favourite fencing master, has worked with me for over a decade in bringing this project to fruition. Our stimulating discussions over lunchtime walks and on road trips motivated me to complete this book when I most needed it. The depth of his expertise considerably enriched my analysis of fencing sources, and his support enabled the project's completion.

Introduction

The word 'device', now associated with mobile phones and tablets, in many ways seems quintessentially modern. However, its long history still haunts its current usage. Coming into Middle English from the Old French for 'desire' or 'intention', *devis*, devices were and are channels for fictional representation, facilitators of communal interactions and even signs of status. This book's title draws from the semantic capaciousness of both 'art' and 'device' to guide its analysis of an important yet understudied area at the intersection of literary criticism, philosophy and cognitive science: the generation of practical knowledge about time through social experiences. *Fencing, Form and Cognition on the Early Modern Stage: Artful Devices* highlights the overlap between two genres of embodied movement in early modern England – dramatic performance and what early moderns termed the art of defence (fencing). I will argue that fencing manuals provide critical new insights into the plots, pacing and characterisation of early modern drama. Even more than enhancing our understanding of early modern drama, attending to the ethical and pedagogical work displayed and accomplished by fencing devices and dramatic devices yields a robust theory of active waiting and brings the imbrications of appropriate timing and ethical decision-making to the fore.

What were devices, and how could they be artful in the early modern theatre? By Shakespeare's time, 'device' most often referred to coats of arms, tricks, or set pieces of movement and/or speech that tell a story. In the latter two senses of the word, the word 'device' often signals metatheatrical commentary. For example, Jonson's Carlo Buffone in *Every Man out of His Humour* (1599) dismisses his mentee's dramatic pretensions by saying 'O, 'tis an old stale interlude device' (4.4.265).[1] Jonson uses Buffone's ridicule of the interlude device (short performance before or after a play, or between acts) pedagogically to invite the audience to critique this foolish and pretentious character's aesthetic judgement, and so to better develop their own good taste.

In addition to referring to a drama in miniature, 'device' frequently connotes dissimulation in English theatre: *Twelfth Night*'s Sir Toby Belch delightedly 'smells[s] a device' in the lead-up to Malvolio's fake love letter, for instance (2.3.151). Devices signal darker modes of dissimulation as well in Shakespeare's revenge tragedies. For instance, *Hamlet*'s fourth act provides one of the most famous examples of a device from the early modern stage when Claudius promises Laertes that he will work Hamlet 'To an exploit, now ripe in my device, / Under the which he shall not choose but fall' (4.7.73). The ambiguous wording ('ripe in my device') leaves it to the playgoer's interpretation if it is the exploit or the king that is ready to bring Hamlet down. It also leaves undefined whether the device Hamlet falls under is that of heraldry, symbolising kingly authority, or a devised scheme. Laertes seems to take it in the latter sense in his response to the king. Given that Claudius's plan involves a fixed fencing match with a poisoned and unfoiled rapier, another usage of 'device' could be understood, however: the fencing device, referring to both the weapon and to the sequence of actions terminating in a hit. Contemporary fencing author and member of the lower gentry George Silver (c. 1550–1620) gives an example of the term in circulation in this sense at the time of *Hamlet*'s composition when he complains about the 'strange vices and devices of Italian, French, and Spanish fencers' – meaning their fencing techniques and the rapier.[2] In an earlier Shakespearean revenge tragedy, the villainous Machiavellian figure Aaron plays upon three of these meanings – device as dissimulatory scheme, as dramatic representation and as a fencing phrase – when he expostulates with the Goth delinquents Chiron and Demetrius to keep a low profile and sheathe their rapiers: 'I tell you, lords, you do but plot your deaths / By this device' (*Titus Andronicus* 1.1.577–8). In this case, Aaron offers his own device of murder, rape and false incrimination to replace the device of Demetrius and Chiron's melodramatic rapier brawl.

The devices treated in *Fencing, Form and Cognition on the Early Modern Stage* are artful in the same sense that Aaron is artful: skilled at verbal and physical dissimulation. Artfulness also has more positive connotations, however, such as the skill involved in collaborative knowledge-making. 'Art' came into English via Anglo-Norman in the eleventh century meaning a technique or a method. In the fourteenth century, it took on the sense associated with the Italian *arte*, which referred to a guild or professional activity.[3] As Pamela Smith explains, during the Scientific Revolution, the distinction between theory and practice proposed by Aristotle came under scrutiny as artisans began casting themselves as knowledge-makers. The art of the artisans, often opposed to the university's science, refers to the kind of knowledge produced through apprenticeships via embodied imitation rather than the kind of knowledge extrapolated from underlying principles.[4] Professional examples of this kind of art are found both in fencing and acting, as practitioners learned through embodied imitation in apprenticeships as well as through books that stressed a connection to science such as Bulwer's *Chirologia* and Swetnam's *The Schoole of the Noble and Worthy Science of Defence*. Finally, the devices of this study are artful in that they carry an aesthetic charge based on the skilfulness or ineptness of application. Given the choice, a spectator would generally rather hear an artful rendition of a soliloquy than a clumsy one and witness a perfectly executed counterattack than a maladroit double hit.

Scholars have noticed before that the art of defence and the art of poesy share many symbols and themes, and that they accomplish some of the same cultural work around setting and enforcing national allegiance and expectations of masculinity.[5] *Fencing, Form and Cognition on the Early Modern Stage* builds on and differs from prior criticism by exploring the shared methodologies and forms of fencing and drama as well as these symbols and themes. Fencing, a ubiquitous cultural practice, provides critical new insights into the plots and timing of early modern drama, which, in turn, can shed light on historical approaches to the skill of timing as it relates to reading and creating opportunity.[6] Literary and fencing devices operate along many of the same principles, requiring the attention of the audience (playgoer or opponent) and the audience's attempt to motivate and interpret the responses of the men on stage. For example, in revenge tragedy the audience's identification with the avenger excuses his embrace of vigilante justice.

Audiences also rely upon fencers to offer legible provocations and responses to provide an entertaining fight where they may critique or admire the decisions made. Within the fencing match itself, a successful fighter must observe the adversary's patterns of movement and think like the adversary to anticipate and foil the opponent's next action. Both theatrical and martial devices construct forms of conflict – antagonistic patterns of movements, gestures and sometimes words. In the performative setting of the theatre, fencing and dramatic devices also serve a pedagogical purpose, as they can implicitly or explicitly develop the students' or spectators' skill in interpersonal timing and at-speed decision making. For example, Jonson famously encourages his audience to decide for themselves, as the play unfolds, their response of laughter or disapprobation. The metatheatrical contract that begins *Bartholomew Fair* requires that 'every man here exercise his own judgement and not censure by contagion' (Induction 86). The theatre's aesthetic judgements are necessarily time-bound as the story moves at the pace of the players. Spectators who 'censure by contagion' have a delayed reaction to the play because they read the body language of fellow audience members rather than authentically interact with the play using their own taste and discernment.

Jonson also expresses this overlap between martial and theatrical modes of teaching discernment and timing when he references English fencing theory on judgement in *Every Man in His Humour*'s fencing lesson scene. Bobadil, the play's *miles gloriosus*, complains to his friend the plagiarising and affected 'rhymster' Matthew: 'I have no spirit to play with you; your dearth of judgement renders you tedious' (1.5.125–6) as Bobadil abruptly ends the lesson. By citing Matthew's judgement as the principle hindrance to a worthwhile match, Jonson expresses the contemporary understanding of fencing competition as a venue for exercising and displaying the skill of judgement. When Matthew, eager to prove himself, asks for another pass, Bobadil responds in more explicitly corporeal terms: 'Why, I will learn you, by the true judgement of the eye, hand, and foot, to control any enemy's point i' the world' (1.5.133–4). Rather than an abstract process of discernment occurring in an individual and bounded mind, judgement here is characterised as what we might today call proprioception – the body's ability to sense the relative spatial and temporal positioning of its members, to coordinate movement, and to maintain a sense of self. The foundational elements of Bobadil's promised lesson combine the judgement of the eye (vision), the hand (touch) and the foot (spatial awareness of the distance between self and adversary). When Bobadil promises to teach Matthew judgement, he draws on the vocabulary of English fencing books of his period. While Italians typically discussed *tempo* (opportunity), *misura* (distance) and *modo* (technique), English authors tended to focus more on judgement, time and space. For instance, Silver names judgement as one of the four grounds, or guiding principles, of fencing because: 'Through judgement, you keep your distance, through distance you take your time, through time you safely win or gain the place of your adversary.'[7] Judgement acts as an overarching capacity to mediate mutually dependent aspects of kinesic intelligence.[8]

Inset displays of fencing, tumbling and singing like *Every Man in His Humour*'s comic scene of inept teaching are pedagogical as well as entertaining in nature.[9] Through such scenes and through repeated exposure, spectators developed the 'skilled vision' necessary to parse at-speed demonstrations of skill and to react in a social setting.[10] Drama and fencing do more than simply share pedagogical goals and methods, however. England's early commercial drama draws from fencing's formal logic in under-recognised but important ways. Playwrights used common fencing sequences as inspiration as they explored methods for visually representing plot structure. Along with precedents in classical and medieval drama, the early modern stage was indebted to non-literary sources for its formal logic. The zigzagging structure of the combat device was one of these non-literary formal influences, coexisting with the more familiar narrative pyramid of rising and falling plot action.

Staging a play

Today, it would be unlikely for a dramatist to draw from the formal structure of the fencing phrase in order to communicate anything so abstract as the sequence and rhythm of a plot. For early moderns, however, the link between fencing and drama was obvious. The etymology of 'play' reflects the historical affinities between combat and playacting. When discussing a dramatic performance now, one rarely needs to qualify that the production in question is a 'stage play' and not some other sort of play. However, in Shakespeare's time, going to see 'a play' was a more ambiguous undertaking. While the sense of play as theatrical performance dates back to the eleventh century, 'swordplay' and similar exercises requiring 'brisk and vigorous action' were, in fact, primary definitions of play for Shakespeare and his contemporaries.[11] Indeed, fencers and actors were known indiscriminately as 'players'. The etymology suggests that medieval and early modern people thought of the activities of the stage and the fencing school in the same terms. The close connection between fencing and drama has largely been forgotten. Yet drama and fencing shared methodologies, training techniques and goals as well as sites and audiences in early modern England. At one point, the Blackfriars Theatre and a fencing school coexisted in the same building, with the theatre upstairs and the school below: the school and the theatre required similar facilities and were situated in the same neighbourhood.[12] The extent of the crossover between dramatic performance and playing prizes requires further exploration, but people such as the early modern celebrity Richard Tarlton, who would have been active on both floors of the Blackfriars building as a famous comic actor and fencing master, demonstrate that the cultures of stage and fencing school were not wholly distinct.[13] As the theatre historian

Andrew Gurr explains, 'Swordplay was already a standard offering on the amphitheater platforms of the 1580s in exhibition bouts and prize fights ... [t]he duel which concludes *Hamlet* was conceived for the open-air stages used for fencing displays.'[14]

Print stabilised ephemeral performances and instructional practices increasingly for both fencing and drama beginning in the 1590s. Due to the nature of their separate enterprises, print worked primarily to record the story and dialogue elements of drama.[15] Printed fencing works were primarily technical, and preserved, instead, the pedagogical and theoretical elements of their authors' work. Masters' pedagogical approaches show through in plates or woodcuts that depict various actions and are accompanied by descriptive text to explain the sequencing of a successful hit or a mistake. Fencing theory incorporates discussions on the status of the discipline as art and/or science, the fundamental elements of fencing, and 'contraries', or sequences of response and counterresponse.

Ridolfo Capoferro's 1610 fencing treatise, published in Siena as *Gran Simulacro dell'Arte e dell'Uso della Scherma* is today one of the most famous examples of these treatises, in part because of the painstaking engravings and the tactically dense layering of action and counteraction (Fig. I.1). In Plate 7, for instance, he walks through an observant fencer (*persona accorta*) and adversary's initial attack, counter to that attack, counter to the counter, and counter to the counter to the counter in a fairly concise description.

Figure I.1 Ridolfo Capoferro. Contraries. Plate 7, *Gran Simulacro*, 1610. Engraving. Vancouver, Academie Duello.

Fencing in England was no less complex than in Capoferro's Siena, but archival material is sparser. Until the waning years of Elizabeth's reign, England was largely isolated from the outpouring of fencing instructional texts that marked Continental fencing discourse, particularly in the Italian- and German-language traditions. Fencing in England had long followed a guild model, with the Company of the Royal Masters of Defence granted the right to train fencers and fencing teachers. Until the late sixteenth century, this largely oral method of instruction left few traces. However, the rise in Italian immigration in the late Tudor period and the heightened interest in Italian cultural productions of that time generated a development of fencing discourse in England and prompted English masters of defence to commit to writing the distinguishing characteristics of their system of fencing.[16] I.G.'s 1594 translation was popular enough to spur imitation from English authors such as George Silver (1599), Joseph Swetnam (1617) and the anonymous author of *Pallas Armata* (1639). In late Tudor and early Stuart England, both Italian and English treatises circulated in England's print marketplace, though it is unclear the degree to which their authors saw themselves as in competition with each other. A year after the publication of I.G.'s translation, the printer John Wolfe continued to capitalise on the success of Italian fencing treatises with the manual *Vincentio Saviolo, his practice, in two books, the first intreating of the use of the Rapier and Dagger, the second of Honor and honorable Quarrels*. Saviolo, an Italian fencing master living in London, looked to the print marketplace in part to attract wealthy students.

By 1599, the Italianate fencing method had gained momentum, but also generated controversy. Most famously, the quarrel between English masters and the Italian master Rocco Bonetti made it into Mercutio's description of Tybalt in *Romeo and Juliet* as 'the very butcher of a silk button' (2.4.23). This description refers to the boast that the Italian master allegedly made that he could 'hit anie English man with a thrust, just upon any button in his doublet'.[17] The quarrels of fencers and fencing masters may seem out of place in Shakespeare's theatre because we have come to expect the separation of pen and sword. In fact, the intersection between these two disciplines was often blurry. The success of these Italian fencing manuals soon spurred imitation as well. George Silver's 1599 *Paradoxes of Defence* urged the English to return to an older and better method of fencing and to shun the new-fangled Italianate fencing system. He followed *Paradoxes* up with a companion volume that was not printed until the nineteenth century, *Brief Instructions* (c. 1605).[18]

Class and national distinctions are encoded in fencing instructional and performance contexts. While we do have records of English fencing performances in courts, English fencers and masters of defence do not occupy the same social role as fencers and fencing masters in the Italian tradition. Traditional English prizefighting is a primarily middle-class occupation regulated by the guild system. Italian fencing focused more on founding schools that often served noble clientele, or in tutoring in individual aristocratic households. During Shakespeare's lifetime, some English parents adopted these practices and introduced Italian fencing tutors, but others like Silver decried Italian influence as unpatriotic and unmanly.

English and Italian fencing masters, adopting both artisanal and scholarly discourses for their instructional texts, leverage technical precision instilled in the body through iterative practice in the work of self-cultivation. For instance, Saviolo claims that the correct ward (position from which to launch an attack or defence) will 'make a Scholler' in much the same way that Spenser promises Raleigh that his poetry will serve to 'fashion a gentleman' (Fig. I.2).[19] Far from a

Figure I.2 Vincentio Saviolo. Engagement. *His Practice*, 1595. Woodcut. Courtesy of Michael Chidester and The Wiktenauer.

marginal extracurricular athletic activity, fencing was a politically and theologically charged mode of *askesis*, self-formation via discipline. The art and science of defence was fraught with significance in terms of one's potential military service abroad and the capacity to preserve life and limb from robbers at home.

Fencing masters use drills to encode a sense of timing and distance within the body through repetition. For example, Saviolo cautions would-be fencers to practise his principles repeatedly 'learning well the time and measure' in order to open one's 'spirits in the knowledge of the secrets of arms'.[20] Joseph Swetnam similarly emphasises practice and repetition in his 1617 manual: '[t]here is no way better to get the true observation of distance, but by often practice, either with thy friend, or else privately in a chamber against a wall, standing twelve foot off with thy hindermost foote'.[21] Spanish, Italian and German strains of fencing pedagogy produced influential writings that were becoming more accessible to the English as they took Continental grand tours or, like Swetnam, served abroad in the military. Even without the benefit of a grand tour, more and more Londoners were becoming acquainted with the religious refugees from abroad, who brought with them their own perspectives on fencing theory and practice.

Fencing pedagogies vary according to each fencing master's theory of knowledge.[22] Those with a more Aristotelian bent favour modelling, abstracting and theorising ideal encounters that are mediated through the fencer's movement. Though the phrases of combat may not proceed according to plan, the assumption is that there is an ideal that should be as closely approximated as possible. The Spanish fencing master and philosopher Jerónimo Sánchez de Carranza (1539–1600) emphasises the important role of theory in guiding decisions and insists on his students understanding primary causes.[23] For example, Carranza dismisses the guard positions of older traditions of Spanish fencing in favour of holding the blade straight out with no bend in the elbow at a right angle to the body with only a slight bend in the knees, since, geometrically speaking, this provides the shortest distance between two points. Another, more widely known philosopher, also felt the lure of combining fencing pedagogy with philosophy. Unfortunately, René Descartes' fencing treatise has been lost. On the other end of the spectrum from these highly theoretical approaches, the German master Joachim Meyer values the situational and contingent more than the ideal, quoting proverbs such as 'only the Market can instruct the Buyer'.[24] He stresses 'daily experience' to note pragmatically that 'no technique, no matter how good it is, may be usefully carried out, if it is not used at its proper time'.[25] Fencing occurs in context between two people, and so the best way to train oneself to recognise openings is to develop reflexes through repetition. This muscle memory allows the fencer to respond immediately to what the opponent does in each moment of combat. Italian authors like Fabris and Capoferro fall somewhere in between these two tactical emphases: though *maestri* like Fabris give general, theoretical advice about how to put the opponent 'into obedience', their abstract principles are firmly grounded in the contingencies of the fight.

The juncture of rhetorical, philosophical and athletic discourses evidenced in English and Italian fencing manuals sheds light on questions of what counts as knowledge and how it is disseminated. For modern readers aware of the scholarly trends of the last few decades to move away from positivism and a strong mind–body dualism, this kind of project may seem obvious and natural. Recent research in philosophy, cognitive science and related disciplines takes seriously the idea of perception as 'a kind of skillful bodily activity', not a passive and incorporeal process.[26] Andy Clark and David Chalmer's influential work on 'extended' minds, for instance, persuasively argues that acting in the world in real time is the purview of the mind, positing an *'active externalism*, based on the active role of the environment in driving cognitive processes'.[27] From this perspective, fencing and thinking are not distinct activities. With training, tactile information gained via blade contact, for example, bypasses linguistic decision-making and develops into what I define as kinesic judgement in Chapter 6. Today's fencing masters, by and large, even if they might not describe themselves as post-Cartesians, teach as if thinking happens outside of the skull, extended through the body and through tools such as the foil.

Because fencing manuals were intended for instructional use in ways that printed versions of plays were not, they allow readers today to see more explicitly the development of a practical knowledge about time in early modern England. The vocabulary and conceptual apparatus that fencing masters developed around the topic of time informed the ways in which dramatists crafted narrative and shaped the figurative landscapes of their plays; conversely, the theatre informed the genre of the fencing instructional manual by setting expectations around masculinity and honour and through the development of performance technologies that influenced the production of fencing spectacles. Fencing masters and instructional writers developed highly nuanced language to describe many different kinds of spatial and temporal dissimulation. Players and playwrights, also specialists in interactive, embodied movement, freely borrowed from such formal structures to stage cunning.

Time, Form, Action

One of the most useful contributions of fencing theory to dramatic practice is the extensive theorisation around time and timing. 'Time' is an almost impossibly capacious term. As the anthropologist Michael Herzfeld notes, the semantic field of the word contains both *kairos* (occasion or opportune moment) and *chronos* (time as linear passage). The word also signifies 'the contrasted senses of Italian *tempo* as "rhythm of action", "weather", or "time-as-passage"' as well as 'duration' and 'period'.[28] With the added complexity of historical distance, *time* becomes an even more slippery concept. These changing conceptions of time take place in an extraordinarily innovative period in the history of the English theatre, as dramatists experimented with methods for representing time and space. As has been widely recognised, during the rise of the commercial theatre a qualitative, corporeal and intellectual understanding of time dominated the dramatic landscape.[29] From Hamlet's vividly embodied imagery of temporal dislocation in a time that is 'out of joint' to the physical representation of Time as a character on stage in *The Winter's Tale*, scholars have become accustomed to thinking of time's dramatic role in flexible and expansive terms. These understandings of theatrical time are incomplete, however, because they are drawn mostly from what drama says about itself, or from cooperative models of tempo such as those found in music and dance. This book completes the picture by bringing drama and fencing discourse together to argue for time as an embodied, antagonistic rhythm of movement.

The emergence of secular, commercial drama in sixteenth-century England offered novel ways to think about time in relation to large-scale political and theological issues, as has been widely recognised. Ricardo Quinones, for instance, suggests that only three 'basic conceptions of Time' come to the forefront in Shakespeare's oeuvre – augmentative, contracted, and extended (328).[30] Frederick Turner explores nine major aspects of time in Shakespeare's plays.[31] Both accounts, and, indeed, the bulk of work on time in Shakespeare, are most interested in the history of the concept of time or how time thematically features in drama. *Fencing, Form and Cognition on the Early Modern Stage* while drawing from the thematical and historical work, will add the dimension of time as corporeal skill. Little has been done to examine the teaching of timing involved in theatrical productions.[32] If, however, as Evelyn Tribble suggests, studying theatre requires a systems-level approach that incorporates attention to the processes of enskilment alongside the physical environment and influence from managers and playwrights, then instructional manuals detailing the performance of skilled activities are vital.[33] This study draws from the interdisciplinary work of Renaissance scholars such as Evelyn Tribble, Gail Kern Paster, Bruce Smith and Allison Hobgood on embodiment to explore the intersection of thinking, feeling and selfhood. Insights from research in historical phenomenology and cognitive science shed light on the ways in which the knowledge-generating practices of the theatre produce embodied knowledge about time.

While Shakespeare and others used poetic meter to explore qualitative and quantitative time, the possibilities opened via interactive performance meant that dramatic productions could tap into a physicality unavailable to lyric, sonnets or other popular forms of early modern poetic composition. By incorporating the positions of bodies in space in relation to platform, props and audience, theatre extends the temporal work of poetry.[34] This complex array of bodies and movement is where fencing theory becomes most useful as a source of inspiration for dramatists. Since fencing time is generated interpersonally, across fencers ('players'), objects and environments, it inhabits a similar context and has a similar purpose. Connecting the practices of fencing to those of the stage to rethink a feeling/cognition divide is not an entirely new enterprise. The British theatre historian David Wiles argues Elizabethan actors used fencing to enhance their 'mind–body awareness' with certain disciplinary skills, including:

> How to hold a firm stance with the legs and avoid any movement that is redundant; how to engage the whole body in actions led by the gesturing right hand; how to rotate the torso fluidly . . . when performing to an audience on all sides; how to interact with a partner in terms of rhythm and proxemics, incorporating height as well as distance; how to build a rhythm and disrupt it without losing control; how to experience tempo as an impulse of the body.[35]

However, where Wiles is most interested in early modern acting's roots in classical rhetoric and its relevance for post-Stanislavskian acting, the early modern model of feeling and thinking expressed in fencing manuals and play texts also speaks to modern-day understandings of embodied cognition in individuals and across groups.

The concept of fencing *contratempo* proved to be an especially important formal appropriation. Salvator Fabris (1544–1618), famous fencing master to the Danish king Christian IV (1577–1648), provides one of the clearest and earliest articulations of fencing *contratempo* in his *De lo Schermo, overo Scienza d'Arme* (1606). When Fabris articulates the thought process involved in setting up traps to exploit the adversary's timing, he warns his readers to be wary of fencers who feign weakness in order to draw an attack that they are then prepared to counter:

> [I]t is easier to take advantage of a tempo when the opponent makes it without realizing . . . it is important to admonish you that there are some who astutely make a tempo to lure you to attack, and as you do so, they will have parried and countered your blow. This is called wounding in contratempo . . . as you can see, this discipline relies in great part on the ability to subtly deceive your opponent.[36]

Fabris believes firmly in limiting the options of opponents, putting them 'into obedience', so that they are always acting in response, whether they know it or not. At the most basic level, one waits for the opponent to make a tempo in measure and then responds with an attack made in a shorter tempo. Once this baseline is established, there is room for extensive subtlety and trickiness. For example, knowing that the opponent wants to launch a counterattack, the attacker might tempt the opponent with giving up a tempo deliberately to draw the counterattack and defeat it with the fencer's own counter to that counterattack.

As Chapter 5 explores in detail, Shakespeare's revenge tragedies turn on this idea of deceptively projecting a weak attack to draw the adversary into a fully committed counterattack. His avengers then defeat this counterattack with a counter of their own. Revenge tragedies with mad avengers often feature a wronged protagonist with no access to legal recourse (usually because the person who has wronged them is in some position of political power over them). In these plays, the avenger feigns madness or infirmity in order to draw the enemy's overextended attack. Timing is especially important in revenge drama: revenge must be condign, and to create the appropriate conditions for revenge requires shrewd planning and precise timing.

The theme of 'time' has been extensively discussed in tragedies of missed opportunity and mistake action such as *Hamlet* and *Romeo and Juliet*, but without the antagonistic, kinesiological dimension that fencing forms can offer. The plots of these plays pivot on the skill of choosing the right time to act. In *Hamlet*, for instance, Richard Halpern persuasively argues that the temporal schemas of an act (individuating, decision-driven) and nature's activity (anonymous, ongoing, productive) come to a crisis in the grave-maker scene. The tragedy, in this reading, depicts a 'crisis of the act [that] is also a crisis of temporality, conceived in part as the simultaneous "too soon" and "too late" that afflicts the play's hero'.[37] Similarly, Vivasvan Soni sees Hamlet's haste and waiting as two 'modes of "action" stripped of judgment'.[38] In this reading, Hamlet is both too hasty and too hesitant, and it is this failure of judgement which leads him to enter the fixed fencing match. James Baumlin and Tita French Baumlin, from a rhetorical perspective, interpret the prince's waiting as a sign of indecisiveness and the play as an example of missed *kairos* since the prince does not act on his chance to murder Claudius. Rather, Hamlet suspends his ghostly revenge mandate until past the time when it is opportune and appropriate.[39]

I agree with these scholars that *kairos* is an important part of *Hamlet*'s revenge drama, but attending to fencing syntax as well as to philosophical and rhetorical elements reveals a fuller and more complex spectrum of the tragedy's rhythms of action and waiting. Hamlet serves equally as a model for good timing as for missed opportunity; this perspective is revealed when the formal logic of sport is applied along with that of law, economics and rhetoric. Hamlet demonstrates a strong grasp of timing by knowing when to act and when to wait in the last act of the play. As early as his first conversation with Rosencrantz and Guildenstern, Hamlet seems preoccupied with projecting weakness. He tells them that he has 'foregone all custom of exercise' – though later, as he confides to Horatio, he has been 'in continual practice' – that is, practicing his fencing every day (2.2.288, 5.2.149). These seemingly casual mentions of his own physical and mental infirmities combine with repeated ineffective verbal attacks upon Claudius designed to showcase a feigned weakness, while pricking the king into injudicious action. These attacks disturb Claudius into action, first as he orders Hamlet's death through Rosencrantz and Guildenstern's letter, then as he arranges the artful device of the fixed fencing match.

When Hamlet tells Horatio 'the readiness is all', as, against his better judgement, he decides to take part in the match, he speaks of the soul's readiness for death (5.2.160). However, his observation could be applied to his behaviour throughout the play. Secular dimensions of readiness are limited not only to Stoic philosophy, but include sportive, technical forms of readiness. In this sense, Hamlet's readiness consists not just in spiritual preparation, but also in the probing actions he has made throughout the play leading up to the moment where Claudius overextends himself. If we consider waiting as part of action, and Hamlet's madness as part of a revenge strategy, then it becomes apparent that *The Mousetrap* staged for Claudius's benefit is a way for the prince to create opportunity. It is, of course, a qualifiedly successful application of *contratempo* strategy: he succeeds in his goal of making Claudius die in a state of mortal sin and, perhaps, in a secondary goal of shuffling off his own mortal coil without committing self-slaughter (afterlife penalties for killing in self-defence or in unpremeditated rage being less onerous than those for suicide), but at the cost of Laertes and Gertrude's lives as well.

The tactics of waiting are also central in the play that founded the genre of revenge tragedy in England, *The Spanish Tragedy*. When the avenging hero Hieronimo realises that he will not get justice from the king for the death of his son Horatio, he feigns madness, gaining the king's sympathy and lulling the murderer, Lorenzo, into inaction. Recognising that 'all times fit not for revenge' (3.8.28), Hieronimo determines to 'dissembl[e] quiet in unquietness' (3.8.30) until he knows 'when, where and how' (3.8.44) to enact his revenge. His tactical madness eventually earns him a kairotic situation in which he convinces his enemies to 'act' in a play with him in which he takes the role of murderer. Rather than the figurative simply becoming literal in a linear progression, the literal murder takes place inside of the figurative encounter of the play.

Anti-revenge dramas, too, trade in the logic of combat when it comes to their pacing and the tactics of their heroes and villains. Where Hamlet successfully draws an attack by feigning weakness and then countering that attack with deadly force, the timing of fencing in *Romeo and Juliet* shows the play's sharp shift towards tragedy in the street brawl between Tybalt and Mercutio. Romeo, attempting to break the antagonistic timing of the fight, is himself dawn into the temporal rhythm of revenge instead of redirecting the brawlers' energies into cooperation. As in *Hamlet*, the tragic logic of this mistimed encounter externalises the temporality of the duel that governs the pacing of the narrative.

Methodology

Fencing, Form and Cognition on the Early Modern Stage couples close formal analysis of both fencing phrases and dramatic plots with a historical exploration of mechanisms of knowledge generation and transmission. Caroline Levine points out that literary critics have developed 'a range of subtle practices for thinking about temporal patterning, addressing such forms as meter, seriality, and plot', which can be put to important socio-political uses.[40] I agree with Levine about the potential latent in reading for form, and with this assumption I abstract the temporal patterning of both stage activities, dramatic and combative. Critical practices for analysing literary forms focus on the cooperative and empathetic aspects of communal interactions with story, emphasising the potential of the object of study to help readers or viewers understand and identify with the internal states of others. These insights, while valuable and important, do not adequately account for an interruptive and combative temporality. By foregrounding the antagonistic temporality latent in the plots of early modern drama, this project aims to recover lost forms that will nuance current models of active waiting and conflict and allow for a richer understanding of seemingly plot-flawed plays.

My methodology follows traditions of applying non-literary forms such as those of law or the grammar school to early modern drama. As Lynn Enterline and others have persuasively argued, drama was fundamentally linked to the grammar school's pedagogical work in developing empathy and identification.[41] The theatre's debt to the grammar school has been more closely examined than the fencing school, though scholars have done extensive work on the history of the duel and personal combat.[42] Many of the insights gained from exploring the connections between the stage and the grammar school are also relevant to the fencing school, however. Humanist pedagogy, particularly the teaching of rhetoric, had investments in how to properly teach temporal knowledge, meaning that fencing and rhetoric shared territory and had similar educational goals and pedagogical claims. Both disciplines deeply influenced how players and audiences engaged in the exchanges of theatre. While rhetorical performances of identification and persuasion swayed audiences to horror, sympathy or laughter, the interruptive and antagonistic timing of the fencing match enfolds layers of surprise and pleasurable suspense for audiences.

In the wake of Gail Kern Paster's work on embodiment and Bruce Smith's influential articulation of historical phenomenology, literary criticism has largely moved past dismissing the body's role in the theatrical experience as peripheral and entirely subordinate to the linguistic elements of plays.[43] However, critics have primarily focused on the static body rather than the body's motion in time.[44] Part of this under-theorisation is driven by the limitations of a literary and dramatic archive, which is not optimised for describing the nuances of temporal learning. Supplementing the literary archives with sources that must record movement, such as fencing masters' specialised vocabulary for physical expressions of deception, provides a rich vein of material to understand how timing, judgement and the sequencing of physical movements impact our understanding of plot and historical sensory experience.

I explore embodied temporality and the transmission of practical knowledge about time in early modern England through this book's principal texts: *The Book of the Courtier* (1528), *Arden of Faversham* (1592), *The Comedy of Errors* (1594), *Every Man in His Humour* (1598), *Titus Andronicus* (1594), *As You Like It* (c. 1599) and *Bartholomew Fair* (1614). These texts are not typically read together, but the *Book of the Courtier* offers a window into a historically situated embodied understanding of time and timing, and the dramatic texts share an important feature: they draw from fencing performance (prizefights) and pedagogy (fencing manuals and lessons) to craft an adversarial sense of theatrical time. I argue that some of the strangest-seeming plot decisions in the early modern canon, such as the seeming aimlessness of the plot after Act 1 of *As You Like It* or the series of jokey digressions that characterise Act 4 of *Titus Andronicus*, echo the formal structure of the device, or phrase of combat I have been describing. I chose these texts because of their potential to illuminate the timing of rhetoric and its relationship to the timing of combat. While *Hamlet* prominently features a fixed fencing match and *Romeo and Juliet* turns from comedy to tragedy through a duel, plays such as *Titus Andronicus* and *Every Man in His Humour* explicitly associate rhetoric with swordplay, articulating the two on a structural as well as a thematic level. While it is certainly possible to find other plays in which duels feature more prominently than the six of this study, the representation of a duel does not teach us as much about how timing was understood and practiced as does the pedagogy that the duel is founded upon. Rather than scouring scanty stage directions to reconstruct the temporal logic of combat, I look to the underlying theory described in fencing manuals to illuminate the embodied skill of timing, described by fencing masters as tempo and judgement.

While both tempo and judgement are faculties of 'knowing-when', I focus on an important distinction. Tempo evokes time's antagonistic and dissimulatory cadences – the ability to manage one's own time and manipulate the time of others. Though grounded in models of *kairos*, or opportune and experiential time, tempo is quantitative as well as qualitative. Over centuries, Italian fencing masters refined the term to develop a flexible and powerful methodology for analysing and teaching lengthy phrases of combat.[45] Qualitatively, fencers choose a moment to dissemble, attack or defend based on the quality of the opportune moments generated throughout the engagement. In this sense, fencers need a sophisticated grasp of *kairos*. Quantitatively, using tempo to numerically define kinds of actions allows for comparison, and to planning several movements deep in a phrase. In these instances, fencing manuals discuss tempo as a unit of uninterrupted movement. An action that consists of one tempo, such as a direct thrust to the opponent's target, is, all things being equal, faster than an action consisting of multiple tempi (that is, striking the opposing steel with one's own sword and subsequently delivering a cut to the face).

Tempo, for my purposes, is time as an embodied and potentially antagonistic rhythm of movement. This model of time was outlined by Italian fencing masters and imported to England near the end of Elizabeth I's reign. While scholars have thought about how individual and group movements inflect early modern theatregoing and illuminate alternate understandings of selfhood, such studies are generally cast in terms of cooperation and joint perception.[46] By centring dissimulation and interruption, this study offers a different model of theatrical time in which players, playgoers and even props are at odds with each other. Fencing, even more than disciplines such as music and dance, captures a range of intersubjective interactions which generate and transmit temporal knowledge. Further, though other endeavours such as wrestling, archery, juggling and tumbling also teach and demand effective timing, fencing featured more frequently in the drama of the period than other competitive sports because of its capacity to represent nuances of class, nation and masculinity through the practice's symbolic centrality in England's history.

Where tempo looks forward to plan traps several intentions deep, judgement is present-oriented and adaptive. If tempo yields itself to long-term planning, judgement excels at describing the skill of at-speed decision making. Judgement is the governing term used in native English traditions of fencing and, earlier in the century, in Italian and German texts. In the late sixteenth century, judgement was understood as a temporal skill as well as a punctual event or a conceptual process, and watching and engaging in fencing or other physical activities was an avenue used to train the ability. 'Judgement' features as a key term in early modern proto-aesthetics as well as in fencing instructional texts. As I explore in Chapter 3, Jonson sees physical training as a way to develop the skill of judgement, useful in both appraising the merits of a play, and in deciding when one's opportune moment has arrived. 'Judgement' as an organising term for the activities of the playhouse has recently received more attention in the wake of scholarship on the relationship between law and drama. For instance, Lorna Hutson, Luke Wilson and Kevin Curran treat the relationship of legal judgment to aesthetic judgement and rhetoric in the early commercial theatre. Hutson argues that changes in dramatic narrative correspond to developments in legal culture: 'these very rhetorical techniques for evaluating probabilities and likelihoods in legal narratives were perceived by dramatists in the London of the late 1580s and 1590s to be indispensable for their purposes in bringing a new liveliness and power to the fictions they were writing'.[47] Similarly, Wilson argues that the legal tradition's methodology for discussing and assessing intention influenced the depiction of forethought in plays like *Hamlet*.[48] Curran focuses on law and subjectivity, arguing that 'law provided Shakespeare with a conceptual language for describing selfhood in distributed terms'.[49] In this reading, judgement is a kind of communal, ethical project, as theatregoers and players collaboratively construct both aesthetic and moral norms. Curran argues that aesthetic judgement becomes the collective responsibility of the theatregoing public, following Sidney's model for good fictional writing. Good literature, as Sidney posits in *Defense of Poesy*, creates good judgement, which goes on to create more good poesy. These analyses provide valuable insight into the role of judgement in the theatre, but, as of yet, they focus more on judgement as the art of deciding *which* (action to take, person is in the wrong, and so on) more than the art of knowing *when* (an action will be successful or appropriate).

Fencing, Form and Cognition on the Early Modern Stage foregrounds the durational and dynamic aspects of judgement and highlights the non-linguistic routes early moderns imagined as available to them to train the faculty. The book's central premise is that the circular relationship between imaginative writing (poesy or drama) and judgement was not confined to literary aesthetics and rhetorical decorums but extended to sportive realms as well. Early modern authors have a long history of thinking of judgement as well as other virtues and faculties as being trained via the body through fencing. For instance, in his *Of Education*, John Milton recommends that students be given an hour and a half of swordplay every day before lunch in order to foster their physical as well as moral characteristics. Practising the 'exact use of their weapon', Milton suggests, 'will keep [students] healthy, nimble, strong, and well in breath' and fencing is 'also the likeliest means to make them grow large and tall, and to inspire them with a gallant and fearless courage'.[50] *Fencing, Form and Cognition on the Early Modern Stage* will argue that the theory of opportunity found in fencing manuals lends itself to a better understanding of this aspect of early modern literary judgement by contextualising how time and motion inhere in processes of judgement.

The evidence that demonstrates how early modern drama appropriated fencing forms is furnished by the dramatic texts themselves, fencing manuals and contemporary writings on prizefighting and duelling. The syntax of the fencing phrase extends beyond the art of defence and permeates early modern drama and scenes that show armed conflict. While there is much to be said about *Hamlet* and *Romeo and Juliet*'s use of the logic of combat, the tragedies themselves do not engage as directly with fencing on a formal level as other plays by Shakespeare and his contemporaries. Though I look at scenes of conflict, by and large the plays I analyse in depth in the following chapters are not strongly linked to fencing in the public consciousness. *Arden of Faversham*, for instance, is not widely regarded as a fencing play. Focusing on plays without an overdetermined fencing association allows me to isolate the logic behind movements of character and plot. My argument homes in on combat scenes because they most clearly externalise the internal logic of the play's devices.

Fencing, Form and Cognition on the Early Modern Stage analyses the writings of Shakespeare and Jonson in domestic tragedy, revenge tragedy, pastoral comedy and city comedy to show how the principles of fencing timing informed the plot mechanics, character interactions and the playwright–audience relationship of early modern English drama.[51] Reading across these genres allows me to highlight the structural use of fencing in varied contexts. I focus on a small subset of early modern drama through Jonson's and Shakespeare's plays in order to provide a consistent point of reference across these different genres. Why these two dramatists? After all, early modern London had many fencing playwrights, and the stage was full of references to fencing. One of our few documents about Christopher Marlowe, for instance, records his participation in a conflict that seemed to be half duel and half self-defence against William Bradley. In *The Roaring Girl*, Middleton and Dekker make the crossdressing heroine Moll Frith's rapier shorthand for her appropriation of phallic power. Middleton and Rowley's *A Fair Quarrel* turn on the intricacies of duelling codes and the cowardice and honour associated with them. I have attempted to separate plays such as these in which fencing, duelling and swords function in a largely symbolic or thematic way from the ones of this study, which I argue share a formal basis of comparison with fencing theory and pedagogy.

Shakespeare and Jonson stand out even in a generation of sword-loving playwrights. Jonson's inclusion is driven by both biographical and formal reasons. He writes extensively in *Timber, or Discoveries* about the intersection of fencing and poesy in teaching aesthetic judgement, for instance. His plays insistently return to scenes of combat in stage prizefights, duels, street brawls, and even competitive gaming and puppet shows. Moreover, he was notorious in his own time for his duel with Gabriel Harvey and his service in the military. Shakespeare's sparser biographical record makes it impossible to say for sure what his own personal relationship was with fencing pedagogy. However, his extensive formal experimentation with fencing on both thematic and structural levels provides a window into the early commercial theatre's innovations and adoptions.

Organisation

Fencing, Form and Cognition on the Early Modern Stage tells the story of how early moderns understood and transmitted practical knowledge about time in six chapters. In Chapters 1 and 2, I analyse two routes through which the logic of combat made its way into the drama of the early English commercial theatre: literary texts and skill-based disciplines. Like the early modern English dramatists and fencing masters whose works this study explores, I turn to Italy for sources and precedents: Castiglione's *Book of the Courtier*, a work of prose verging on drama due to its many characters and dialogic structure. The book was highly influential throughout Europe and became especially important in England after Thomas Hoby's 1561 translation made it more widely available. Castiglione uses the courtier's chief profession – armed combat – to describe his embodied conception of tempo, which is central to *sprezzatura*. I argue that Castiglione provides a model for the literary deployment of the timing of combat that influenced English dramatists.

Embodied, skill-based disciplines as well as literary texts influenced the dramatists of the early commercial theatre. As an internationally acclaimed literary masterpiece showcasing the best of court life, *The Book of the Courtier* (1528) may seem like an odd companion to the focal text of Chapter 2, *Arden of Faversham* (1592), a brutal and titillating domestic tragedy. While divided by tone, audience, genre, language and nearly every other metric, these works together represent two significant routes through which the logic of combat made its way into the drama of the early English commercial theatre. Playwrights drew from Castiglione's literary model as they deployed elements from fencing into the formal structure of their works. *Arden of Faversham* shows another way in which fencing influenced the early English stage through its adaptation of contemporary theories of judgement and tempo, faculties of kinaesthetic reasoning governing one's time and position. Chapter 2 explores *Arden of Faversham*'s use of the affordances of the playhouse and the fencing phrase to convey underlying information about characterisation and plot. Opportunity, rather than linear narrative, is the driving force of the domestic trage-dy's many 'plots' – of land, of action and of scheme. Through repeated stagings of ineptness and skill, the tragedy illuminates a spatially charged and antagonistic timing, as objects in the play act as techno-logical extensions of the players but are also adversarial to them.

After I have established what early moderns considered to be 'time' and how they went about learning and teaching it, I shift to the playwright who is arguably Castiglione's most direct English dra-matic heir, Ben Jonson. Chapter 3 extends my exploration of fencing as a literary-aesthetic influence through a reading of *Every Man in His Humour* (1598). I argue that the comedy uses fencing discourse and practice to justify and explain Jonson's innovative comic prose. At this intersection of blows and prose, Jonson places a thinly veiled version of Silver, who was notorious for his anti-Italian polemics and advocacy for the 'downright blow' as a manly, English attack. I argue that he is an unrecognised source for the comedy's Squire Downright. These underexplored historical connections both provide insight into Jonson's developing model of judgement and set the stage for a more granular analysis of the interplay between fencing strategy and dramatic pacing. Alongside *Every Man in His Humour*, I analyse Shakespeare's *Comedy of Errors* (1594). Where *Every Man in His Humour* details the embodied capacity of judgement as it is taught via fencing practice, *The Comedy of Errors* explores how knowledge about time and identity is generated through touch. *The Comedy of Errors* differs from the other, more fencing-specific scenes of con-flict in its slapstick encounters that feature slaps, pinches and kicking rather than thrusts and blows. However, it illuminates contemporary understandings around how antagonistic touch creates knowledge, which is useful for analysing the fencing touch.

Having excavated the lost historical connection between litera-ture and the fighting arts over the shared ground of tempo and judge-ment, Chapters 4 and 5 move to a formal and historical analysis of how this influence plays out in revenge tragedy and pastoral comedy with Shakespeare's *Titus Andronicus* and *As You Like It*. Where this introduction and the first three chapters establish theatrical timing as antagonistic rhythm of movement and explore the provenance of the early theatre's model of timing, Chapters 4 and 5 analyse the technical details of specific fencing tactics such as the counterattack, *contratempo* and the feint. Through a reading of English and Continental fencing manuals, Chapter 4 fleshes out the ways in which *Titus Andronicus* exemplifies the uniquely disruptive and antagonistic properties of fencing right-timing. These insights reveal a richer, more motivated play than one in which a baffled avenger enacts, by sheer happenstance, a condign revenge.

Continuing this exploration of specific fencing strategies Shakespeare adapts to the English stage, Chapter 5 shifts focus to comedy, asking what happens to this antagonistic, interruptive temporality when it is transposed to a pastoral setting. I argue that where Titus employs a *contratempo* strategy common to revenge drama, Rosalind uses the comic mode of feints and feigning to take Orlando's time and leave him flat-footed. In contrast to *contratempo*, feigning relies not on a pretended weakness to lure the adversary to attack, but on distraction. Like the conditional *if* that structures the comedy, feints posit in their first movement a hypothetical. The subsequent movements hold in suspense many possibilities at one time until the action is concluded with a touch to the open line. I find that the structure of the comedy reflects this movement in both its non-verbal cues (the play's blocking) and in its verbal ones. The play's temporal themes – poor social timing, indifference to opportunity, the conditional 'if' and its pausing of time – are caught up with questions of disguise and misdirection.

The final chapter and coda of *Fencing, Form and Cognition on the Early Modern Stage* suggest future research applications of this analysis of tempo, judgement and dissimulation. In Chapter 6, I argue that Jonson uses metatheatrical techniques, experiments in plot structure, and the players' complex interpersonal timing patterns to explore what I term 'kinesic judgement', a subset of the kinesic intelligence theorised by Spolsky and others. Kinesic judgement is built on a logic of constructive antagonism that is crucial for Jonson's understanding of theatrical experience, as in his complaints about emotional contagion – the audience's tendency to 'censure by contagion' rather than developing and using their own aesthetic judgement. Jonson's competitive approach to the interactions among players, playgoers and the playwright shows through most clearly in a scene of gameplay (the 'game of vapours') and a scene of performance (a bawdy puppet show). Through these antagonistic interactions of groups and individuals Jonson posits a largely non-cooperative mode of theatrical distributed cognition. The coda explores further ramifications of the model of antagonistic timing explained by fencing masters and brought alive by playwrights. Combat, as a conceptual category, adds to conversations in philosophy, disability studies and education as well as literary studies and cognitive science. For instance, while fencing is often cast as the activity of the normate elite male body, its archive has much to offer disability scholarship as well. The embodied temporality I explore in *Fencing, Form and Cognition on the Early Modern Stage* chimes with other recent work in disability studies on crip time and kairotic spaces. My coda points to a generative intersection between early modern disability scholarship and modern-day discussions in education research. Margaret Price's work on classroom *kairos* shows one way in which theories of time and space are relevant to understanding the institutional challenges faced by students with disabilities. My research has further implications for crafting hospitable learning environments because it works to illuminate the historical complexity of time and timing as experiential and constructed through its analysis of early modern judgement as a trainable, temporal process rather than an act of a single moment.

The devices of the early modern stage may seem far afield from our own, and, in many respects, they are; however, the employment of fencing devices and dramatic devices has more to say to our contemporary moment than is at first apparent. Through the ethical and pedagogical work these devices display and accomplish, we can more readily recognise the imbrications of appropriate timing and ethical decision making, developing skills that are becoming progressively more urgent in light of global economies, philosophies and ecologies where our decisions ever more impact those around us and on the other side of the world.

Notes

1. See the Bibliography for the play editions cited in this chapter. Throughout this book, quotations from the plays under discussion will be cited parenthetically by act, scene and line numbers.
2. Silver, *Paradoxes of Defence*, 29.
3. See 'art, n.1'. *OED Online*. Oxford University Press. That fencing in England and Italy was alternately described as 'art' or 'science' or 'art and science' further suggests the discipline's engagement in questions of

theory and practice. From the Latin for 'knowledge', the word 'science' was imported into English in the early fourteenth century.

4. See Smith, *Body of the Artisan*.

5. On fencing and gender, see Ira Clark, *Comedy, Youth, Manhood* and Low, *Manhood and the Duel*. On fencing and subjectivity, see Feather, *Writing Combat and the Self*. Unlike the above sources, my discussion will focus upon the pedagogical strategies of fencing masters and the formal adoption of fencing techniques to dramatic plot structure as well as literary representations of combat.

6. Whether one's fencing technique is hidden or displayed depends upon the context. For young aspiring gentlemen in training for duels, the craft was often practised secretly. For example, in 'Cowardice, the Mother of Cruelty', Montaigne writes: 'When I was young, gentlemen avoided the reputation of good fencers as injurious to them, and learned to fence with all imaginable privacy as a trade of subtlety, derogating from true and natural valor' (*Essays*, 491). For the more middle-class fencing spectacles common on the English stage, public displays required the audience's interpretation.

7. Silver, *Brief Instructions*, 82.

8. The concept of kinesic intelligence is explored in detail in Chapter 6. The term, originally coined in 1996 by Ellen Spolsky, refers to bodily knowledge and the ability to reflect on that knowledge.

9. For more on skill and ineptness in early modern drama, see Tribble, 'Skill'.

10. The concept of educated attention is explored in Grasseni, ed., *Skilled Visions*.

11. The *Oxford English Dictionary* records as entry I.1.a of 'play, n.' as 'Active bodily exercise or movement; brisk and vigorous action of the body or limbs, as in fighting, fencing, dancing leaping, etc.' and I.1.b as 'The action of lightly and briskly wielding or plying a weapon in fencing or combat.' These usages date from c. 800 in the former instance and to c. 1000 in the latter (*Beowulf*). *OED* entry III.16 records 'A dramatic or theatrical performance, and related senses' from the eleventh century.

12. See Borden, 'The Blackfriars Gladiators'.

13. Herbert Berry transcribes the record of Tarlton's master's prizefight in *The Noble Science*. According to this account, 'Mr tarlton was a lowed a mr the xxiijth of octobere vnder henrye nayllore mr – ordinary grome off her majvstes chamber' (53).

14. See Gurr, *Playgoing in Shakespeare's London*. On prizefights, see pp. 162, 177–80.

15. I do not mean to suggest that typographical innovation and creativity were not important elements of the change from a performance medium to a print medium. As Claire Bourne argues persuasively in her *Typographies of Performance in Early Modern England*, the innovative

typographical page designs developed in theatrical texts of the fifteenth through the eighteenth centuries were used intentionally to re-create 'extra-lexical effects of performance' such as the interaction of bodies on stage (1). I do wish to highlight how different rhetorical contexts led to different aspects of the embodied material, both fencing and performing, being emphasised.

16. See Wyatt, *Italian Encounter* for more on the cultural commerce between England and Italy and the immigration of Italian artists and artisans to England in the Tudor period.

17. Silver, *Paradoxes of Defence*, 16.

18. Published in the *Works of George Silver*, ed. Cyril Mathey. London, 1898.

19. Saviolo, *Vincentio Saviolo, his practice*, 8r; Spenser, Prefatory Letter to Sir Walter Raleigh, in *The Faerie Queene*.

20. Saviolo, *Vincentio Saviolo, his practice*, 3v.

21. Swetnam, *Schoole*, 83.

22. Printed treatises do much to illustrate the theory of knowledge held by their authors, but we know far less about the on-the-ground instructional context of the fencing school than we do of the grammar school. Student notes and lesson plans from the turn of the seventeenth century are sparse, so the instructional environment for fencing during Shakespeare's and Jonson's lifetimes is a matter of some debate. A generation later, however, as the students of famous seventeenth-century masters like Capoferro and Fabris become teachers themselves, these instructors become more explicit about how the theoretical is applied in the context of a lesson. Their notes allow for a closer approximation of how masters transmitted the practical knowledge about time so important to their discipline. The master communicates theoretical principles to students during lessons that focus on techniques, while practising with other students allows for the students to apply the concepts they learn from the master in a practical context. In 1610 Capoferro urges those who would 'become a perfect fencer' (literally a *giocatore*, or player) to 'play daily with different fencers' (28) in addition to taking lessons from a master.

23. Sydney Anglo writes 'Carranza assumed that, in order to achieve mastery of the sword, it was necessary to understand primary causes. Unfortunately, since he considered almost every kind of knowledge (mathematic, perspective, anatomy, medicine, astronomy, and music) relevant to fencing, it was inevitable that his book should grow into a vast, rambling and, ultimately, rather crazy edifice' (*Martial Arts*, 67). This assessment is, perhaps, biased by Anglo's understanding of the role of fencing pedagogy in a person's holistic education. Where Carranza sees fencing as a vehicle to teach philosophy, Anglo privileges 'all in' fighting and street smarts.

24. Meyer, *Art of Combat*, 44.

25. Ibid. 69.
26. Noë, *Action in Perception*, 2.
27. Clark and Chalmers. 'The Extended Mind', 1.
28. Herzfeld, 'Rhythm, Tempo, and Historical Time', 180.
29. See Harris, *Untimely Matter* and Wagner, *Shakespeare, Theatre, and Time* for two examples of critical engagement with embodiment and theatrical time.
30. Quinones, 'View of Time in Shakespeare', 328.
31. Turner's nine aspects include historical, objective time; the experience of time; time as agent; time as realm or sphere; natural, cyclical time; time as medium of cause and effect; particular moments or periods of time ('right' or 'wrong' times to do something); time as revealer or unfolder; time as rhythm or timing.
32. Wiles, *Players' Advice to Hamlet* is a notable recent (2020) exception to this trend.
33. See Tribble, *Cognition in the Globe*.
34. For another recent work exploring Shakespeare's poetics of temporality and embodiment, see Chapman, 'Lucrece's Time', which discusses the relationship between rape and time in Shakespeare's *Rape of Lucrece,*
35. Wiles, *Players' Advice to Hamlet*, 318.
36. Leoni, *Art of Duelling*, 17–18.
37. Halpern, 'Eclipse of Action', 46.
38. Soni, 'Judgment and Indecision in *Hamlet*', 62
39. See Baumlin and Baumlin, 'Chronos, Kairos, Aion'.
40. Levine, *Forms*, 5.
41. See Enterline, *Shakespeare's Schoolroom*. See also Knecht, *The Grammar Rules of Affection*.
42. For historical research on the social history of the duel and its construction of masculinity and national identity, see: Bryson, *The Sixteenth-Century Italian Duel*; Peltonen. *The Duel in Early Modern England*; Manning, *Swordsmen*; Hughes, *Politics of the Sword*; Kiernan, *The Duel in European History*; Frevert, *Men of Honour*; and Anglo, *Martial Arts*.
43. While both Paster and Smith have written extensively about embodiment and literature, I am thinking in particular of Paster, *Humoring the Body* and Smith, 'Pre-modern Sexualities'.
44. Jonathan Sawday, for instance, explores the immobile anatomised body in *The Body Emblazoned*. Francis Barker, in *The Tremulous Private Body*, sees in early modernity the beginnings of a tendency to transform bodies into texts that is fully realised in bourgeois modernity. There are certainly exceptions to this tendency, including Evelyn Tribble's work on skill and cognition, Gina Bloom's *Gaming the Stage* and Stephen Kolsky's work on dance in 'Graceful Performances'. In general, however, the body still features most prominently as a site for the application of power.

45. For English fencing masters, too, the granular analysis of relational times was of fundamental importance, but they differed in whether or not they translated *tempo*, and in the theory of opportunity they reference when they use the word 'time' instead. For instance, the anonymously authored *Pallas Armata* (1639) leaves *tempo* untranslated and glosses the term for an English audience as '*tempo* is, that thou takest heed never to make a thrust or blow at thine adversarie, without thou hast a faire opportunity to hit, or requisite measure, that he be within thy reach', whereas George Silver in his *Paradoxes of Defence* (1599) and *Brief Instructions* (c. 1603) uses 'time' in a subtly different way, as I will explore at length in Chapter 2. Joseph Swetnam in *Schoole of the Noble and Worth Science of Defence* translates *tempo* as 'time' but conceptually retains a traditionally Italian way of using the term.

46. See Hobgood, *Passionate Playgoing* and Tribble, *Cognition in the Globe* for recent approaches to the early modern theatre that emphasise emotional contagion and joint perception.

47. Hutson, *Invention of Suspicion*, 2.

48. See, specifically, 'Hamlet, Hales v. Petit, and the Hysteresis of Action', ch. 1 in Wilson, *Theaters of Intention*, 25–53.

49. Curran, *Shakespeare's Legal Ecologies*, 3.

50. Milton, 'Of Education', 234.

51. As I discuss in Chapter 3, Shakespeare likely had a hand in writing *Arden of Faversham*.

Chapter 1

The 'maister of al artificiall force and sleight': Castiglione's Literary Tempo

Introduction

The first word of Baldassare Castiglione's *Book of the Courtier* (1528) – *quando* – expresses an interest in time and timing that is sustained throughout the book. Because of a semantic shift in which 'time' has become unmoored from 'timing', Castiglione's writings have become less legible to modern-day readers, however. Castiglione's debt to orators such as Cicero is well established, but he also draws from other modes of conceptualising and teaching time from disciplines closer to Cinquecento Urbino, such as contemporary practices of music, dance and fencing. Fencing in particular provides an underexplored and promising avenue to understanding how Castiglione's model of time signifies in his larger projects because fencing, like the court, relies on the antagonistic and dissimulatory rhythms of interpersonal interaction rather than on the cooperative rhythms of music and dance. *The Book of the Courtier* expresses an interplay between two modes of expression – literary and combative – that would have been taken for granted in Renaissance Italy and England. Castiglione's contemporary fencing masters, Pietro Monte and Antonio Manciolino, can illuminate how fencing pedagogy informs Castiglione's investment in this historically particular model of tempo.

Thomas Hoby's translation of *Il cortegiano* was well received by his contemporaries. The translation was published in 1561 and reprinted in 1577, 1588 and 1603. Hoby modestly downplays the importance of the translation, since 'this Courtier hath long straid about this realme' in the 'three principal languages, in the which he hath a long time haunted all the Courtes of Christendome' before settling in to 'dwell in the Court of Englande'. The translation was immensely popular, and the book was well known even before its translation. Much ink has been spilled attempting to definitively link Shakespeare's drama to Castiglione's influence, but documenting direct influence has proved difficult. However, a wealth of scholarship traces possible allusions, formal adaptations and more between *The Book of the Courtier* and Shakespeare's Henriad, *Hamlet*, *Love's Labour's Lost*, *Much Ado about Nothing* and other plays. The case of Castiglione's influence on sixteenth-century English drama is more conclusive in Jonson's case, as he not only owned a copy of *The Book of the Courtier* but also directly references Castiglione in *Discoveries*. It is safe to say, however, that the book's immense popularity ensures that it was not far from the minds of playwrights and many members of their audiences in the late sixteenth century.

The Book of the Courtier is famously hard to place in a single genre. The idyllic account of courtly debate set in the Urbino of Castiglione's youth has been read as political allegory, as literary game and as courtesy manual, to name just a few interpretations.[1] The book participates in a larger Renaissance interest in rules and classification through its exploration of the behaviours and attributes which compose the ideal courtier. Because it uses a dialogue form, it avoids tedious didacticism and retains an open and fluid tone. Peter Burke characterises the great achievement of the work as 'adapt[ing] humanism to the world of the court, and the court to the world of humanism' during a period of social reorganisation and religious and political unrest.[2] This delicate task motivated Castiglione over the course of almost two decades to craft his text to comment on a number of conventional dichotomies. Throughout the four books that comprise *The Book of the Courtier*, Castiglione's characters (drawn from his real-life acquaintances) weigh in on such pressing contemporary questions as the hierarchy of sword and pen, noble birth versus meritorious deeds, the question of the future of the Tuscan language, and the relative importance of painting and sculpture. The book concludes on a philosophical note, with Pietro Bembo's famous rhapsody on ideal love.

The ambiguity of the book's genre and its dialogue form leave readers free to imagine Castiglione's voice issuing from any number of his characters with their different perspectives and values. In Bembo, one can see Castiglione the philosopher and poet, in Lady Emilia the organiser of genteel pastimes, and in Federico the arbiter of courtly conduct. To my knowledge, however, no one has yet considered how the court fencing master, Pietro Monte, embodies Castiglione's views. Monte's perspective would have had much to recommend itself in the view of Castiglione's original audience, however, as Castiglione was described by contemporaries as a man of arms as well as a man of letters.[3] For instance, King Charles V famously called Castiglione 'one of the best knights of the world', and Castiglione's friend Jacopo Sadoleto also praised his knightly qualities, saying that Castiglione's military prowess was coupled with liberal arts as well as a proper understanding of theology.

In part, Pietro Monte's role is underexplored because the 'maister of al artificiall force and sleight' is present but largely silent and is given relatively few moments in the sun.[4] More importantly, I believe, we do not perceive Monte as commenting on the book's larger themes because of a lost historical connection between literature and the fighting arts. Though the logic of combat has been largely forgotten in twentieth- and twenty-first-century scholarship, it played a major role in the education of the early moderns and in their entertainments. Renaissance humanism prized balance over extremes. The ideal courtier is one whose physical prowess is complemented by learning, and vice versa. A modern privileging of art over war can sometimes lead to projecting an anachronistic antagonism between arms and letters on to authors of the past. However, the conventional arms-versus-letters dichotomy ultimately leads to a balance between the two, rather than a real victory of one over the other. Poets like Tasso displayed their familiarity with the sword by incorporating detailed technical discussions of fencing manoeuvres in their work, and fencing masters took up pens to dignify their professions and to show that they, too, could take part in both the burgeoning print marketplace and the court.

The deference with which Monte is treated points to the special role of the court fencing master.[5] By Castiglione's death, these *maestri di scherma* were just beginning to make use of the medium of print.[6] In prior generations, manuscripts were written and dedicated to noble patrons. Fiore dei Liberi (c. 1340s–1420s), one of these authorial *maestri*, wrote the first extant Italian-language treatise on arms around 1409 or 1410 for Niccòlo III d'Este. The master, true to a medieval fighting tradition, emphasises battlefield and tournament fighting as well as duels. Flourishing mostly after Fiore, a series of masters from Bologna who used a common set of terminology also produced several influential fencing treatises. The Bolognese (or Dardi) school of fencing uses many of the same descriptive names for guard positions as Fiore, such as *Coda lunga* (long tail) and *Porta di ferro* (iron gate). This school published manuals from the early to late sixteenth century. However, the trajectory of fencing practice followed another branch, and the Bolognese tradition died out in the seventeenth century. In Rome, Camillo Agrippa's 1553 *Trattato Di Scienzia d'Arme* codified a new terminology and pedagogy. Agrippa's new classification allowed for more detailed atomisation of fencing movement by departing from descriptive guard names and moving to a numbering system with guards and hand positions of first, second, third and fourth.[7]

The Bolognese fencing master Angelo Viggiani (d. 1552) shares Agrippa's interest in the science and philosophy of fencing – his fencing manual stages a debate of several days' length between a representative scholar and soldier, Boccadiferro and Rodomonte, on the distinctions and commonalities between their two disciplines. Viggiani and Castiglione, contemporary soldier-authors with ties to Charles V (Viggiani served under Maximillian II, Charles V's nephew, in the Italian War of 1542–6) may well have been known to each other personally. Both authored works using a multi-vocal dialogue format treating graceful and effective physical expression, and both used the conventional conversation game of sword and pen to explore larger topics. Book 1 of Viggiani's *Lo Schermo*, like *Il Cortegiano*, attempts to dissolve distinctions between arms and letters, but from the perspective of the fencing master rather than Castiglione's perspective of the courtier.

When Castiglione takes up the conventional debate between sword and pen, he does not reinforce a division between the two but rather uncovers the many common skills such as tempo which are shared by scholars and soldiers. Reliance on interpersonal models of timing and training that focus on repetition are central to both sword and pen. Fencing time incorporates one's own speed, the relative time elapsed between fencer and adversary, and the intentions of the fencers. The measurement of these dynamic potentialities is referred to as 'tempo'. Because of the limitations imposed by a strictly chronological description of a bout, fencing discourse developed terms to classify and teach complex temporal practices. For example, an action *di tempo* (in time) can simply mean an action that is performed while the opponent is moving. With greater nuance, the term can signify that the fencer has read the adversary's timing and begun to anticipate his or her movement. In contrast, an action *fuori di tempo* (out of time) denotes a failed action, one that misses its opportune moment. By training fencers to induce their adversaries' errors and force them out of tempo, these manuals teach how to master proper timing.

On a thematic level, Castiglione uses fencing to illustrate larger points about comely dissimulation and his characters describe it as the chief profession of the ideal courtier. Less obviously, *l'arte di ben maneggiare la spada* (the art of handling the sword well) works on a structural level as well, driving Castiglione's pacing and his conceptualisation of *sprezzatura* as artful, planned spontaneity. I aim to contextualise the literary dimensions of swordplay and the combative aspects of literature in this chapter. In so doing, I will show how Castiglione draws on contemporary fencing pedagogy to construct his own influential notion of social timing, which made its way into England and English drama.

Modo, Maniera and Tempo: The Temporality of Sprezzatura

In *The Book of the Courtier*, tempo is a way of being in relation to others continually in flux based on age, status and company, and it features as an important part of graceful comportment. As Eduardo Saccone notes, grace 'signifies not so much a particular quality as a modality, an ability: the graceful using of qualities so as to provoke grace'.[8] Castiglione hints at such a modality when Lady Emilia decrees that Federico Fregoso should continue the account of the ideal courtier. She asks him to shift from Lodovico's description of the necessary knowledge and qualities of the courtier to the practical application and development of these attributes; to explain 'in what sort, maner, and time the Courtier ought to practice his good condicions and qualityes' (99). When Federico responds to Emilia, he denies an easy separation between activity and essence. *Modo*, *maniera* and tempo administrate the ontological (qualities) and the circumstantial (conditions) in the practice of courtiership: 'where ye will sever the sort, the time and the maner of good condicions and qualityes and the well practisinge of the Courtyer, ye will sever that can not be sundred: for it is these things that make the condicions and qualityes good and the practicing good.' Federico's distinction highlights an important, but often overlooked, aspect of Castiglione's project. Even in scholarship that takes seriously the skills of courtiership, this dimension of tempo is neglected in favour of *modo* and *maniera* because the latter terms speak more directly to how identity is often understood as behavioural and ontological more than temporal.[9] Burke's seminal *Fortunes of the Courtier*, for instance, points out that it is the temporality of *sprezzatura* that separates it from earlier concepts of negligence. *Sprezzatura*, he notes, is 'a new sense given to an old word, the basic meaning of which was "setting no price on" . . . it also involves giving the impression of acting "on the spur of the moment" (*all'improviso*, 2.34). This contrived spontaneity is a more dramatic version of the *neglegentia diligens* which both Cicero and Ovid advocated for in their different ways.'[10] However, Burke turns immediately to a discussion of self-consciousness and performance after making this fascinating point. I would like to linger for a moment on the spontaneous temporality of Castiglione's coinage: a quality of time as much as a mode of behaviour is at the centre of Castiglione's *sprezzatura*.

A long line of scholars have agreed that Hoby's decision to render *sprezzatura* as 'recklessness' was unfortunate. The longer phrase, 'recklessness to cover art' (368), is a little better, but still a far cry from more recent translations' emphasis on affected ease. His otherwise excellent translation captures pre-modern sensibilities about the organisation of knowledge and spheres of disciplinary authority, however.[11] For example, Hoby's rendering of words like 'artful' and 'artificial' suggest the manual, concrete sense of deceit as craft or a kind of handiwork.[12] However, in a post-Cartesian context Hoby's translation of *tempo* as 'time' becomes somewhat inadequate. The shift towards a strong mind/body dualism tended to separate 'time' and 'timing' into the provenance of physics and philosophy on the one hand, and athletics, music and dance on the other. Thus, what Castiglione means by *tempo* is no longer conveyed by the English 'time'. As has been well established, 'time' signified differently in the Renaissance, before the advent of fields like human factors and ergonomics and before the standardisation of clocks, when different churches knolled out the hours in cacophonous disagreement. In this transitional period, describing the passage of time was the provenance of rhetoric, not the stopwatch.[13] To understand the major reconfigurations around how early moderns thought about time, it is helpful to look at how contemporaries defined the term in their dictionaries.[14]

Early Italian dictionaries such as the 1526 *Le tre fontane di Messer Nicolo Liburnio in tre libri divise, sopra la grammatical, et eloquenza di Dante, Petrarcha, et Boccaccio* used quotations from the works of exemplary authors to define words as part of a project to elevate Italian vernacular.[15] Glosses from these dictionaries are centred on eloquent deployment of vernacular language rather than systematic definition. These dictionaries would have been quite useful to a reader or poet evaluating the linguistic potentialities of the vernacular, but are less helpful in giving a precise and concise sense of how tempo was conceptualised. Similarly, early English monolingual dictionaries focused on 'hard words' rather than systematic and complete coverage. Fortunately, we can clarify the changing definition of tempo by consulting the English–Italian dictionary of the Italian expatriate and lexicographer John Florio. A major shift occurs in the term's definition between the 1598 and 1611 dictionary editions. The 1598 *World of Words* defines tempo as 'time, season, leasure, opportunitie or occasion, the state of time, commodity or necessitie of the time present. Also weather foule or faire.' The 1611 *Queen Anne's New World of Words* glosses tempo as 'time, the space of time, measure of motion, season, leasure, while. Also occasion, opportunitie or necessitie of the time present. Also the weather be it foule or fair.' In just over a decade, the entry has changed to de-emphasise time-as-opportunity (*kairos*) by introducing a more mathematical understanding of time as measurement, or *chronos*. This is not to say that measurement had no place in earlier temporal models – *chronos*, the linear and progressive model of time is ancient.[16] However, in early modernity, a growing interest in incrementalisation, optimisation and efficiency brings the measurement of time to new prominence and displaces the qualitative time of *kairos* into a secondary, marginal realm of bodily timing.

Maestri di scherma, like their counterparts teaching rhetoric, treat this embodied and qualitative mode of time as one of the foundational principles of their art. Giuseppe Pallavicini in his 1670 *La Scherma* argues that fencing is founded on time, and that the fencer who understands time the best will be called the best fencer.[17] Similarly, Nicoletto Giganti (c. 1550–1622) writes in 1606 that one can only claim to understand defence and offence if one understands time and measure first.[18] These masters follow a greater Renaissance trend away from examples embedded in context and towards the theoretical. Fencing represents a confluence of theory and practice, science and art.[19] Different temporal and geographical conditions produce fencing masters who stress either theory or practice more in their approaches. For example, Giganti and other sixteenth- and seventeenth-century masters tend to emphasise the theoretic and appeal to underlying principles, while earlier masters such as Fiore use exemplary models.[20]

The Disports of Urbino: Games and Temporal Skill

Castiglione engages both more theoretical and more practical questions, as he discusses the utterly mundane alongside the ideal. Hoby gravely presents a long prescriptive checklist of lessons to take away

from *The Book of the Courtier* in the first pages of his English translation, extracting all the advice given by the various characters of the
book. Castiglione himself begins in a more playful way. *The Book
of the Courtier* is organised in temporal terms by four days of gameplay, each of which is interrupted by the attention of the party being
called to the lateness (or earliness) of the hour. Castiglione catalogues
in careful detail numerous moments of distraction, digression, lateness and earliness such as when a discussion of aesthetics is interrupted by the late arrival of the Prefect who hurries as fast as he can
to be in time to hear what everyone else is talking about.

Castiglione's literary game of fashioning the court of Urbino contains within it many concentric rings of game and gaming. The gen-
dered arrangement of participants, 'devyded a man and a woman, as
longe as there were women' (34), who discern where and how to sit,
is itself a social game that occurs before the proposal of any specific
verbal game. In this sense, the court of Urbino becomes what the
Dutch historian and cultural theorist Johan Huizinga terms a 'play-
ground' – a zone that is 'marked off beforehand either materially or
ideally' to create order.[21] The circle is reminiscent both of the perfect
circle of Euclidean geometry and of the precedents of ancient games
designed for groups of players. Not coincidentally, the shape also
denotes networks of alliance – the inner circle of elite intellectuals,
politicians or, in this case, courtiers. Albury maps the multiple rings
of audience forming the Urbino courtly circle, from outsiders like the
papal courtiers to peripherals like Pietro Monte and Unico Aretino,
to insiders such as Federico Fregoso and Pietro Bembo.[22]

Castiglione's preoccupation with timing first emerges in a verbal
game, and later is introduced in relation to non-linguistic practices
like fencing and dance. The opening scene of *The Book of the Courtier* introduces tempo as one of the courtier's key traits by contrasting
Unico Aretino's virtuosic display of good timing with Fra Serafino's
flat-footed and mistimed attempt at humour. The courtiers and court
ladies join in a circle to play the meta-game of each proposing a
game for the evening's entertainment. Amid general pleasantry and
laughter, a jarring note sounds when Fra Serafino bungles his turn.
His failure is made even more striking because it comes immediately
after the suggestion of the masterful crowd-pleaser, Unico Aretino.
Aretino proposes a game where each player guesses what the jew-
elled 'S' on the Duchess's forehead means. When, as he anticipated,
he is asked to provide his own explanation, he feigns a moment of
reflection and then recites a sophisticated and seemingly improvised
sonnet, impressing the other players. The later suspicion that he had

already composed the sonnet does not seem to impinge upon the audience's enjoyment of Aretino's management and seizure of opportunity: 'bicause it was more witty and better knitt then a man would have beleved the shortnes of time required, it was thought he had prepared it before. So after mens favourable voice geven in the praise of this rime . . . Fregoso whose tourne was then next, began' (31).

In contrast, Lady Emilia interrupts and skips over Fra Serafino in the midst of his 'trifling tales': one can almost see the collective eye-roll of the congregated courtiers when he breaks into 'his usual nonsense' to suggest a game that is not really a game – for every man to 'tel his opinion, how it cummeth that (in a maner) all women abhorre rattes, and love serpents' (37). These unplayed games, coming as they do prior to the pastime that occupies the rest of the book, may seem unimportant and digressive. However, they actually perform the work's central concern: how *sprezzatura* and other public displays of artful deceit turn on the courtier's careful cultivation of temporal skill, trained through disports such as word games and fencing.

Aretino's strategy is later echoed by Federico in his discussion of fencing and *sprezzatura*. Fencing is an apt vehicle for discussing the ins and outs of court life because court, like the field of combat, not only allows trickery but calls for it.[23] For instance, Federico contends that the artful courtier should create an illusion of wide-ranging competency by avoiding activities in which he 'hath but a meane skill'. Instead, he should plan out his seemingly spontaneous public displays of skill 'before hande, showyng notwithstanding, the whole to bee done ex tempore, and at the first sight' (149). Federico's advice here echoes Aretino's strategy by feigning improvisation with a pre-composed sonnet: only by painstaking planning can the courtier be sure of displaying *sprezzatura*.

Federico's carefully managed argument enacts the good tempo he prescribes for the courtier. He provokes a predictable objection from Gaspare Pallavicino, who argues: 'I thinke not this an art, but a verie deceite, and I beleave it is not meete for him that will bee an honest man to deceive at anye time' (151). Federico's ready counter suggests that he is following his own advice and that the question of skilful dissimulation is one to which he has given some thought. Federico resists the reading of deceit as opposed to honesty through the analogy of a fencing competition:

> [dissimulation] is rather an ornament that accompanyeth the thinge he doeth, then a deceite: and though it be a deceite, yet it is not to be disallowed. Will you not saye also, that he that beateth his fellow,

> where there be two playing at fence together, beeguyleth hym, and
> that is bicause he hath more art than the other? . . . We saye not then
> that this art or deceite (in case you wyll so terme it) deserveth anie
> maner blame. Also it is not ill for a man that knoweth himself skilfull
> in a matter, to seeke occasyon after a comelye sorte to showe hys
> feat therein, and in lyke case to cover the partes he thynketh scante
> woorthye praise, yet notwithstandinge all after a certain warye dys-
> symulacion. (151)

Federico's analogy highlights the adversarial timing of court life. It is, crucially, not enough to have good *modo* and *maniera*, or 'sort' and 'manner', because the self is not fixed and essential but rather something that must be administrated through wise foresight. Court life, even constructive and ideal court life, is not predicated on coop-eration among courtiers, but rather their skilful antagonism. As W. R. Albury points out, the pastime of 'provoking the folly of those in whom it is latent' is part of how court insiders entertain each other.[24] This delight in dissimulation is often hidden by a shift from Renaissance to Baroque notions of artifice. Contra Harry Berger, I argue that Castiglione's *Book of the Courtier* displays and celebrates deceptive skill rather than participating in a culture of paranoia regarding the discrepancies between surface and interior. Scholarly discussions of Renaissance dissimulation often take Pallavicino's perspective, focusing on anxiety, closed bodies and surveillance. In these terms, *askesis* is closely equated with ascetic denial or nega-tion. However, to take Federico's part, the elegance of deceit is an equally important concern, and selves are formed through the ludic as well as disciplinary practices.[25]

Poiesis and the Feint

As we have seen, fencing is a useful analogy for court life because of the shared characteristics of danger, antagonism, playfulness, display and deception. Even more than fitting analogy, however, according to the consensus of Book I, fencing should be the courtier's chief medium of graceful expression. As Ludovico explains, 'the principall and true profession of a Courtyer ought to be in feates of armes' (51). Further, the ideal courtier must

> [S]hewe strength, lightnes, and quickenesse, and to have understan-
> dyng in all exercises of the bodie, that belonge to a man of warre. And

herein I thinke the chief point is to handle well all kynde of weapon both for footeman and horseman, and to known the vauntages in it. And especially to be skilfull on those weapons that are used ordinarily among gentlemen, for beside the use that he will have of them in warre, where peradventure nedeth no great connyng, there happen often times variaunces betwene one gentleman and an other, whereupon ensueth a combat. (52–3)

As this quotation suggests, the history of fencing is also a history of ideal aristocratic masculinity, which was indebted to the duel as an intersection between a self-fashioning humanism and medieval chivalric culture.[26] Stance and movement advocated by fencing masters differs dramatically based on the aesthetics of the period and the context of the match. The earlier Bolognese school of fencing stresses performance and grace as a means to spatial control. Their approach resonates with that of the English masters a generation later, which, as we will see in *Arden of Faversham*, similarly emphasises spatial mastery, though without the same emphasis on graceful performativity. *Sprezzatura* and display feature as techniques of self-formation in the Bolognese tradition. In later texts, such as Capoferro's 1610 *Gran simulacro*, the fencer establishes spatial mastery through efficiency and minimal movement. The risk of giving one's opponent a free tempo means that asserting masculinity no longer comes through large, flashy movements performed out of measure, but rather through precise, decisive and practical motions. In accordance with the earlier fencing tradition, Castiglione's courtier does not simply handle weapons well, but he performs *feats* – that is to say, he displays qualities such as speedy and correct decision-making under pressure while maintaining good form. Men of war use weapons; gentlemen use weapons which require cunning. For Ludovico, cunning means the ability to deceive the adversary by communicating misleading messages through bodily cues. Castiglione represents gentlemanly cunning as an essential part of the courtly self rather than denouncing deception as a sign of dangerous, fallen times in which exteriors no longer reliably map to interiors.

Federico and Ludovico evoke with their behaviour and assertions a specific deceptive fencing technique, the feint, as well as gesturing to the competitive sport of combat in a general sense. An underlying tropology of combat runs through many early modern literary works, as authors like Castiglione co-opt the vocabulary and dissimulatory techniques of fencing. The poetic uses to which the activity of swordplay has been put are well known. Love and rhetorical contests head the list of such figurative appropriations. While it is common to read of a lover vanquished by his beloved, or of a brilliant riposte in an argument, the family of fencing tropes related to deception is not as frequently invoked today.[27] However, the alliance of these two faculties of *poiesis* is illustrated in Florio's expansion of his definition of *finta*, used as a technical term for the feint in fencing, from the 1598 to the 1611 version of his dictionary. The first defines *finta* as 'a faigning, an offer, a proffer to do any thing', and the second adds to this definition 'a fiction' as a derivation. In this period, 'fiction' generally refers to fashioning or imitating, but as early as 1599 it bears with it the generic sense of 'species of literature' which is 'concerned with the narration of imaginary events and the portraiture of imaginary characters'.[28] Florio connects the kinds of feints found in fencing with those found in fiction writing. The link is not original to the Italian expatriate, however, but stems from authors like Castiglione who, a generation earlier, make extensive use of the feint as a figure for social dissimulation.[29]

On a technical level, masters define feints as those movements that distract the opponent from one's true intentions. For instance, Filippo Vadi (1425–1501) writes in his manual dedicated to Guidobaldo:

> When you enter into half-sword measure
> Strike from every direction
> Creating openings with artful blows
> Those misleading blows are called feints
> Which trick others into defending the wrong side.[30]

Feints occur in at least two movements. The first is a simulated menace – the strike which can come from any direction. The second movement is a replacement of the blade in a different line so that the fencer can strike the uncovered target of the adversary. Later, in the section of his manual on individual techniques, Vadi gives a specific example (Fig. 1.1).

The fencer on the right fakes a rising diagonal blow to the opponent's side. Misled by the unexpected change in angle, the fencer on the left unsuccessfully attempts to parry. As the opponent parries, the fencer withdraws and turns his blade to clear the parry, then hits the jaw. The feint holds open multiple possibilities in a single moment.

In 1639, an anonymous English university student attempting to represent the Italian rapier system of fighting to his peers in an English manual (*Pallas Armata*) makes the connection between literary device (metaphor) and fencing technique explicit, writing: 'Finda is

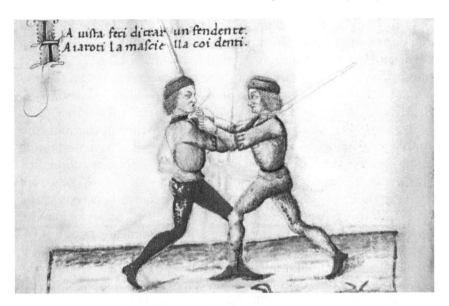

Figure 1.1 Filippo Vadi. The feint. *Arte Gladiatoria Dimicandi*, c. 1485. Rome, Biblioteca Nazionale Centrale, MS Vitt.Em.1324. Wikimedia Commons.

called in the Italian tongue a deceit or cozenage, and metaphorically brought into fencing' (6). The feint is a problem of timing that exists on the border between playfulness and earnestness. For masters like Giganti, it represents the most playful and poetic aspect of fencing tactics. Giganti highlights the fluidity between the school and the space of the theatre or fencing hall by entitling his 1606 fencing book *Scola, overo teatro*. He describes feints as the most elegant form of fencing, appropriate for a schoolroom or game: 'I am only going to describe those actions which to me seem the most beautiful, artful, and useful . . . Among all the ways in which you can artfully strike your adversary, the feint, in my opinion, is the best. The feint is when you imply that you will do one thing and then you do another.'[31] Masters like Capoferro who focus more on the duelling field and less on a student's performative ability warn against using the feint except in very restricted situations. His reasoning is that feints surrender a tempo and expose the fencer to the risk of falling prey to a counterattack: 'Feints are not good because they lose tempo and measure . . . if you feint outside of measure, it does not convince me to move, but if you feint in measure I will hit you while you are feinting.'[32] The feint's riskiness is part of its elegance, but its successful execution requires a careful reading of the context and its stakes.

As this advice about when to feint suggests, fencing, like literature, occurs in different genres: the point-of-honour duel, the tavern
brawl, and the public display of skill in a contest all have different
conventions and solicit different advice from masters. Agrippa's 1553
Trattato uses a lethal, thrust-oriented and streamlined system. Saviolo advises fencers never to spare the life of a friend when they go to
the duelling field. Many masters writing at the turn of the sixteenth
century de-emphasise performance, labelling flashy, entertaining
actions as too risky. The play element is never completely eclipsed by
this increased interest in efficiency and lower-risk actions, however.
In 1619, Giovanni Gaiani discusses the difference between school
and field, raising such questions as what to do when performing in
front of a monarch or how to fence one's own student in front of his
friends and family.[33] Gaiani's English contemporary, the puritanical
Joseph Swetnam, though not a playful author by any stretch of the
imagination, advises a number of non-lethal tactics to avoid imperil-
ling one's soul – and potentially getting arrested for murder.

Some fencing genres, such as the point-of-honour duel, follow a
similar temporal logic to that of revenge tragedy with an emphasis
on drawing attacks through feigning an opening that one is then prepared to counter. Revenge drama employs a recursive and amplifying
temporality – avengers suspend action to wait for the best moment
for condign revenge, which they actively prepare for by recreating the
original scene of the crime in some way. This recreation varies from
Hamlet's *Mousetrap* play to Vindice's elaborate poisoned skull in *The
Revenger's Tragedy*, but they all incorporate an element of return
with excess. Feints, in contrast, tend to occur in non-lethal training
bouts at fencing schools and at public performances. They are risky,
flashy manoeuvres which rely on misdirecting the opponent's attention so that the fencer can hit in an unexpected play. In this way, they
tend to follow the comic mode. Deceptive temporal manipulation in
comedy more often relies on misdirection than pretended weakness –
the crossdressing heroine rather than the mad avenger. Castiglione
draws from the logic of the feint to exemplify pragmatic and artful
courtly behaviour, binding together feints, tempo and self-formation.

Good tempo, for Federico and for Monte, means knowing how
to live – that is, both in the narrower sense of staying alive during a
duel and also in terms of time management and spending one's life
wisely. This is why tempo assumes a fundamental role in processes
of self-formation, and why fencing occupies such a prominent role
in self-rehearsal. Self-formation as a kind of *poiesis* engages both
with creative world-making and with deceptiveness as one performs

identity in multiple ways by adopting various characteristics. Ludovico gives voice to a common contemporary understanding of fencing as a means to self-formation. A generation later, the Italian expatriate fencing master Vincentio Saviolo (d. 1598/99) writes of how to 'make a scholler' in much the same way. Students (and gentlemen) are crafted through disciplinary techniques in a kind of human *poiesis*. Reflecting *poiesis* as a model of creation, self-formation is bound up with dissimulation.

Fittingly, it is the fencing master most known for his liberal use of feints in his tactics who makes part of the gathering at Urbino.[34] Monte published widely, from treatises on the Immaculate Conception to works of early empirical science detailing experiments relating to cannon range and velocity. Monte is characterised by Count Ludovico as 'oure M. Peter Mount, who (as you know) is the true and only maister of al artificiall force and sleight' (58). Hoby's word choice in translation is germane: the 'art' of 'artificiall' is a major feature of Monte's legacy. Throughout, he maintained an interest in the aesthetics of athletic expression, its art in the sense of a craft perfected into beauty through patience and exercise. Monte and Castiglione's Ludovico share a preference for smaller builds to heavier ones. Monte condemned painters of his time for favouring heavy musculature, asserting that true gracefulness is found in lithe, flexible bodies rather than bodies knotty, rigid and distorted by overbuilt muscles:

> [O]ld pictures and frequently modern ones follow this common error. Indeed, they advised to represent the greatest form, yet by changeable and monstrous measure . . . arms for all that ought to be free and pleasant, not knotty or hilly. But what should seem to be almost just as from nature, without swellings by exertion.[35]

Similarly, Castiglione asserts through Ludovico that it is best if the ideal courtier is

> neither of the least, nor of the greatest sise. For bothe the one and the other hath with it a certayne spytefull wonder, and suche men are marveyled at, almost, as muche as men marveile to behoulde monstrous thynges. Yet if there must needs be a defaulte in one of the two extremities, it shall be lesse hurtfull to bee somewhat of the least, then to excede the common stature in height. (52)

Monte and Castiglione's shared athletic aesthetic is about more than attractive demeanour and goes to the heart of how they conceptualise the *sprezzatura* of comely dissimulation. As Sydney Anglo summarises,

Monte advises 'your approach work should be swift and without any apparent effort (that is what we should term "telegraphing"), so that your opponent never has time to prepare his counter'.[36] The effortless grace of *sprezzatura* serves a tactical purpose. Fencing exercises the relaxed posture and effortless footwork necessary to deceive one's opponent. In this way, dissimulation for Monte happens at the level of footwork and blade mechanics before the first blow is thrown. *Sprezzatura* obscures intention and denies the opponent a tempo of opportunity. While Monte focuses on the psychology of combat, the mind games played by the fencers, his contemporary Manciolino emphasises spectacle.

Manciolino's *Opera nova* (1531) casts fencing as artful performance and provides a valuable point of reference for the kind of fencing in practice during the composition of Castiglione's book. The treatise stresses elegance and gentlemanliness, upright posture with the sword held high, light and energetic footwork, and a spectacle that is a feast for the eyes as well as accomplishes its goal. Manciolino redefines the terms of the fencing game to claim that, in the school, ugly fencing cannot win and elegant fencing cannot lose:

> We shan't therefore call him victor who wins by chance and throws random blows like a brutal peasant; nor shall we call vanquished him who proceeds according to the correct teachings. It is indeed more respected among knowledgeable men to lose with poise than to win erratically and outside of any elegance.[37]

These words echo Federico's contention that deception, in the context of court life, is an occasion for artful and admirable aesthetic creation rather than a mere dishonourable ruse. The fencer's responsibility to his spectators to give a graceful and visually pleasing performance is made clear here.

Where courtiers use 'ornaments' to beautify their courtly performances, Manciolino describes an 'embellishment', or *abellimento*. He uses the refrain 'you will embellish the play' repeatedly in his training *assalti* – long drills with a set of prescribed footwork and bladework used to teach groups of students in the fencing school. Every few actions, fencers break distance and pause to show off their elegant flourishes in relative safety. The embellishment is a sequence of non-threatening actions that involves striking the buckler with the weapon and performing a sequence of footwork from out of distance (too far away to be hit by the adversary in a single movement). Embellishments serve practical purposes: they denote when a new phrase of action is being introduced, train students to recognise when they are safely out of distance, and cue new rhythms of movement. Repeating these patterns encode fencing technique into muscle memory and train appropriate and reflexive responses. Importantly, they also shift students into the realm of aesthetic performance. For Manciolino, fencing becomes an elegant dance rather than a simple, utilitarian aesthetic of machinic efficiency.

Manciolino, like Castiglione, plays with genre as part of his creative enterprise. Manciolino's style is briskly technical in the sections of his treatise that deal with describing the bodily movements of fencing training. However, in the introductions to the six books that make up the treatise, he often allows himself poetic liberties. That Manciolino imagines his system of swordplay in poetic terms should come as no surprise to readers by the time they reach his description of the *assalti*, as his text is sprinkled with assertions such as the one opening Book II describing footwork:

> [J]ust as rich fabrics adorn the charming and lovely Nymphs lightly treading on Mount Menalus or in the Lyceum, so does supple stepping embellish the blows of the dazzling sword. Were our weapon despoiled of its proper steps, it would fall into the darkness of a serene night being orphaned of the stars.[38]

While Manciolino seems to be saying that a technical treatise cannot be written and enjoyed in the same way as the fine subjects of classical poetry, the *assalti* that the 'rough-haired Satyrs conduct toward hunting Nymphs in the pages of poetry books', his repeated and insistent combining of the two formally reflects the movement of the *assalti* themselves in a playful and literary way.[39] At the beginning of each book, he steps out of measure – away from his topic – and performs some sort of ornamentation of the work through an apostrophe about how impossible it is to write a beautiful technical fencing treatise. He then steps back into measure and resumes the technical register of discourse to describe the execution of the actions he teaches. Castiglione's *Book of the Courtier*, like Manciolino's *Opera nova*, draws from common cultural strains around what constitutes a good time. For both, the choice of genre speaks to an interest in interruptive and cooperative inter-relational moments. This emphasis on relational timing adapts itself readily to the stage, which may explain why *The Book of the Courtier* exerted greater influence on Italian vernacular drama and, in turn, English dramatists like Shakespeare than other works treating court life and deception composed in different genres.[40]

Recent years have seen extensive scholarship on the legibility of the body, but there has been far less work done on the body in motion than on the static body. When the static body dominates scholarly conversation, we miss important aspects of Renaissance aesthetics of performance. Specifically, the tempo of courtly interaction opens on to larger questions of time and timeliness. Early modern understandings of time foreground *kairos*, an ethically charged opportune, or appropriate, time.[41] Early moderns taught and learned the skilful seizure of opportune moments via embodied social practices such as fencing. Aretino's skilful dissimulation in the book's opening choice of game foreshadows Castiglione's interest in courtly *virtú* as 'an adversarial and dissimulatory power'.[42] The adversarial nature of this encounter is encapsulated with the logic of feinting transposed to the court of Urbino. A judicious application of various types of deceit is central to Castiglione's perfect courtier, and to ludic enterprises in general. As Saccone notes, both *sprezzatura* and irony are dissimulatory practices essential to courtiership as envisioned in *The Book of the Courtier*. Where authors such as Aretino and Ariosto highlight the negative social consequences of deceitfulness, Castiglione explores the kind of feigning necessary to a courtly context on a playful rather than paranoid register.[43]

Castiglione posits 'time' as a question of identity and literary aesthetic when he describes the tempo, *modo* and *maniera* of the ideal courtier. The word 'tempo' can do so much work for him because it is a robust and expansive definition of time which incorporates embodied, antagonistic interactions. The full range of Castiglione's tempo is indicated by literature's debt to fencing discourse and fencing discourse's literary commitments. Castiglione and his friend Monte take different routes to develop and teach a sense of tempo, but they were united in their assessment of its centrality to values, conduct and poise.

Notes

1. See Albury, *Castiglione's Allegory*; Greene, '*Il Cortegiano* and the Choice of a Game'; Berger, *Absence of Grace*.
2. Burke, *Fortunes of the Courtier*, 34.
3. J. R. Hale cautions readers not to overstate Castiglione's skill and experience as a military leader in 'Castiglione's Military Career' (57). For my purposes it is enough that he cast himself and was described as both soldier and scholar.
4. Castiglione, *Book of the Courtier*, trans. Hoby, 66. Subsequent English translations of Castiglione are also drawn from Hoby, with page numbers given parenthetically in the text.

5. For more on Pietro Monte's life and work, see Forgeng, *Pietro Monte's Collectanea.*

6. The first extant printed Italian book on fencing was Antonio Manciolino's, which was printed in 1531 (though there is some evidence that an earlier, lost version of this book circulated prior to the 1531 printing). The newness of the print medium for fencing treatises may suggest why Castiglione's library tended towards classical sources on combat such as Vegetius's *De Re Militari* rather than contemporary works on fencing. Also, Castiglione spent much of his adult life in courtly contexts with famous fencing masters like Monte and presumably learned much of the art of defence in person. For more on Castiglione's possessions, including his formidable collection of swords and armour, see Rebecchini, 'Pietro Bembo e Baldassarre Castiglione'.

7. This numbering system is still in use in Italian fencing today, but with refinements designed to allow for even more precision in describing the positioning of the body and the sword and their articulation together.

8. Saccone, '*Grazia, Sprezzatura, Affettazione*', 51.

9. For example, see criticism on Castiglione that reflects on performance and self-construction. Burke in his seminal text, *The Fortunes of the Courtier,* calls the book 'an "open" work' that is 'not only ambiguous but deliberately so, in the manner of a play' (37). Lanham similarly argues 'The central self is a skill, instinctive good drama' and asserts that 'Urbino knows no leisure at all, just as self-conscious man knows no leisure in the world. He is either making or unmaking himself' (*Motives of Eloquence*, 156–7). More recently, Berger focuses on behavioural skills and strategies of self-representation in the court, arguing that *The Book of the Courtier* 'depict[s] sprezzatura not only as a representational technology but also as a normative demand: a demand for the performance of exemplary inwardness that's assumed to be inauthentic by the performers no less than by their audiences' (*Absence of Grace*, 4).

10. Burke, *Fortunes of the Courtier*, 31.

11. See Wyatt, *Italian Encounter* for the differences in goals and politics between Hoby's translation, which Ascham praises, and Castiglione's original Italian text.

12. See Wolfe, *Humanism* for an in-depth consideration of courtly dissimulation and 'the collateral, mutually legitimating discourses of courtliness and mechanics' (56).

13. For more on the material conditions of timekeeping in early modern London and on chronographia, the artful depiction of time in rhetoric, see Stern, 'Time for Shakespeare'.

14. See Quinones, *The Renaissance Discovery of Time* for more on this conceptual shift from the perspective of literary history. Michel Foucault engages with the shift in temporal understanding at great length throughout his career, beginning in *The Order of Things*. More recent works that engage with materialist history and the history of ideas in relation to late

medieval and early modern temporal practices include Harris, *Untimely Matter* and Dinshaw, *How Soon is Now?*

15. See Beltrami and Fornara, 'Italian Historical Dictionaries', for a survey of Italian lexicography.

16. As Rudolf Wittkower notes, for Greeks of the classical age, '[t]ime was a series of propitious moments – and as such could be represented in the figure of the god *Kairos*' ('Chance, Time, and Virtue', 313). In contrast, *chronos* refers to a linear and progressive model of time, one that can be incrementalised and segmented.

17. Pallavicini, *La Scherma Illustrata*: 'tutta la Scherma stà sù'l tempo fondata, e chi meglio lo conosce, l'accetta, e titolo di meglio Schermitore asseguisce' (21).

18. Giganti, *Scola, overo, teatro*: 'ma per conoscer il tempo, & la misura, le quali chi non conosce, benche ripara, & benche ferisca, non si può dire di sapere e riparare, e ferire' (4–5).

19. See Pamela Smith, *Body of the Artisan* for more on early modern reconfigurations of knowledge and embodied epistemology, in particular her statement that 'this confluence of theory and practice can also be found in Prince Maurits's study of fencing as a combination of science and art, his reorganization of the army on mathematical principles, and the meticulous record-keeping of his equine breeding program, which recorded the servicing of mares, the birth of their foals, and the foals' characteristics' (164–5).

20. In this sense, Fiore and other early fencing masters follow what Foucault terms an exemplary approach to disciplining the body, where later masters take on a more elementary approach, breaking the body and its movements down to ever more precise movements. For more on the shift from exemplary to elementary methods of teaching, see Foucault's discussion of docile bodies in *Discipline and Punish*, 135–69.

21. Huizinga, *Homo Ludens*, 10.

22. Albury, *Castiglione's Allegory*, 20.

23. Castiglione uses many other activities such as goldsmithing to defend courtly dissimulation. Fencing is the most prominent and the only one also said to be specifically the chief domain of knowledge of a courtier, his 'principal and true profession'. Hoby's list de-emphasises fencing by burying 'to play well at fense upon all kinde of weapons' in the middle of his list, underneath drawing, dancing, singing and playing the lute, and before tennis, hawking and riding.

24. Albury, *Castiglione's Allegory*, 23.

25. Bernardo's analysis of how to make good jokes articulates the place of playful, positive dissimulation in court life. It is 'an honest and comelie kinde of jesting that consisteth in a certain dissimulacion, whan a man speaketh one thinge and privilie meaneth another' (180). For all kinds of jokes from the off-colour to the sarcastic to the flattering, 'the chief matter is to deceive opinion, and to answer otherwise than the hearer loketh for: and (in case the Jest shal have any grace) it must nedes be

seasoned with this deceit, or dissimulacion, or mockinge, or rebukinge, or comparison' (189).

26. See Low, *Manhood and the Duel* on the duel and aristocratic masculinity. For spatial mastery via games, see Bloom, '"My Feet See Better Than My Eyes"'.

27. The French word for 'answer' or 'reply' used in a technical sense in fencing to refer to the attack directed at the opponent immediately following one's own parry is 'riposte'. This term has been conspicuously co-opted to refer to a quick, clever retort. Similarly, in German, the *Vorschlag*, or first strike, was adapted into rhetoric to describe a suggestion or attempt to persuade.

28. 'fiction, n.', *OED Online*, Oxford University Press, September 2015. Web. See definitions 1a, 2 and 3b in particular.

29. The connection between feigning and fiction reaches back to the Latin *fingere* which incorporates both the sense of invention and composition and that of counterfeiting.

30. Vadi, *De Arte Gladiatoria Dimicandi*, 12v, n 1.

31. Giganti, *Scola, overo, teatro*, 23. Translations of Giganti are drawn from Tommaso Leoni's *The Complete Renaissance Swordsman*.

32. Capoferro, *Gran Simulacro dell'Arte e dell'Uso della Scherma*, 29.

33. For more on Gaiani and non-lethal contests, see Terminello, 'Giovanni Battista Gaiani (1619)'.

34. Of Monte, Sydney Anglo writes: 'unlike other masters, he bases his entire system upon feints . . . He likes to keep opponents guessing at all times' (*Martial Arts*, 133).

35. Monte, *Collectanea*, II.i.

36. Anglo, *Martial Arts*, 264.

37. Manciolino, *Opera Nova*, 95. Translations of Manciolino are drawn from Tommaso Leoni's *The Complete Renaissance Swordsman*.

38. Manciolino, *Opera Nova*, 95.

39. Ibid., 109.

40. See Clubb, *Italian Drama* on how Castiglione's humanism influenced Italian vernacular drama of the sixteenth century and ultimately Shakespeare's as well.

41. See Paul, '*Kairos* in Political Philosophy' for a recent account of *kairos* in early modern English political theory and literature.

42. See Wolfe, *Humanism*, 40.

43. Harry Berger argues the opposite in *The Absence of Grace*, saying that the subtext of *Galateo* and *Il Cortegiano* is one of deep paranoia born out of a culture of surveillance, and that readers are not permitted to ignore 'the latent ethical consequence suffered by those who master the technology of sprezzatura and submit to its normative demands' (226). However, I believe that Berger's reading dismisses the animating sense of play at work in *The Book of the Courtier*, regardless of how accurate his insights may be to the political context of court life in general.

Chapter 2

Arden of Faversham: Tempo and Judgement on the English Stage

Introduction

Generations of playwrights found inspiration in Castiglione's *Book of the Courtier*, but they did not need to look to the Continent or even to the long-ago past for compelling sources. They also availed themselves of other, more proximate accounts, such as the 1551 murder of Thomas Arden, which was recorded in Holinshed's *Chronicles of England, Scotland, and Ireland* (1577, 1587). *Arden of Faversham* (1592) enacts the real-life murder of a wealthy landowner by his wife, Alice.[1] The crime was sensational enough to draw an unusually detailed five pages of description and analysis in the *Chronicles*, and this account was then adapted to the stage as England's first domestic drama. The anonymously authored play was likely penned in part by Shakespeare, perhaps as the junior member of a master/apprentice playwrighting pair.[2] In both the *Chronicles* version and the play, a variety of murder conspiracies spin into escalating violence and complexity. Alice plots with her lover, Mosby, to murder her husband, Thomas Arden. They enlist the help of another farmer (Greene), a painter (Clarke), a disloyal servant (Michael) and two ruffians for hire (Black Will and Shakebag). After a number of failed attempts, this large group of conspirators finally manages to murder Arden. Alice forces her maid, Susan, to help with the cover-up, and they are all caught and executed.

The play follows its source text quite closely and incorporates many details, such as the specific love favours Alice and Mosby exchanged. However, in one surprising move, the adaptors add an additional murder attempt right before the final successful ambush in Arden's home over a game of backgammon. Given the repeated and repetitive failures of the previous five assaults, why add one more?

I will argue that the added attack encapsulates the play's engagement with *place*, which in contemporary parlance encompassed aspects of opportunity and time as well as location. The relationship between props, players and audience illuminates the spatially charged, antagonistic timing of the theatre. In *Arden of Faversham*, the objects of the play enact divine agency and act to thwart the intentions of the characters who interact with them. The series of attempts on Arden's life formally follows the class of dissimulatory actions termed 'second intention'. In these attacks, the fencer does not intend to hit on their first attack. Instead, the first movement of the attack works to draw a defensive response. The attack is then renewed until the blow lands. The logic and structure of renewed attacks shed light on the ways in which place and time interact with the material structures of the playhouse.

The renewed attack represents a potent structural tool, but *Arden of Faversham* also more broadly speaks to the ways in which English playwrights understood cognitive processes and drew from other disciplines to represent spatial and temporal dissimulation. As a growing body of scholarship illuminates, a variety of sources beyond classical and medieval dramatic traditions and texts were fundamental to the development of the professional theatre as playwrights experimented with non-verbal ways to communicate important aspects of plot and character. Scholars have extensively explored several of these other disciplines – including dance, tumbling and music – to study the potential offered for embodied communication, but fencing remains underexplored.[3] Fencing, however, is the discipline with the most to offer a study of antagonistic and dissimulatory timing, particularly in terms of how fencing masters wrote about and taught judgement. In the play, as in early modern fencing manuals, the faculty of judgement circulates thematically as a variety of spatial awareness – kinaesthetic reasoning governing one's time and position, the capacity to evaluate intersubjective time and space. However, even while the contributions of legal modes of judgement to the rhetoric of the early commercial theatre have been well documented, judgement as a corporeal and temporal skill has received little attention.[4] Displays of cunning are understood, through the lens of English fencing theory, as attempts to 'gain the place' of the adversary.[5] Through a reading of Silver's tactical advice alongside the botched and successful murder attempts in *Arden of Faversham*, I will articulate the play's engagement with plot as both pace and place.

But would early modern spectators really have read patterns of movement adopted from other disciplines closely enough to infer information about character or action? Research at the intersection of anthropology, historical phenomenology, cognitive science and literary studies suggests that they would have. Early moderns viewed public and private performances via a field of visual practice alternate to our own, as scholars of theatre such as Tribble argue, building on earlier work of anthropologists. For the average citizen in London, acculturation involved developing the ability to analyse fencing phrases as long sequences of non-verbal action. The development of this 'skilled vision' allowed the playgoing public to evaluate and interpret 'inset skill displays' using a common vocabulary.[6] *Arden of Faversham* adapts the shared visual coding of embodied action and takes advantage of the educated attention of its public. With the shift from a readership of the prose *Chronicles* to spectatorship, the play looked to adjacent performances such as fencing matches for models of how to encode non-verbal antagonism and deception. Several moments, such as when the would-be murderers describe a lengthy fight sequence to Alice, hint at the entertainment value in analysing non-verbal sequences of action. This and other aesthetic preferences may not recommend the play to a modern-day audience that has come to expect different forms of plot and exposition. *Arden of Faversham* has been criticised for its repetitiveness – the plot, after all, is a seemingly endless series of murder attempts that grow steadily more violent and spectacular until Alice finally succeeds in stabbing Arden to death. However, the play's narrative structure and use of stage properties demonstrate an important moment in the early commercial theatre's use of props and development of plotlines through violent conflict.

Along with the productive possibilities of the 1590s theatre, the transition from earlier, more religiously centred drama to a secular commercial context raised its own challenges. Playwrights found that they needed to channel the skilled vision of their audiences in new ways as they moved from telling well-known stories such as Noah's Flood or the Visitation of the Shepherds. Audiences were accustomed to being themselves co-opted into various storylines as tavern-goers, feast attendees and other kinds of spectators as dictated by the needs of the pageant or mystery play's plot, but the requirements of the commercial theatre also meant that other cues were needed to orient the audience. Playwrights used the audience's pre-existing knowledge and expectations surrounding timing and movement, as established in the familiar spectacle of fencing prizefights. In the case of *Arden of Faversham*, several moments of bodily conflict work together to produce the spiralling formal effect of the tragedy's plot.

'But give me place and opportunity': Attempting Arden

It hardly seems fair when Susan Mosby is dragged off to be executed with the rest of the perpetrators of Arden's murder at the end of *Arden of Faversham*. Though compelled by her mistress to assist in the cover-up, she is innocent of the planning and execution of the murder itself. As Susan puts it, 'wherefore should I die? I knew not of it till the deed was done' (18.19–20). Susan illustrates the theme of being in the wrong place at the wrong time that runs through the theatrical version of *Arden of Faversham*. While in one sense, as the play's final scenes suggest, the tragedy is a reflection on determining culpability and judgement, human and divine, it ultimately reflects on such prudential matters of placement and timing more than the cautionary morality tale of its source text. The death sentence, meted out to guilty and innocent alike, does not portray a triumphant judicial system: the play leaves the impression of incomplete justice, thwarted providence and bungling criminals. This emphasis reflects the interest of the playgoing public in displays of skill and ineptness. Alice's skill and the ineptness of her co-conspirators reflect the dual, interrelated themes of scheming and place which run throughout the play, united by its deployment of the term 'plot'.

In *Arden of Faversham*, 'plot' joins together the opportunistic and the positional. From the 'plot of ground' Arden greedily acquires to the 'complot' laid by Mosby and Alice, to Franklin's final meditation about the mysteriously blighted grass under Arden's corpse, the 'plot' in which 'Arden lay murdered', the word circulates within the play in key positions (13.33, 14.89, Epilogue 10). Joined with these definitions of place and scheme are the senses of 'plot' as a method of visualising abstract space. 'Plot', or 'platt', referred to the structure of the stage itself as well as to the reduction of objects in space to abstract, two-dimensional representations. As Henry Turner notes, 'plot' at the time of *Arden of Faversham*'s composition was still heavily indebted to its roots in artisanal discourses.[7] Makers of all sorts relied on plots of one kind or another to plan their projects, and playwrights were no exception. Their 'plots' were documents hung backstage that gave players the details of each scene and listed the characters appearing on stage at each juncture. To plot a play is to time it – to determine the play's storyline and the pace at which its action occurs, how events follow one another. *Arden of Faversham*'s plot is unique in its series of amplifying failures which are driven by displays of comic ineptness and slapstick as Alice tries and fails repeatedly to make the tempo (create the opportunity) for Arden's murder.

Many elements of Holinshed's prose account of the murder persist into the dramatic retelling with surprising faithfulness. The alterations made to the sequences of events illuminate how the play was designed to appeal to an audience as a live performance. *Arden of Faversham*'s relationship to its source text adds a valuable dimension to a study of timing on the Elizabethan stage because, as Bakhtin points out, the generic status of a work and its relationship to time are deeply connected.[8] In this sense, the play's 'plot' is a change in sequence and speed of actions as it is adapted from prose history to live performance. With the shift from prose narrative to stage, the timing of Alice's story changes in significant ways. The story moves on the chronotopic spectrum towards an emphasis on space (*topos*) as it is staged, but the spaces of the play are organised by and in service to its timing. While Bakhtin's model of the chronotope is most interested in the imagined spaces and times that play out in novels, it provides a useful frame of reference for drama as well. *Arden*, in particular, is invested in timespace through the connection of good or bad timing to specific places.

Criticism on *Arden of Faversham* has noted the play's intimate engagement with questions of space and place from several different angles. Gina Bloom and Garrett Sullivan take up the places of the play in terms of spatial mastery and the ethics of land ownership. Sullivan argues that land, particularly the 'plot of land' that is the land grant of Faversham Abbey, is 'positioned variously in relationship to intersecting feudal, religious and familial discourse'.[9] Bloom connects the thematic strands of gameplay with those of space and place. She explores the ways in which '*Arden* deploys the topos of gaming to query the fantasy of scopic and gnostic power', how characters navigate spatial and visual limitations.[10] She uses the game of backgammon's formal properties to model contestation for space and spatial mastery both in the Elizabethan theatre and in the themes of the play itself. Indeed, spatial mastery and temporal mastery go hand in hand as locked doors, windowsills, inopportune company and mystical mists work to suppress kairotic moments for the would-be murderers. However, in current scholarship, timing is typically treated separately from the artful manipulation of space, a subject which is actually central to the tragedy.

Arden of Faversham's interest in artful manipulation and inept failure comes to the surface early in the first scene. Arden confides to his friend Franklin that he is sure that his wife is cheating on him with a neighbour of lower social standing: a 'botcher' who '[c]rept into the service of a nobleman' to become 'steward of his house' (1.25–9).

Mosby is a botcher in several ways – the primary sense of the word in this period refers to a mender of broken things, often clothing or shoes. It is likely that Mosby mended clothing based on the taunts Arden hurls at him later in the scene when he takes Mosby's sword away and sends him back to his 'pressing iron' and 'Spanish needle' (1.313). Holinshed writes that Mosby was 'a tailor by occupation, a black swart man, servant to the Lord North' (1062).[11] A botcher is of even lower status than a tailor, so Arden's transformation of Mosby's occupation is a calculated insult. The sense of 'botcher' as 'one who does things bunglingly' is also operant in this period, and Arden's contemptuous use of the term ironically foreshadows the many botched attempts that Mosby makes upon Arden's life. The sword, figured here as a 'Spanish needle', symbolises Mosby and Arden's relationship in their two moments of physical conflict in Scenes 1 and 14. In Scene 1, the sword takes on phallic characteristics, as Arden equates sword ownership to one's social status, and, by extension, appropriate love objects. Arden is allowed by contemporary social codes to have a sword (and its entailed capability to penetrate) while Mosby must be more circumspect about whom he penetrates. Later, Arden's sword allows for the play's most impressive display of physical skill, as Arden and Franklin defend against Mosby and two other attackers. While swords represent staged and skilful cunning late in the play, at this early moment, swords and swordplay are connected with 'botching'.

If Mosby ineptly botches his part in the conspiracy, Alice's continually evolving strategy and her virtuoso rhetorical abilities showcase skill. Alice's skill has drawn comment from scholars such as Richard Helgerson who claims that Alice is the play's 'most brilliant and troubling poet-rhetorician',[12] and Carol LaPerle, who contends that the play 'represents an effective rhetor as capturing the full potential of *kairos* – a moment of rhetorical prowess and control completely dependent on the context of the situation'.[13] Her ability to adapt to continually shifting circumstances is evident in her first sally into murder plotting. She conspires with the painter, Clarke, promising him Susan in marriage in return for an effective poison. Though Clarke offers to paint a poisonous picture, instead the conspirators settle for a more traditional poison administered through soup. Upon tasting it, Arden remarks, 'I am not well: there's something in this broth, / That is not wholesome. Didst thou make it, Alice?' (1.365–6). Alice responds by throwing the broth on the ground and melodramatically crying, 'There's nothing that I do can please your taste. / You were best to say I would have poisoned you' (1.368–9). Arden asks for mithridate, a poison antidote. He is clearly concerned about the nature of his sudden illness. However, despite the obviousness of the attempt, her overwrought response to his question manoeuvres him into placating her: 'Be patient, sweet love; I mistrust not thee' (1.390). Alice, through this probing action, establishes that, even with great provocation, her husband will not become suspicious of her. This realisation emboldens her to set in motion a new plot.

Alice's adaptability is an opportunistic skill that would have been familiar to audience members from watching expert fencers as well as great orators. To generalise, while Italian fencing masters emphasise stealing the adversary's tempo, English fencers think more in terms of taking the place (the positional advantage) of the adversary. For instance, when Silver lists the grounds of fencing (judgement, distance, time and place), he includes two terms for spatial awareness. Silver goes on to elaborate 'Through judgement, you keep your distance, through distance you take your time, through time you safely win or gain the place of your adversary'.[14] To 'win' place resonates with the interest of *Arden of Faversham* throughout in games and gambling. Silver first introduces both 'distance' and 'place' so that he can nuance discussions of position. Where judgement acts as an overarching capacity to mediate different kinds of kinaesthetic reasoning, distance is an intersubjective and dynamic function of the space between self and adversary. Alternately, place trades in the language of opportunity. It refers to gaining the position of advantage or taking away someone else's position of advantage.

Italian sources typically have only one term for relational space in such lists of fencing's fundamentals – measure (*misura*).[15] Silver also uses the term measure later in his treatise. Shortly after Silver defines these four grounds of fencing, he transmutes them into 'four' governors: judgement, measure and the twofold mind. Measure in this sense takes on the role of distance as a way to discuss the intersubjective space between fencer and adversary: 'measure is the better to know how to make your space true to defend yourself, or to offend your enemy'.[16] Place at first seems to fall out of this discussion, but Silver clarifies that he is actually expanding on its work in recognising and exploiting opportunity: 'the third and fourth governors are a twofold mind when you press in on your enemy, for as you have a mind to go forward, so must you have at that instant a mind to fly backward upon any action that shall be offered or done by your adversary'.[17] Mind, in Silver's sense, is a variety of *habitus* rather than an incorporeal cognitive processor. He describes this foundational fencing element as the ability to safely press into your enemy's distance.

Silver uses the 'twofold mind' to describe the state of readiness one must inhabit when one attacks in order to drawn an opponent's reaction, but the world also reminds us of another similar contemporary usage – to have a twofold mind is to be double-minded. Indeed, while in the King James Version it is the double-minded man who is 'unstable in all his ways'. In the Lambeth Bible this distinction belongs to the 'twafalde Mon'.[18] Double-mindedness refers to the negative side of adaptability – the 'double-minded man' is unstable because he exists in a state of continued vacillation. In Alice's case, her double-mindedness gives her the tools to prosecute attacks and turn on a dime. When an attack fails, she is ready to distract her husband by feigning pretended rage and resentment of his unspoken suspicion. The connection between dissimulation and adaptation play out both in common parlance and in more specialised fencing vocabulary.

In Alice's next move to win Arden's place, she enlists the help of the bitter Greene, a farmer disenfranchised by her husband's new land grant. As her strategy evolves, she places herself at more of a remove from the crime, allowing Greene, Shakebag and Black Will to close distance and gain Arden's true place instead. In Black Will and Shakebag's first four attempts – St Paul's bookyard, Arden's London residence, Rainham Downs and the ferry crossing – they are not successful even at coming into measure (striking distance), much less at gaining place. Arden has the sound strategy of defence and retreat throughout. His tactical conservativism makes it difficult to win his place – as Silver explains, the best way to gain place from someone is to wait for them to close the distance between you: 'you can strike or thrust at him at that instant when he has gained you the place by his coming in'.[19] In this formulation it is through the adversary's imperfect coming into measure that allows for the strategy to succeed rather than any technique of one's own. Arden is careful. Since he has the upper hand – his marriage to Alice, his newly enlarged wealth, and his own physical health and strength – he will not expose himself to risk by making the first move to attack, even at great provocation. Ultimately, Alice realises that she must convince him to make a tempo so that she can win his place. Before she does, however, her cutters mount a series of what Silver might term 'doubles' and modern fencing knows as renewed attacks – assaults that fail a first attack only to be immediately transformed into a new attack.

While the *Chronicles* simply records that Black Will and Shakebag miss their chance in the St Paul's bookyard because Arden is surrounded by too many people, in the tragedy the windowsills and shop stalls conspire to create comically inopportune moments. Greene offers to 'lay the platform for [Arden's] death' and is emphatically turned down by Black Will, who exclaims, 'plat me no platforms!' (2.93–4). Black Will exhibits unusual wisdom in his rejection of Green's offer – it seems that the entirety of Green's plan is to have Black Will wait in a crowded area to kill Arden. This plan is abandoned because, unsurprisingly, Arden is not alone. The double meaning of plot/plat here resonates with the play's greater thematic interest in dissimulatory scheming and spatial manipulation. Greene points out Arden and urges Black Will to 'stand close and take you fittest standing, / And at his coming forth speed him' (3.36–7). These lines emphasise the disposition of bodies and space and use the metaphor of speed, a body's movement through space to refer to Arden's murder. This choice of euphemisms ironically employs a temporal metaphor, as Arden's death is comically mistimed and ultimately anything but speedy. As Black Will stands in the doorway of a stall, ready for his ambush, an apprentice decides to shut up the stall to keep thieves at bay during an anticipated crowd: he lets down his window and it 'breaks Black Will's head'. In the furious ensuing exchange between Black Will, who demands 'amends' for his broken head, and the apprentice, who threatens them with prison, Arden and Franklin enter, see the fracas, and ignore it, determining that it is a trick 'Devised to pick men's pockets in the throng' (3.53).

The space of the bookyard and the actants of bookstall, apprentice and crowd take an active role in robbing Black Will and Shakebag of their tempo and in preserving Arden's true place. These exchanges between human and non-human agents show how the lively artefacts of the theatre can enhance or impinge upon a player's performance, often in surprising ways. The bookyard attempt most clearly of all the attacks illustrates how good timing is spatially dependent – the space of the bookyard and the assemblage of bookstall, apprentice and crowd take an active role in creating an akairotic moment. The slapstick comedy generated by this unexpected intervention of the bookstall on one register dramatises the back-and-forth between the dramatic retelling of Arden's murder and its prose narrative, with the books' home defending their territory against the incursions of shady characters with evocative names of 'Will' and 'Shakebag'. On another, it reflects the antagonistic environment of the Elizabethan theatre. Slapstick as a comic technique works towards a flattening of human/non-human relations as the player's body becomes something acted upon by objects. This comic moment's effect is to call our attention to how the stage generates meaning through the arrangements of human and non-human configurations of matter and their means and moments of contact.

In another moment of antagonistic contact with a portal, Black Will and Shakebag again fail in their attempt to close the distance between themselves and Arden. However, while the first attempt used slapstick to enact the windowsill's surprise ambush, in this case the door stands in for the defensive interstitial space between murderers and victim. Shakebag and Black Will arrange with Michael, Arden's traitorous servant, to leave the door to Arden's London residence unlocked overnight. Approaching the entry, Shakebag and Black Will attempt to outdo each other with their courage. Shakebag notes, 'This is the door – but soft, methinks 'tis shut. / The villain Michael hath deceived us' (5.34–5). Black Will leaves his quarrelling with Shakebag to confirm 'Soft, let me see. Shakebag, 'tis shut indeed. / Knock with thy sword; perhaps the knave will hear' (5.36–7). These lines, and the action immediately preceding them, make the door into the focal point of the scene. This prolonged encounter with the entryway manifests the combative logic of the scene and the play as a whole. The door is the pivot around which the audience perception of public and private space moves. The same space is imagined as interior, as Arden locks the door from the inside, and exterior, as Shakebag and Black Will subsequently draw near.

Symbolically, the locked door represents denied opportunity and foreshadows the final murder scene in which Shakebag and Black Will are granted entry into another of Arden's houses. Black Will's suggestion that Shakebag knock with his sword reinforces the element of lively and antagonistic props – the sword transforms into a doorknocker, or, alternately, the door transforms into a buckler shielding Arden. The repeated 'soft' is both an exclamation of surprise and an injunction to move cautiously and quietly. The exclamation draws attention to the tactile and auditory dimensions of the encounter and connotes speed of movement, a redeployment of the temporal in this inopportune space and time. Renewing their attack, Shakebag and Black Will withdraw so that they can corner Michael as he emerges from the house the next day. Michael, by way of reparation, offers his master's itinerary, suggesting Rainham Down as 'A place well-fitting such a stratagem' (7.19). Ultimately, Michael's attempt to lay a platform does not prosper any more than Greene's, as Arden runs into a friend during his trek across the lonely uplands and cannot be ambushed.

When the playwright(s) decided to adapt the prose chronicle to the stage, one of the most significant changes made was to introduce a new murder attempt just before the successful ambush. Given the sheer number of attacks and the level of detail involved in describing each, it is a surprising decision to add one more. After all, what purpose does it serve in moving the plot along? In fact, the added attempt illustrates the play's investments in time, judgement and the relationship among players, props and audience. Instead of having Shakebag and Black Will miss their way and get lost as they attempt to set up an ambush for Arden, a 'mystical mist' develops and hides Arden and his friend Franklin from view on their way to an appointment. In the *Chronicles*, nothing is said about Arden's return trip, but in the play this is the most spectacular of the attacks. It is the only attempt in which Arden fully participates, fighting back against his aggressors. As such, it most clearly offers an example of antagonistic timing.

To close the distance, Alice takes the more extreme measures that her first probing attack has assured her are safe. She provokes her husband directly by kissing Mosby in front of him and Franklin. Her attack represents a particular fencing strategy – the second-intention attack – adapted to the stage to represent an embodied display of cunning. Alice's attack does not depend upon hitting in the first motion but can exploit Arden's reaction to the attack to gain advantage if the initial attack misses. Second intention differs from the *contratempo* strategy we will see in *Titus Andronicus* because *contratempo* lures a counterattack by using a dissimulated failed attack – it relies upon an opponent who wants to attack. Second-intention actions are more suited to the adversary who, like Arden, prefers to defend.[20] Capoferro describes this kind of action in his section on sword and dagger (Fig. 2.1).

In Figure 2.1, Capoferro describes a scenario in which the first attack is successfully parried by the fencer on the left. Immediately, the fencer on the right passes forward with the left leg to strike the opponent in the chest with the dagger instead. Formally, this tactic resonates with the ways in which Arden successfully parries the larger, more obvious attempts on his life – the threat of the sword on his way home – only to be brought down by Alice's dagger in the end. Second-intention actions are appropriate for Alice's rhetorical abilities because they are 'eyes-open' actions, which rely on adaptability in the moment more than making a plan in advance. These actions are distinct from the kind of adaptive feint referenced by Giganti in that the first attack is a real one, not a simulated thrust or menace. The first strike may or may not necessarily fail, and Alice is prepared for either contingency.

Figure 2.1 Ridolfo Capoferro. Second intention. Plate 41, *Gran Simulacro*, 1610. Engraving. Vancouver, Academie Duello.

In their attempt to draw Arden out, Alice and Mosby set off to intercept Arden on his way home, linking arms to taunt him into action. As Mosby jeers at Arden for his 'horns', Franklin declares ''tis time to draw!' Arden and Franklin draw their swords and attack Mosby. Black Will and Shakebag jump into the fray in pretended concern for Mosby. Alice, presumably, stands on the sidelines and watches. The six bodies on stage, five of which engage in the altercation, encapsulate the larger temporal rhythms of the play and reflects the characterisation of the combatants: Alice continually delegates; Arden intimidates Mosby; Franklin, the mediator, comes between Arden and his assailants on the field as in life; and Black Will and Shakebag compete with each other and belittle each other's efforts. With Alice, the audience witnesses the assault and is later given a summary of the action. Alice's frustrated question is 'How missed you of your purpose yesternight?' (14.49). Because she saw the whole fight unfold, it is most likely her question is rhetorical. Regardless, Greene, who did not see the fight, eagerly attempts to fill her in: ''Twas long of Shakebag, that unlucky villain' (14.47). Collaborating, Black Will offers a blow-by-blow playback of the fight in an attempt of his own to 'reimplot' the events and his failures:

BLACK WILL: When [Shakebag] should have locked with both his hilts, he in a bravery flourished over his head. With that comes

Franklin at him lustily and hurts the slave; with that he slinks away. Now his way had been to come in hand and feet, one and two round at his costard. He like a fool bears his swordpoint half a yard out of danger. I lie here for my life [*he takes up a position of defence*] If the devil come and he have no more strength than fence, he shall never beat me from this ward; I'll stand to it. A buckler in a skillful hand is as good as a castle; nay, 'tis better than a sconce, for I have tried it. Mosby, perceiving this [Shakebag's retreat], began to faint. With that comes Arden with his arming-sword and thrust him through the shoulder in a trice. (14.52–64)

Black Will's summary is rife with temporal terms. He accuses Shake-bag of engaging in frivolous movements with the sword, raising it in a flashy and threatening manner over his head rather than rushing in and presenting a threat through circular cuts aimed at the head. Because Shakebag is unable to deprive his adversary of place – advantageous positioning – Shakebag is injured, and his injury frightens Mosby so much that Mosby does not attack. For Black Will, the spatial mis-calculation of raising the sword rather than closing measure is also a timing mistake that causes Shakebag to lose the element of surprise.

If Shakebag's spatial-temporal error is one of misplacing the weapon, Black Will's is on the opposite extreme of placing the weapon but never prosecuting the attack. Black Will, comically oblivious, demonstrates to Alice how he stood, showing off his skilful sword and buckler ward. However, the metaphorical castle his ward forms does different figurative work than he presumably intends. While Black Will wishes to highlight his power and stability by casting him-self as a castle, he really emphasises a castle's complete immobility as he apparently stands still and misses the whole encounter. His role, as assassin, is not to hold off a siege, but instead to press an assault on the keep. The castle and the sconce, as they stand in for the technological unit of skilful hand and buckler, reflect, like the earlier door and knocker, a way of thinking about props in terms of their antagonistic potential. However, where the door and sword-knocker evoke the 'places' (and their positional opportunities) of the home and the street, inside and outside, the hand and buckler bring attention to the skilful interaction of prop and player.

Alice's brief response to this interpretation of events is telling: 'Ay, but I wonder why you both stood still' (14.65). With the marker of agreement, she signals that she, too, understood the logic behind the flurry of action. Like the play's contemporary spectators, Alice can be assumed to have a high degree of visual competency for ana-lysing phrases of action – the explanation heightens the audience's enjoyment rather than filling the character in on vital information. Alice condenses the story down to its real point: neither Mosby nor Black Will moved into measure to attack. In his defence, Black Will offers that he was so stunned by Shakebag's incompetent fencing that he was immobilised: 'Faith, I was so amazed I could not strike' (14.66). Unlike Alice's alert, adaptive waiting, Black Will's variety of waiting is frozen and passive. He is double-minded in the biblical sense of having an unsteady and deceptive character but does not display the adaptability of Silver's twofold mind.

This scene reflects an Elizabethan understanding of time as spatially and ethically charged. In terms of Silver's four grounds of fencing – judgement, distance, time and place – Black Will has judgement but no time – he knows precisely what actions should have been taken, but too late to do anyone any good. Arden, in contrast, has time but no judgement. He is able to wound Mosby but does not understand the larger stakes of the game. Adept at seizing tempo here, Arden fails in the bigger picture of recognising his own vulnerability. Thinking of the assaults of the play in terms of fencing phrases and the antagonistic environment of the playhouse brings into focus the chaotic ending scenes. While Alice is skilful at fencing with human antagonists, when it comes to her interactions with antagonistic objects she falls apart.

'Why, how long shall he live?': Running Out of Time

The stage play's hectic energy features one event tumbling over another. To create the impressively despicable and capable villainess of England's first domestic tragedy, the play made several changes to the story's timeline. The *Chronicles* account, in contrast to the rapid succession of events that marks the tragedy, unfolds in a more orderly manner and over the timeframe of two years. This slower timing leads to a difference in character motivations and sympathies. The chronicler, in foregrounding the longer duration of Mosby and Alice's affair, makes of Thomas Arden an altogether less sympathetic figure. According to Holinshed, Arden allowed the familiarity between Mosby and Alice to continue, not because of his love for his wife and dislike of confrontation, as in the play, but rather because he did not want to 'offend hir, and so loose the benefit which he hoped to gaine at some of hir freends hands in bearing with hir lewdness'.[21] His long-suffering attitude is driven by greed rather than affection – the affair 'continued a good space, before anie practise was begun by them against maister Arden' (1025). Alice, 'at length inflamed in love with Mosbie, and loathing hir husband, wished and after practised the meanes how to hasten his end' (1025).[22] Alice's disgust at her husband's failure as head of household figures at least as importantly as her love for Mosby. The focus is less on Alice's lewdness and more on Arden's delay in setting his household to rights. Because Arden does not act in a timely manner, he is murdered.

Arden's wilful desire to turn a blind eye also features in the stage play, but because the events unfold so quickly it is easier to excuse his negligence, as he does not have time to properly consider the implications of his wife's behaviour. Alice seems to be impetuously hurling herself headlong into vice and murder: in Scene 14, Alice rages that 'these mine eyes, offended with [Arden's] sight, / Shall never close till Arden's be shut up / This night I rose and walked about the chamber / And twice or thrice I thought to have murdered him' (14.81–4). Mosby remonstrates with her for the ill-conceived idea, which Alice turns to her advantage to directly press 'Why, how long shall he live?' (14.86). The shift in dramatic timing works to engage audience sympathies for Arden more than for Alice, but it also shows off Alice's skill as orator and changes the providential narrative at work. For the *Chronicles*, the focus is on God's punishment of Arden for his greed. In the play, while Franklin does speak some final lines condemning Arden's cupidity, the focus ultimately is more on place and opportunity.

The mounting frustration of Arden's murderers accounts for the ludicrously violent murder sequence. Arden is, in turn, strangled with a towel, bludgeoned with a pressing iron and stabbed by Shakebag and Alice. The excess of the murderers' violence gives way to a perplexing lack of direction in covering up the crime. Arden's blood on the floor stubbornly refuses to be washed away, Arden's purse hangs accusatorily on the bedpost, belying Alice's assertion that her husband did not return home, and Michael forgets to dispose of the murder weapon and bloody towel. Given Alice's abilities as a conspirator and smooth-talker, how does she come to be at such a loss in the aftermath of the murder? Though many parts of the play highlight Alice's skilfulness, in the sequence following the murder the blood of her victim and other pieces of evidence take on active roles in condemning her. As in the bookyard scene, at Alice's home the props are at war with the characters represented on stage. The play, in closing, reflects upon this combative relationship in its characterisation of Arden's blood, purse and girdle.

Blood works as an especially expressive prop in *Arden of Faversham* because it is caught in a transitional moment between its status as a favoured symbol of supernatural events and its more mundane expression as evidence to be considered along with other types of evidence. In both models blood assumes agency, the capacity to bear witness. Witnessing in *Arden* still retains the legacy of the judicial duel and trial by ordeal as a shared domain of combat and speech. The legal reasoning surrounding Arden's spilled blood that motivates the final scenes is still closely tied to the play's overall interest in combat. Alice and Susan find the blood stains to be indelible. Susan washes the floor and discovers that the blood 'cleaveth to the ground and will not out' (14.264). In a similar vein, Alice declares 'But with my nails I'll scrape away the blood' only to find '[t]he more I strive the more the blood appears' (14.265–6). When Susan asks for an explanation, Alice gives the stubborn bloodstains their own appetites and desires, saying the blood will not wash out because 'I blush not at my husband's death' (14.267). The rushing of blood to the face in shame and guilt is absent and replaced by Arden's blood stuck stubbornly to hands and floor, a play of resemblance between signs. Here, as in the bookyard scene, props arrange themselves against characters.

Mosby's attempt to hide the blood stains with rushes last only until the Mayor and Franklin arrive and interpret the signs of murder: blood on a knife and hand-towel, footprints in the snow, rushes in the dead man's slipper that match the rushes at the scene of the crime, and blood spots next to Arden's favourite seat. When the Mayor declares, 'See, see! His blood! It is too manifest' (14.399), he articulates how he and Franklin rely on evidence gathered through the senses. Their detective work suggests a nascent empiricism as they read the scene of the crime. However, the blood still assumes the role of witness here, and as such is invested with power and agency. Blood continues to speak as Alice denies the crime. When she is faced with the corpse of her husband, she finds that 'The more I sound his name the more he bleeds. / This blood condemns me, and in gushing forth / Speaks as it falls and asks me why I did it' (16.4–6). As Simon Barker and Hillary Hinds point out, the fresh bleeding of a corpse when confronted with its killer was a popular belief at the time of *Arden*'s performance.[23] Blood's self-evident speech in this moment is interpreted in gushing and falling. This moment of tension, with the body and blood behaving in unexpected ways that undercut Alice's claims of innocence as she speaks them, reflect another experience common to playwrights and players: the disruption of unruly props. The misfiring of a canon during a performance of *Henry VIII*, leading to the destruction of the Globe Theatre, is still several decades in the future, but the anxiety of misbehaving props is evident in this early domestic tragedy.

Mosby's guilt is attested by stage properties that also steal the show from him. When the Mayor asks Mosby why he committed the crime, Franklin intervenes, saying 'Study not for an answer, look not down / His purse and girdle found at thy bed's head / Witness sufficiently thou didst the deed' (16.13–15). Purse and girdle join blood as active witnesses of a crime as the three together work to silence Mosby. While both bleeding corpse and misplaced purse are said to speak for themselves, their interpretations are importantly different. Whereas Alice's interpretation of her husband's bleeding corpse relies on the play of resemblance (between absent blush and streaming blood), the witness of the purse comes from deduction. These scenes in the aftermath of the murder shift from the logic of combat to that of the courtroom. Both strains of evidence-bearing, the empirical and the vibrant material, are present in the prose account and the stage play.[24] The *Chronicles* tends towards the latter, highlighting the role of blood and hair as forensic evidence. The investigators find the evidence and reconstruct what happened, showing it to the criminals to force a confession. The grass of Faversham leaves a supernatural testimony in the form of an imprint of Arden's body visible for two years after his murder (the length of time for which he winked at his wife's lewdness) as a sign to others about how God punishes greed. The prose account highlights the themes of God's judgment and the signs of the murder. With the stage version, questions of theatrical experience and the interactions, often hostile, of spaces and configurations of matter inhabiting them come to the fore.

In the shift from prose history text to performed domestic tragedy, the added attempted murder scene and the changes in the speed of events create a compelling dramatic structure. The play uses the logic of the second-intention action to structure displays of cunning and antagonism. Alice begins with the probing attack of her bowl of broth, and then Shakebag and Black Will launch an attack and several renewed attacks. When Alice realises that simple attacks will not work on her defensive and cautious husband, she lures him into making the first move so that she can 'win' his place as he comes into measure – it is because he feels guilty for striking Mosby that she can counter with her own from the advantage of her own place, the domestic space.

Going to the theatre – an exercise in learning judgement, for good or bad – produces its own kinds of skill-based knowledge, which I have argued is intrinsically temporal. The multiple layers of contestation over time and timeliness in *Arden of Faversham* suggests a version of theatrical time in which human skill at navigating the time of one's adversary (*tempo*) joins with the fortuitous temporality of non-human forces and events in a relationship between player and prop. Opportunity, rather than linear narrative, is the driving force of *Arden of Faversham*'s many 'plots'. In the next chapter, Jonson and Shakespeare will illustrate the ways in which judgement was trained and taught in the theatre, as exercises in judgement continued to be the provenance of both playwright and fencing master into the highly productive decade of the 1590s.

Notes

1. All references to *Arden of Faversham* are taken from the New Mermaids edition. Hereafter, quotations from the play will be cited parenthetically by scene and line numbers.
2. Studies using computational stylometry, stylistic analysis and verbal tests suggest that Shakespeare had some hand in its adaptation. For example, Kinney argues that 'we can be confident in our conclusions: *Arden of Faversham* is a collaboration; Shakespeare was one of the authors; and his part is concentrated in the middle section of the play' (99). See Kinney, 'Authoring *Arden of Faversham*', and Jackson, 'Shakespeare and the Quarrel Scene'.
3. On dance, see Kolsky, *Courts and Courtiers*; on tumbling, see Tribble, *Early Modern Actors*; on music, see van Orden, *Music, Discipline, and Arms*.
4. See Lorna Hutson's *Invention of Suspicion* for her argument that changes in dramatic narrative correspond to developments in legal culture. See also Luke Wilson's *Theaters of Intention* for his argument that the legal tradition's methodology for discussing and assessing intention influenced the depiction of forethought in plays such as *Hamlet*.
5. Silver, *Brief Instructions*, 2.
6. On 'skilled vision', see Grasseni, *Skilled Visions*. On 'inset skill displays' and the 'education of attention', see Tribble, 'Skill'.
7. In many ways, my argument resonates with Henry Turner's work on the spatial arts and how artisanal discourses and the field of geometry came to inform some of the most crucial aspects of stagecraft: the arrangement of action and the impact of its 'spatial disposition' on the 'methods of reasoning' modelled by the play (*English Renaissance Stage*, 23). However, where Turner focuses on the spatial element of plots and plotting, I am interested in both the spatial and the temporal dimensions.
8. Bakhtin's chronotope connects time and space in the literary aesthetic: 'Time, as it were, thickens, takes on flesh, becomes artistically visible;

likewise, space becomes charged and responsive to the movements of time, plot and history' (*Dialogic Imagination*, 84). For Bakhtin, in the literary aesthetic the temporal takes on more importance than the spatial.

9. Sullivan, '"Arden lay murdered in that plot of ground"', 232.
10. Bloom, '"My feet see better than my eyes"', 11.
11. Holinshed, *Chronicles*, 1062
12. Helgerson, *Adulterous Alliances*, 140.
13. LaPerle, 'Rhetorical Situationality', 177.
14. Silver, *Brief Instructions*, 82
15. Sometimes in Italian sources even measure is folded into tempo because tempo encompasses opportunity, broadly defined. Italians may have never developed the technical language around 'place' because they evolved a different terminology for describing positional advantage, which included counterguards, finding the sword, enumerating different kinds of tempo, or moments in which to attack, and more.
16. Silver, *Brief Instructions*, 83.
17. Ibid.
18. 'twofold, adj. (and n.) and adv.' *OED Online*. Oxford University Press.
19. Silver, *Brief Instructions*, 84.
20. Nineteenth- and twentieth-century pedagogy has classified and clarified many aspects of this tactic that are implicit in the contemporary texts. For instance, it differentiates between the renewed attack and the second intention as two instantiations of the same tactic used in slightly different situations. The renewed attack is a class of second-intention actions in which the fencer, having fallen short, replaces the weapon with whatever footwork is necessary to reach the opponent's target. It is used against a passive opponent who parries (with or without a retreat) but does not riposte. Alternately, one is said to be acting in second intention when one lures the other fencer into a parry–riposte sequence. Anticipating the opponent's parry, instead of feinting and not allowing the opponent to deflect the incoming steel, the fencer allows the adversary to deviate the sword. In the aftermath, the fencer is prepared to counter-parry and riposte the adversary's parry and riposte. This action would be used against fencers who will not bite for anything less than a real initial attack. *Arden of Faversham* makes use of both of these varieties of second-intention tactics as well as preliminary probing actions in its sequence of five murder attempts.
21. Holinshed, *Chronicles*, 1024.
22. Ibid. 1025.
23. Barker and Hinds, eds, *The Routledge Anthology of Renaissance Drama*, 111.
24. I use the term 'vibrant material' in Jane Bennett's sense of distributive agency to highlight the ways in which the human and non-human elements of *Arden of Faversham* complicate a traditional subject/object split (Bennett, *Vibrant Matter*).

Chapter 3

Exercises in Judgement

[T]he exercising of weapons . . . gives a perfect judgement.
George Silver, *Paradoxes of Defence*, 2

Introduction

Early modern playgoers loved to see players attempting to make decisions based on unclear evidence; the more obscure the evidence and the higher the personal cost to characters, the more thrilling it was for the audience. The proliferation of courtroom scenes in early modern drama testify to the voyeuristic delight playgoers felt as they watched characters flounder, probing to learn more, acting on imperfect knowledge, and rationalising their verdicts. From Shakespeare's *Merchant of Venice* and *Measure for Measure* to Jonson's *Volpone* and Tourneur's *Atheist's Tragedy*, judges and magistrates provide a source of suspense and entertainment that exceeds their prescribed role of recapitulating plot points and providing an outside perspective on the events of the play. Scenes of judgment continue to captivate audiences even today in reality court shows like *Judge Judy* and countless crime dramas such as the long-lasting *Law and Order*. It is easy to overstate the similarity between these modern-day forms of judgement and those in the early modern theatre, however. The former is indebted to a post-Enlightenment philosophy of judgement while the latter emphasises a subtly different model in which judgement is a type of skill. The skill of judgement speaks to the physicality of decision-making, as understood by early modern playwrights, pedagogues and fencing masters.

Thomas Wilson, the Elizabethan diplomat and judge, uses judgement and skill interchangeably in his *Rule of Reason* (1551): 'Hitherto we have treated of the former parte of logique called in latine *Iuditium*, that is to say, judgment, or skill, to declare the nature of everye worde severallie, to set up the same words in a perfecte sentence, and to knitte them up in argument.'[1] An early Anglo-Norman borrowing from French, the earliest senses of 'judgment' in England are forensic or theological – the judicial decision or the judgment of God.[2] A more general sense of judgement as a faculty of discernment quickly followed. Though aesthetics as 'the science of art' was not yet fully articulated in Shakespeare's day, by the turn of the seventeenth century the field of aesthetics' forerunner, a literary-critical judgement, was central to Jonson's poetics. Soon thereafter followed the more general sense of judgement as a faculty of discernment.[3]

In this skilful sense, judgement prominently features in various disciplines including theology, fencing and rhetoric. Masters of divinity, fencing masters and rhetoricians expended considerable ink on whether judgement is inborn or trained. Like the conventional debate between sword and pen, both extremes are straw-man arguments and the truth lies somewhere in between the poles of the false dichotomy. Instinct, in which judgement has its origins, is less important than the process by which judgement is learned and exercised. Because early moderns understood judgement as an embodied capacity, they sought somatic ways to train it. For instance, in another London gentleman's effort to reform native fencing instruction, George Hale's 1614 pamphlet, *The Private Schoole of Defence*, argued that men should learn to fence for three primary reasons: necessity at home (self-defence), public good abroad (war) and exercise. Hale's explanation of the last reason captures a historical sensibility regarding disciplines of mind and body: '[N]o other recreation carries so generall imployment both of body and minde, as this doth: for here the Feete labour equally with the Hands, the Eye and the Judgement walke together.'[4] Perception and decision are not simply sequential or acting in concert, but they are mutually engaged in a quotidian physical activity (walking) with implications of motion, speed and direction. In fact, Hale grounds his entire definition of his subject matter in terms of judgement:

> [T]he Science of Defence is an Art Geometricall, wherewith the body is guarded with a single or double weapon from wrong of the Offender, or the greatest disadvantage of his Offence. The Parts thereto required are Strength and Judgement. Under Strength are comprehendeth swiftnesse of motion and quicknesse of eye . . . Under judgement falls the considerations of Time, Place, and Distance.[5]

Judgement, in Hale's (and, I will argue, Jonson and Shakespeare's) sense, is a specifically corporeal and temporal skill. It is corporeal because, trained via physical exercise as embodied knowledge, judgement functions as more than an abstract, conceptual activity. Judgement is temporal because it operates as a skill of timing as well as one of discerning.[6] Bringing the *when* to the fore allows for a clear view of judgement's role as an ongoing process of sorting and discerning among particularities.[7] More than a verdict or an innate characteristic of critic or magistrate, judgement is an ability trained through a variety of linguistic and non-linguistic means.

This chapter considers two comedies that conclude with scenes of legal judgment and that deal with judgement as an embodied, cognitive process throughout. Both plays represent earlier-career successes building upon the structural blueprints of the comedies familiar to Elizabethan schoolboys who would have grown up on Plautus and Terence. Unlike the other plays explored in this book, *The Comedy of Errors* and *Every Man in His Humour* are not remarkable for their experimental plot structures, but for their illumination of how the theatrical staging of slapstick violence creates certain kinds of knowledge.[8] These types of knowledge – subjective, temporal, aesthetic – show how the term 'judgement' circulates specifically via the sense of touch. Shakespeare's beating scenes in *The Comedy of Errors* showcase antagonistic timing and judgement. In Jonson's *Every Man in His Humour*, this imbrication of timing and judgement is manifested via sword brawls. Jonson and Shakespeare both use the threat or the realisation of violent contact extensively to evoke laughter, build suspense or reveal important plot and character information. Both comedies are rife with comic slapstick scenes where violent touch is used to propagate self-knowledge and the plot's development, but the characters' level of self-awareness differ substantially. That is, Jonson's humours characters do not know themselves – Bobadil is unaware he is a blowhard *miles gloriosus*, while Squire Downright is similarly ignorant of himself as an irascible and straightforward country gentleman type. In contrast, in Shakespeare's early city comedy, the characters know who they are, but others do not. Antipholus of Syracuse is bewildered when he is showered with gifts and attention meant for Antipholus of Ephesus. Antagonistic touch, subjectivity and judgement, coming together as they do in these two plays, raise questions such as 'What kind of knowledge is produced through touch?' and 'What way of knowing is it to touch and be touched?' in the context of the early modern theatre. While these questions have been addressed by scholarship on the epistemology of touch, attention has primarily focused on cooperative models, where intersubjectivity is implicitly or explicitly linked to synergy. Fencing demonstrates how adversarial and inter-ruptive rhythms of words and bodies work to create these effects across individuals and their environments.

Touch becomes especially important in terms of aesthetic judge-ment because of its relationship to taste. Jonson and Shakespeare treat taste as a metaphor for the capacity to judge drama. While the evolution of the meaning of taste in an aesthetic register has lost much of its early modern connection to the bodily sense, in the early modern period taste is decidedly corporeal and often cast in contem-porary medical treatises as a subspecies of touch. Early modern med-ical theory, which drew on Aristotelian teaching, equated the two terms. As Carla Mazzio points out, 'the ideas and the vocabularies of taste and touch were deeply entwined in anatomical theories of [the Renaissance], and this partnership extended into the domain of met-aphor in the realms of music, rhetoric, and theology'.[9] In fact, Shake-speare and Jonson's contemporary, Thomas Tomkins, draws from Plato's *Gorgias* in his 1607 *Lingua, or the Combat of the Tongue and the five Senses for Superiority*, where 'cookery (as opposed to medicine) is established as an art of deception and explicitly aligned with the deceptive powers of rhetoric'.[10] Shakespeare capitalises on metaphors of taste and touch, with violent words seasoning the dis-appointing meals of marital harmony in *Comedy of Errors*. These connections between deception and cookery also suggest why Jonson imagines his plays as banquets, with different dishes to tempt dif-ferent palates. Jonson certainly thought of deception in connection with his art, as he defines a poet as a 'maker, or a feigner' and argues that 'he is called a poet, not he which writeth in measure only, but that feigneth and formeth a fable, and writes things like the truth'. The activities of cooking and eating in this deceptive Platonic register capture an important aspect of Jonson's literary theory in its antago-nistic corporeality.

The body's central role in Shakespeare's poetics is well-established, but critical history around Jonson's writings is more divided. While more recently Jonson scholars have attuned to Jonson's gleeful cor-poreality, earlier critics stressed his relationship to Stoic philosophy and considered Jonson's goal to be to elevate the ideal and critique the material. As Ross Knecht observes, Jonson's continual blurring of the roles of satirist and object of satire throughout his career speaks to the body's place in his poetics.[11] That is, it raises the question of whether Jonson envisions the body as essentially base, only discuss-ing its sensations in order to correct and critique, or whether Jonson, in his vivid descriptions of bodies and bodily functions, depicts the body as more than an object of censure. If the latter, others have argued, the division between word and flesh is not absolute. Instead, Jonson's 'linguistic practice' could be seen as 'partaking in, rather than distancing itself from, the life of the flesh'.[12] In what follows, I will explore the ways in which the bodily sense of touch leads to knowledge around the self and around the temporal skill of judgement.

The epistemology of touch has been approached in a variety of promising ways, from the perspective of post-structuralist philosophy in Jean-Luc Nancy's *Noli me tangere* to David Linden's recent work in neuroscience *Touch: The Science of Hand, Heart, and Mind*. The inherently relational nature of touch provides a valuable framework for thinking about how knowledge is generated and transmitted in a post-humanist context invested in the porosity of boundaries. Rather than expanding the current discourse that addresses questions of touching and being touched largely through cooperative models of contact, fencing theory and practice illuminates how the adversarial and interruptive rhythms of words and bodies create effects across individuals and their environments. These adversarial relations, intersubjective antagonism, in early modern theatre, evoke Daniel Heller-Roazen's meditation on what it would mean for touch to be 'the root of thinking and for thinking, in turn, to be the most elevated form of a kind of touch'.[13] However, where he ends *The Inner Touch* with a meditation on Aristotle's theory of friendship, describing the sense of being alive and taking joy in existence as a kind of touch transferrable to others through the joint perception of friendship, this chapter deals in different kinds of knowing touches: the episodes of corrective, diagnostic or violent touch that animate *The Comedy of Errors* and *Every Man in His Humour*. These scenes show that the ways in which the early modern theatre conceptualises intersubjective antagonism is a valuable supplement to current work focusing on empathy and cooperation in joint activities and their embodied knowledges.

Twins in a Pinch: Touch, Time and Teaching

The Comedy of Errors, like *Arden of Faversham*, explores the dramatic potential of slapstick humour. Its plot structure, in contrast, is more traditional and recognisable to those educated in the late Tudor grammar school, using source material and a five-act structure borrowed from Plautus's *Menaechmi*. *The Comedy of Errors* begins in tragedy, as a hapless elderly man (Egeon) recounts his tragic story to the Duke Solinus, the ruler of Ephesus. Solinus presides as judge over Egeon because Egeon unwittingly broke a travel ban on visitors from Syracuse. Solinus, while rigidly enforcing this rule, is nonetheless moved by Egeon's tale of his search for his missing son and wife. According to Egeon, he and his wife were separated in a shipwreck many years ago, along with their twin sons and the twin servants they adopted to serve their sons. Egeon has been searching for his lost son and wife since. Grieving for the loss, one set of twins adopts the same name as the other set of twins – leading to an Antipholus of Ephesus, an Antipholus of Syracuse, a Dromio of Ephesus and a Dromio of Syracuse. Solinus gives Egeon one day to pay a steep fine but adds that, if the fine remains unpaid, then Egeon will be executed, regardless of Solinus's personal sympathy. Unbeknown to Egeon, his missing son, servant and wife have ended up in Ephesus. The comedy shares much with Plautus's *Menaechmi*. Both feature twins with interchangeable identities and roles. Both use farce and slapstick to create an atmosphere of hectic trading, irony and misunderstandings. Shakespeare exponentially complicates the confusion of mistaken identities by adding a second set of twins, the Dromio servants.

Recognition – society's of the individual, the individual's of the self – is a key theme of Shakespeare's early comedy. The foreign twins, Antipholus and Dromio of Syracuse, wander happily around Ephesus as they are treated with the respect afforded to their Ephesian twins by the townspeople who mistake them for their brothers. They are given gold chains, affectionately hosted family meals by Antipholus of Ephesus's wife Adriana and sister-in-law Luciana, and other tokens of what they take for extreme and somewhat eerie hospitality. In contrast, the goldsmith treats the rightful Dromio and Antipholus of Ephesus as mad thieves because Antipholus refuses to pay for the gold chain that his twin mistook as a gift. Antipholus is further embarrassed by being denied entry into the feast prepared by his wife Adriana, who has locked the doors as she thinks her husband is secure inside. When the wrong Antipholus tells Adriana he does not know her, she looks for medical help to correct his seeming madness. Adriana contacts Pinch, a character variously referred to as a doctor, a cleric and a schoolmaster, to treat her mad husband, who has apparently entirely forgotten her and their life in Ephesus. In the end, all is reconciled as the characters congregate at a nearby abbey where the Abbess reveals she is the Antipholus twins' long-lost mother and the brothers meet each other. Solinus presides but does very little judging, except to comment on the characters' probable madness and to ask questions. After all is resolved, they remove to Solinus's house for a feast. Throughout, scenes of corrective, diagnostic or violent touch illuminate the theme of recognition by revealing the play's theory of knowledge and its adversarial model of subjectivity. Two moments are particularly noteworthy: an interaction between Pinch and Antipholus of Ephesus in which the medico-pedagogue attempts to take Antipholus's pulse, and a complaint from Dromio of Ephesus in which he likens himself to a ball punted between his master and mistress.

In the penultimate act of *The Comedy of Errors*, the schoolmaster-turned-leech appears to diagnose and treat the seeming madness of Antipholus of Syracuse. His name, 'Pinch', appropriately gathers together associations of the sensory organ of touch, skin, in terms of pain, malicious and/or erotic touch, and juvenile petty cruelty. This pleat of meaning and flesh reflects the logic of the play: what seems smooth and unified to the characters (their own singular identity) is pulled up sharply with the creation of a ridge of flesh that now has two sides, the doubling of the two sets of twins. The touch of the pinch serves as a figure for the play's engagement in the contexts of the schoolroom and the bedroom as well as for the characters' hyper-managed and organised senses of time that nevertheless melt down when they are squeezed up against the temporal schemas of other characters. Personal identity is collected and dispersed by the pleasure and pain of a schoolroom-style violence and erotics. Literal human embodiment, but also the figurative embodiment of Time on stage, shows the ways in which temporal cycles and directionality are posited and thwarted in the comedy. Ultimately, temporal and subjective knowledge are caught up together, both mediated by the sense of touch.

Subjective Knowledge: 'I am an ass indeed'

The Comedy of Errors' engagement with identity has long been of interest to critics, but more recently the perspective of cognitive science in sensory experience and subjectivity has been brought to bear on the play's representations of doubles and selves. For Mary Crane, the spatial configurations of homes, bodies and theatres act as 'containers for different forms of subjective interiority', with alienation and integration both representing possible trajectories for the self.[14] Touch produces subjective knowledge in her framework of cognitive theory because cognitive theory uses touch and tangible experiences perceived inside and outside the body to create an integrated perception of embodiment. Carla Mazzio, too, analyses the relationship between touch and epistemology in English Renaissance drama.[15] For her, touch is uniquely situated to trouble traditional worldviews and categories of knowledge because the haptic sense crosses boundaries and resists categorisation. She argues that the rhetorical deployment of 'touch' in all its metaphorical valences destabilises our ways of knowing and organising the world. In Mazzio's framework, the violent touch such as the mortal *touche* of Hamlet and Laertes's fencing match, ultimately closes down meaning: when touch moves from the metaphorical to the literal through the realisation of tangible blows, its destabilising properties are reduced into a single punctual act. That is, for Mazzio, while a literal blow occurs at a singular moment in time, the metaphor of touch is mobile and multifaceted. The implications for *The Comedy of Errors* are that touch moves along a continuum from linguistic to corporeal violence in which the corporeal shuts down linguistic possibilities. Where Crane argues for a self realised by its containment in spaces and Mazzio argues that the epistemological complexity of touch is contained when it is materialised in the form of hurt, attending to the more sportive mode of physical contact illuminates the ways in which Shakespeare uses the painful touch to create new associations and metaphorical resonances in *The Comedy of Errors*.

Though the importance of hands and subjective knowledge in this play has been noted, as of yet the play's violent touches have yet to be considered in the context of knowledge creation. For instance, Raphael Lyne's recent work on mirror neurons focuses on touch, knowledge and experimentation. Taking one example, he describes the final handclasp between the Dromio twins as creating and disseminating affective knowledge among characters and between the players and the audience. Indeed, feeling and knowledge generation might at first seem to be most comfortably aligned with the affectionate gesture of the final scene. However, the beating scenes are also explicitly tied to the mission of knowledge generation through the metaphorics of pedagogy and learning. Floggings are used in the schoolroom as a technology to enhance student memory. In *The Comedy of Errors*, any linear progression of pedagogy, building on remembered knowledge with new knowledge, is frustrated because the students are continually substituted for each other. One Dromio is sent out with money to secure lodgings, the other innocently wanders by immediately after and denies all knowledge of the transaction. The subsequent beating will not help him stay on task when the task is not actually his own. Consequently, rather than reinforcing memories the beatings convey the false reality to each Dromio because they are being punished for an action they did not do and cannot remember, which directly thwarts Pinch's later intent to enhance their memory.

Feeling and striking are humorously conflated and related to experiential knowledge, though it is important not to confuse 'pain' with 'touch' and so lose the specificity of each. Admittedly, the act of flogging and the sense of touch are not equivalent, yet *The Comedy of Errors* asks the audience to think of them in the same way. For example, in Act 4 Pinch, the play's medico-pedagogue, ministers to the unwilling Ephesian Antipholus, illuminating the convergence of schoolroom discipline, diagnosis, touch and temporality in this telling exchange:

> PINCH: Give me your hand, and let me feel your pulse.
> ANTIPHOLUS OF EPHESUS: There is my hand, and let it feel your ear.
> (4.4.47–8)

Antipholus imitates Pinch's medical language, using 'feel' as a way to discover and investigate. By feeling Antipholus's wrist, Pinch expects to be able to diagnose Antipholus's malady through an evaluation of the tempo of the pulse. Antipholus, in a different kind of feeling, instead strikes Pinch, 'giving' his hand to Pinch in a different way than the schoolmaster/doctor intended. The humour is further heightened by the hand being given its own detached agency, through the use of the third person (let 'it' feel, not let 'me' feel) because Antipholus, for comic effect, verbally distances himself from an act that he clearly does not intend to disavow. The moment represents a resistance to a type of knowledge-gathering by self-important but deluded medical dabblers. Pinch, by observing Antipholus's bodily signs, generalises and de-individualises him by labelling him as mad and prescribing a general, set course of treatment. In fact, this treatment is radically levelling because it is also prescribed for Dromio when Pinch orders that they together should be 'bound and laid in some dark room' (4.4.89). Antipholus's more experiential and particular form of knowledge, generated by striking, is substituted, with the aggressive touch opposed to the medical touch.

Pinch's name is laden with rich associations in the period, from the narrow part of a bow to the folding together of layers of skin in a painful, sudden grasp between fingers. Pinching, a violent touch, is mostly often found in the schoolroom as children torment each other with petty, though relatively harmless, acts of violence. The connection between skin, the schoolroom and pain in this scene recalls earlier moments in the play where its engagement with the realm of pedagogy is not limited to its schoolmaster, but extends to the other relationships among characters as well. Consider an early servant beating in the play, the second of five. Dromio of Ephesus compares himself to a ball kicked between his master and his mistress. When he is beaten, he asks:

> Am I so round with you as you with me,
> That like a football you do spurn me thus?
> You spurn me hence, and he will spurn me hither
> If I last in this service, you must case me in leather.   (2.1.81–4)

Dromio transforms his beating at Adriana's hands into a moment of identification with the football, collateral damage in the game between her and her husband. The football is made of dried skin – an object made to be kicked out of a formerly sensing material that has lost its sensitivity. This imagery resonates with the play's repeated ass imagery in several ways. The deadened skin of the leather reminds us of the donkey's loss of sensitivity through beatings, of its hardened hide. Other equine associations are at work as well – the root for the thrice-repeated verb is the same as the noun, 'spur'. The word 'spurn' is in transition during this period. Its literal meaning, 'to strike against something with the foot' or 'to kick', dates back to around the turn of the first millennium. A more figurative usage evolves alongside it and has overtaken it in modern parlance: 'To reject with contempt or disdain; to treat contemptuously; to scorn or despise.' That is, where spurning today involves a turning away from in rejection, spurning in Shakespeare's day could mean either this tactile driving on through techniques of managed pain (spurring) or a rejection. The football neatly captures both associations, as Dromio is driven away from one master, motivated by pain, to be punted back by the other master.

Just as the literal props in *Arden of Faversham* assume agency, in *The Comedy of Errors* Dromio controls the comedy of the scene by linguistically transforming himself into a metaphorical prop. Dromio's identification with the football across the boundaries of human subjectivity operates according to the logic of negative human exceptionalism that Laurie Shannon explores in her work on *King Lear*. Shannon argues when humankind becomes more beast-like it is through a process of 'subtraction and weakness'.[16] In this comic mode, what is imagined to be subtracted by Dromio is his very vulnerability to blows and kicks. Dromio of Ephesus asks to be covered in a second, more effective skin. Like Adam and Eve divinely clothed in animal skins, Dromio desires 'some beastly addition to perfect a shortfall in the terms of human embodiment'.[17] However, unlike *King Lear*, the tragedy Shannon principally draws on for her analysis, the football analogy in *The Comedy of Errors* shows us a less ponderous and morally weighty version of human negative exceptionalism. Cast in terms of a game, Dromio's complaint about his beating playfully figures Adriana and Antipholus as the school-children who compete.[18]

Through his identification with a ball, Dromio projects a different potential subjectivity created through touch. He reasserts performative control over the situation by drawing the football conceit from the blows. His comic responses shift audience attention from his masters to himself and narrative of the events. This moment shows an opposite movement from what Mazzio describes in her analysis of *Hamlet*. Mazzio argues that, in the tragedy, the multiple associations of being 'touched' give way to the single, punctual and mortal touch of the fencing match. In this scene of *The Comedy of Errors*, a beating with single, punctual blows gives rise to an intersubjective identification made via the sense of touch rather than collapsing and reducing the linguistic register to the blow.

Though the obvious class dimensions in *The Comedy of Errors* should not be glossed over, the Dromio twins, with their rhetorical performances and jokes about beatings, do more than evoke the stock saucy servant archetype. They also reflect the popular grammar schoolroom laments of Elizabethan London's schoolboys, with their football games and the comic brutality of their masters. This identification with education reinforces the theme of dispersed subjectivity that the Dromio twins enact. As Lynn Enterline argues, 'the grammar school's theatrical demand for mimicry performed in public under the threat of punishment' does not work to reify a singular, stable subject, but rather to produce a subject who expresses rhetorical capability through continual displacement.[19] Part of the Dromios' humour is achieved through identifications with objects and animals. These identifications serve to displace subjectivity in response to the schoolroom's demands for theatrical performance in practices of *actio* and *imitatio*.

Thus far, I have described the pinch's associations with pain, but the play's touches are erotically charged as well. From the perspective of the schoolroom, the erotics of the beatings similarly emerge at the intersection of 'rhetoric, pain, pleasure, and power'.[20] The connection between these elements is made explicit when Luciana tells Dromio of Syracuse that he is an ass. He responds in an aside to Antipholus of Syracuse:

> 'Tis true, she rides me, and I long for grass.
> 'Tis so, I am an ass; else it could never be
> But I should know her as well as she knows me.   (2.2.200–2)

Though his explicit meaning is to wonder at this stranger giving him commands, to express confusion over how Luciana can know him without him knowing her, the controlling verbs of riding and knowing are sexually charged. While the schoolroom is only specifically invoked through the profession of Pinch, its logic of pleasure is at work in the interactions between the Dromios and those in power over them. The Dromios take pleasure in producing rhetoric from the pain inflicted on them by the power of their masters and mistresses.

The play's ass rhetoric is echoed later in the play and applied to Dromio of Ephesus. Their acceptance of the title and the rhetorical use they make of it creates a mirroring effect. The Ephesian Dromio's meditation also speaks to the themes of embodiment and cognition the play engages:

> ANTIPHOLUS OF EPHESUS: Thou whoreson, senseless villain!
> DROMIO OF EPHESUS: I would I were senseless, sir, that I might not feel your blows.
> ANTIPHOLUS OF EPHESUS: Thou art sensible in nothing but in blows, and so is an ass
> DROMIO OF EPHESUS: I am an ass indeed. You may prove it by my long ears. I have served him from the hour of my nativity to this instant, and have nothing at his hands for my service but blows.
> (4.4.23–30)

Senselessness and sensibility suggest in these lines a working together of cognition and feeling. Antipholus invokes the 'senseless' in its intellectual dimension, castigating his servant for insolence and stupidity. Dromio, as usual, comically brings out unintended associations with the word, wishing that he were indeed senseless but, on a bodily register, unable to feel pain. Antipholus reuses the word, this time with both connotations in play – sensible as responsive, receptive and teachable, and sensible as bodily feeling. 'Sensible' in these lines brings out the difficulty of separating embodied, experiential knowledge from seemingly abstract and theoretical knowledge. As

Elizabeth Harvey notes in *Sensible Flesh*, Lucretius's emphasis on sensation as the basis for all knowledge brings together epistemology and perception in the skin's work of mediating between the subject's body and the world.[21] The slipperiness of this divide resonates both in terms of a materialist view of the cosmos, and, as Lyne points out, in twenty-first century cognitive science research on mirror neurons.[22] Ultimately, touch provides the conditions for knowledge generation. Tangible blows themselves are seized by the Dromios in order to identify across the boundaries of the human.

Temporal Knowledge: 'A time for all things'

Temporal knowledge, as well as subjective knowledge, is a key concern of *The Comedy of Errors*. But what does temporal knowledge mean in the context of the Elizabethan playhouse? What kinds of knowledge about time can one have, and how can this knowledge be taught? As Matthew Wagner argues in *Shakespeare, Theatre, and Time*, in early modernity there is a rising interest in methods of mastering and measuring time. Personal clocks and watches bring time down to an individual level in a way that is unprecedented. It is perhaps this temporal knowledge we are most familiar with today. Indeed, entire fields of study such as human factors and ergonomics involve helping create the optimally efficient movements and procedures that squeeze every bit of potential productivity out of each minute. However, equally (or even more) important to early moderns was the mastery of time represented by a grasp of *kairos*. While today timing tends to be emphasised more for athletics, music and dance than as part of a core curriculum, for the Elizabethans the rigorous training of timing was a part of daily life in grammar school rhetoric classes. Having good timing, knowing the opportune moment to act, and situating oneself appropriately in life for one's age was a major concern for the Greeks and for their eager imitators, the Elizabethan humanists.[23] *Kairos* involves not just passive waiting for an appropriate moment to come, but actively making an opening for oneself to exploit. The term occurs in classical rhetoric, and the concept would have also been encountered in the fencing training practices of the period that made up an important part of the life of (mostly) men in Shakespeare's time.

The second form of temporal knowledge, timing, is at least as important in *The Comedy of Errors* as the market-driven optimisation of each minute. The staccato back-and-forth rhythms of dialogue, especially between the Dromios and their masters and mistress, make the audience conscious of the tempo of their debates. The Dromios are shown to be master manipulators of timing, as they continually seize the comic opportunities opened to them by their straight (wo)men throughout the play. Flatfooted use of dead metaphor and cliché by Adriana, Antipholus and Luciana continually gets taken up, refashioned and redeployed into new humorous images that show off the Dromios' verbal skill. Even though the Dromio twins excel at rhetorical timing, Antipholus of Syracuse tries to teach Dromio of Syracuse that very skill through a beating. In what follows, we see the comic irony of a stern schoolmaster who is not, in fact, as in control of the lesson he teaches or the situation he is in as he might think.

In the exchange between Dromio and Antipholus of Syracuse, the touch of the beating and the erotic touch come together to teach good timing or to undermine time's trajectory. Beatings are designed to teach timeliness, as we learn from Antipholus of Syracuse when he beats Dromio of Syracuse for what he considers to be ill-timed humour regarding the (supposed) loss of a thousand marks. He demands, 'learn to jest in good time. / There's a time for all things' (2.2.63–4). In the playful exchange that follows, Dromio contests his master's platitude, using the material presence of Time, depicted as a bald man:

> DROMIO OF SYRACUSE: I durst have denied that [there is a time for everything] before you were so choleric.
> ANTIPHOLUS OF SYRACUSE: By what rule, sir?
> DROMIO OF SYRACUSE: Marry, sir, by a rule as plain as the plain bald pate of Father Time himself.
> ANTIPHOLUS OF SYRACUSE: Let's hear it.
> DROMIO OF SYRACUSE: There's no time for a man to recover his hair that grows bald by nature.   (2.2.65–72)

As Wagner suggests, Time develops 'definable embodiments in the daily and theatrical life' of Shakespearean England.[24] Bearded and winged, 'Time in Shakespeare often inhabits a codified and widely recognizable body'.[25] In this sense, Dromio of Syracuse's words not only appeal to an abstract metaphor for Time, but also in fact conjure up a specific, bodily image. Representations of Time often depict a bearded man with long hair, with or without the top of the head being bald.[26] Father Time's baldness also reminds us of another famous allegorical figure's hair loss, as Antipholus of Syracuse insists on timeliness in the lines prior to this moment. The proverbial baldness of

Fortune behind, in reference to grabbing the entity by the forelock and not allowing the timely moment to pass, is conflated with the cyclical passing of time, ageing from young to old and losing hair.

While Antipholus attempts to teach Dromio good timing by beating him, and Dromio evokes timing as a grasping touch, it is the erotic touch that has the potential to interrupt and subvert linear time. As their exchange continues, Dromio brings up syphilis as a fast track towards hair loss – the embodiment of Time ultimately allows for its embawdiment:

> ANTIPHOLUS OF SYRACUSE: Why, but there's many a man with more hair than wit.
> DROMIO OF SYRACUSE: Not a man of those but he hath the wit to lose his hair.
> ANTIPHOLUS OF SYRACUSE: Why, thou didst conclude hairy men plain dealers, without wit.
> DROMIO OF SYRACUSE: The plainer dealer, the sooner lost. Yet he loses it in a kind of jollity.   (2.2.82–9)

Though men go bald 'by nature', venereal disease also plays a part in the process, turning young men bald and confusing a linear passage of time and natural pattern of hair loss. While the baldness of Fortune behind proverbially stands as an admonition to seize opportunities in a timely manner, some opportunities, when seized, produce unwanted effects. For Dromio, worms may try virginity, but venereal disease tries concupiscence. Dromio's anti-*carpe diem* joke highlights the interconnections of touch and temporality in the play. While lineage and generation figure as the household-building positive consequences of the erotic touch, Dromio here is equally concerned with the capacity of touch to short-circuit the linear workings of time. Beatings figure pedagogically as memory aids in the schoolroom, but latent within the schoolroom's touch is the erotic touch that we see here brought to bear on processes of experiential learning.

Like his brother, Dromio of Ephesus connects beatings to time and then materialises that time on stage. Where Dromio of Syracuse calls to mind the literal embodiment of Time/Fortune as an allegorical character, Dromio of Ephesus conflates the striking hands of his master with the striking hands of the clock.[27] He argues that the blows actually work to thwart comprehension:

> ADRIANA: Say, is your tardy master now at hand?
> DROMIO OF EPHESUS: Nay, he's at two hands with me, and that my two ears can witness.

> ADRIANA: Say, didst thou speak with him? Know'st thou his mind?
> DROMIO: I? Ay, he told his mind upon my ear. Beshrew his hand. I could scarce understand it.
> LUCIANA: Spake he so doubtfully thou couldst not feel his meaning?
> DROMIO: Nay he struck so plainly I could too well feel his blows, and withal so doubtfully that I could scarce understand them.　(2.1.44–53)

When Dromio of Ephesus returns to Adriana after unsuccessfully attempting to persuade Antipholus of Syracuse to come back to the house for lunch, he gleefully spins out a series of puns to finally recreate the scene for Adriana and Luciana. Adriana uses the dead metaphor 'at hand', which Dromio then takes up, literalises and redeploys in a more intentional metaphorical register. Antipholus's hands become the hands of the clock and the clapper of the bell, and Dromio substitutes himself for the bell. Dromio's pun that Antipholus 'tolled/told' his mind creates a double meaning that confuses aural and tactile communication. Luciana's choice of verb, 'feel', in her attempt to clarify Dromio's meaning continues the indeterminacy of the two modes of apprehension. Dromio's response suggests an excess of stimulation, which leads to the inability to understand the lesson – a net loss in learning. With the erotics of schoolroom encounters emphasised, as we have seen, the beatings between Antipholus and Dromio takes on an underexplored sexual dimension. When Dromio casts Antipholus as the quick-tempered schoolmaster and himself as the beaten pupil, he evokes the phallic associations with the teacher's rod so commonly used in poetry from and about the schoolroom.[28]

Part of the humour of *The Comedy of Errors* comes from the incompetence of the Antipholus twins and Adriana as schoolmasters. They attempt to teach lessons to the Dromios via blows, but their lessons are comically ineffective. The Dromios are irrepressible, and they are also the wrong Dromios. Their masters are slow on the uptake and respond to being confused with the impotent (but still painful) violence that characterised the early education of many members of Shakespeare's audience. Antipholus of Syracuse marvels 'What now? How chance thou art returned so soon?' when he mistakes Dromio of Ephesus for his own Dromio immediately after having given him the thousand marks to secure a lodging (1.2.42). The mystery deepens when Antipholus finds out that 'by computation and mine host's report, / I could not speak with Dromio since at first / I sent him from the mart!' (2.2.6–8). Antipholus's time calculations and his wonder at the impossibility of Dromio being in two places at once do not save Dromio of Syracuse from a beating, however. Faced with a confusing situation, Antipholus's reaction is to blame Dromio in anger, much like an incompetent and choleric teacher. In contrast to fencing lessons, which emphasised dissimulation, these moments of violent contact are humorous precisely because of their seeming directness. Dromio does not intentionally trick Antipholus, regardless of what his master might believe. Antipholus rains direct blows down upon Dromio.

I have argued that *The Comedy of Errors* is interested in the production of subjective and temporal knowledge through touch. Thus far, I have mostly considered separately the subjective and the temporal. However, the two are not completely distinct. To return to the scene of diagnosis I opened with, the temporal and embodied experience of subjectivity that the play returns to is encapsulated in the moment when Pinch tries to take Antipholus's pulse. In a Galenic context, the tempo of the pulse-beat is imagined to reflect an inner state, to reveal to what extent the patient is 'touched', or mad. Time is generated from the body's rhythmic pumping of blood, but it is the highly individualised time of each patient's body. The speed of a person's pumping blood provides doctors with vital information as to the appropriate treatment. Mistaken identity engenders mistaken times, as one Antipholus's rage born from being blamed for the other Antipholus's actions creates symptoms that are taken for madness. Similarly, while the pedagogical use of flogging is built on a logic of correction and retention, because the Dromios continually substitute for each other, this logic is frustrated. Instead, floggings become what many schoolboys may have already felt them to be – irrational expressions of spleen without a real instructional purpose.

Touch brings together the bodies and temporalities of the characters, each pair of whom is stuck in their own day's logic and cycle of time. When conflicting time cycles come together, explosive and humorously ineffective violence erupts. As Jonathan Gil Harris puts it, Shakespeare's model of time is 'a progressive line that follows the arc of the sun, but . . . also counterintuitively a plane in which the future is behind and the past ahead, and a preposterous folded cloth in which before and after are coeval'.[29] Such coevality is modelled in the wrinkles of each character's timescape. However, in *The Comedy of Errors*, as I have suggested, the folded flesh of the pinch, with its tactile associations, is a more apt figure for the play's colliding temporal schemas than the folded cloth.

Shakespeare's model of time has garnered more attention than that of Jonson, but the two men collaborated in a later play to explore the intersection of embodiment, cognition, temporality and swordplay.

Four years after *The Comedy of Errors* was first performed, Shakespeare found himself once again immersed in a Plautine tangle, but this time as an actor rather than a playwright as he performed in Jonson's *Every Man in His Humour*.

Judging Jonson

Every Man in His Humour is often regarded as one of Jonson's most successful early plays. The comedy, perhaps taking a cue from his colleague Shakespeare's earlier work, ironises scenes of knowledge transmission and posits a kind of temporal knowledge generated via touch – specifically slapstick and painful touch. For Jonson, wildly out-of-balance humours characters rather than the established cast of Roman city comedy provide the vehicle for teaching and learning self-awareness. Characters, with varying degrees of self-awareness, encounter difficulties (jealousy, rage) based upon their predominate humoral configuration. A fencing lesson and a sword-fight bookend the comedy's engagement with learning, affectation, and dissimulation.

The comedy's plot is mostly important for introducing an ensemble cast and allowing them to showcase their follies. It centres on a competition between two young men, one native to the city and the other visiting from out of town. The game is to see which man can produce the most affected and ridiculous people to laugh at. The out-of-towner brings his country cousin who looks to gain some town polish. The city-dweller produces for his contribution a self-proclaimed fencing master and a bad amateur poet-plagiarist. A further wrinkle occurs in the form of a well-off older merchant who is jealous of his young wife and resentful of the partying guests he unwillingly hosts. The merchant's brother, an irascible country gentleman, further adds to the tension and is obsessed with his own deep irritation with the false fencing master, which develops into an explosive conflict. Throughout, a clever servant character wends his way pranking the other characters and conspiring with his master, the city-dweller. These pranks include exacerbating the folly of the humours characters through techniques such as tricking the city-dweller's nosy but well-meaning father. An eccentric justice listens to everyone's case at the end of the play, passes judgment, and adjourns for a feast.

Jonson retains this plot when he undertakes major revisions to the play between its quarto (1598) and folio (1616) versions.[30] While the quarto version featured Italian characters peopling Florence, for the folio version Jonson transplanted his characters to the streets of London and gave them appropriate English names – Mattheo became Matthew, Prospero became Wellbred, and Musco retained his name's vermin-like connotations as Brainworm. In arguably the most complete character makeover, the play's 'choleric older half-brother', Giuliano, became a 'plain squire'. This change is abrupt compared to the other, more parallel re-christenings. Why foreground the squire's directness over his irascibility? This change in character name reflects both Jonson's attempts at connecting with audiences using topical and contemporary references as well as his increasing interest in the theme of judgement.

In the years that elapsed between the quarto and the folio publications of *Every Man in His Humour*, Jonson made several changes to foreground the theme of judgement, including the addition of a prologue and the alteration of a soliloquy on education. The folio's new prologue takes up questions of taste, as Jonson questions his audience's literary judgement. It is possible that the play's newly anglicised characters and location were due to Jonson's realisation, as his career progressed, that the comedy's strength lay in its 'social immediacy'.[31] The change in setting augments the connections audiences might draw between the behaviour of the humours characters and that of recognisable people in the playgoers' neighbourhoods. The plot is minimal in both quarto and folio, acting primarily as a catalyst for the actions of the play's out-of-balance characters. These characters, and their comic imbroglios, became a centrepiece of the play's new direction.

Several scenes from the quarto and folio versions of *Every Man in His Humour*, paired with contemporary fencing treatises, support the suggestion of a corporeal and temporal model of judgement at work in the early modern English theatre.[32] Three moments of reflection on judgement are particularly salient: Knowell Senior's reminiscences about his own school days; Kitely's soliloquy on jealousy as a pestilence infecting imagination, judgement and memory; and the fencing lesson through which Bobadil claims to teach Matthew judgement of the eye, hand and foot. This last reflection on judgement will open to broader questions about Jonson's sources, which, as I argue, point to the methodology used in fencing pedagogy for judgement inculcation.

Knowell Senior displays Jonson's interest in the corporeality of judgement early in the play through his musings on his son. A nosy father who typically 'knows well' how to behave, Knowell Senior has a serious character flaw: he does not perceive his son as an adult and does not respect his son's privacy. He opens the play by surreptitiously reading a letter addressed to his son, and his grumbling about its contents first introduces the theme of judgement in the folio version of *Every Man in His Humour*. Knowell reminds himself that his son is a scholar of 'good account' in 'both our universities', but admits that he is not blind to his son's faults. He reminisces:

> Myself was once a student and, indeed,
> Fed with the self-same humour he is now,
> Dreaming on naught but idle poetry,
> That fruitless and unprofitable art,
> Good unto none, but least to the professors,
> Which then I thought the mistress of all knowledge;
> But since, time and truth have waked my judgement,
> And reason taught me better to distinguish
> The vain from th'useful learnings.   (1.1.15–23)

Knowell Senior uses 'judgement' to differentiate among fields of study, and it is one of the most rarified senses in which the word circulates. However, the embodied and temporal complexity of judgement is present even in this context. The folio's introduction of judgement early in the play represents a significant departure from the character's lines in the quarto version. In the quarto, Knowell Senior reminisces about his schooldays and remembers how he subsequently dismissed poetry as an important discipline by saying 'But since, experience hath awaked my *spirits* / and reason taught them how to comprehend / The sovereign use of study' (1.1.19–21, emphasis mine). By the folio revision, these lines have been reworked: 'But since, time and truth hath waked my *judgement* / And reason taught me better to distinguish / The vain from th' useful learnings' (1.1.22–4, emphasis mine). While in the quarto experience is a causal agent which awakens the spirits and works alongside the capacity of reason to educate, in the folio it is not Knowell's spirits but his judgement that is awakened. Knowell imagines judgement in biological terms, asleep and dreaming of poetry versus awake and productively at work on important topics. The spirits-to-judgement shift retains the same effect because 'spirits' and 'judgement' both carry a psychosomatic charge. Spirits, in a humoral medical framework, have much in common with the concrete workings of an embodied judgement. As Paster and others have noted, the spirits of the early modern stage are embodied, responding to material pressures and exerting their own influence within the body.[33] The two terms – spirits and judgement – also carry distinct connotations. When Jonson pairs spirits with reason in the older man's education,

Knowell is directed to a singular 'sovereign' use of study. When judgement is paired with reason, Knowell takes a more pluralistic approach to worthwhile knowledge. Reason's development in this case allows Knowell to engage in active, ongoing processes of discernment across multiple topics. This on-the-ground, contingent characterisation of judgement reflects the ways in which it acts in a forensic capacity, mediating the many different kinds of cases that join together to form common law. When Jonson shifts from a singular, sovereign study to this dynamic and multifarious context of distinguishing vain from useful, he begins to align judgement with an emerging early modern proto-aesthetic sensibility that valued the particular.[34]

Where Knowell Senior's soliloquy on education presents judgement as a capacity for discerning among particularities, the play's *senex amans*, Kitely, highlights judgement's temporality. Kitely's judgement is not binary, awake or asleep, but rather it engages in constant activity as a psychophysiological process and is therefore susceptible to sickness. Memory is similarly subject to all the same vulnerabilities as a plague-infected body – it is not a recorded set of past perceptions stored in a mind safely separated from the body's vagaries. Unlike many ageing and jealous husbands in literature, Kitely is fully conscious of his own contaminated judgement. He complains (in the same language in both quarto and folio versions) that jealousy infects:

> The houses of the brain. First it begins
> Solely to work upon the fantasy
> Filling her seat with such pestiferous air
> As soon corrupts the judgement: and from thence
> Sends like contagion to the memory,
> Still each to other giving the infection,
> Which, as a subtle vapour, spreads itself
> Confusedly through every sensitive part
> Till not a thought or motion in the mind
> Be free from the black poison of suspect.   (1.4.211–20)

Jealousy, for Kitely, is a vaporous disease that sickens first fantasy, then judgement and finally memory. By the final phase of the 'pestilence', fantasy, judgement and memory are engaged in an endless recursive loop of poisonous suspicion. Jealousy engages in a kind of destructive athletic training. Where good exercises encode efficient reflexes into the body's muscle memory, this circuit from perception, to discernment, to remembrance amplifies the pestilence's power through repeated training.

By casting jealousy as a vapour, Jonson brings to the fore an adversarial quality he sustains throughout the play. Kitely is the only character in *Every Man in His Humour* to use the word, but elsewhere in his oeuvre Jonson uses 'vapour' as a near synonym for 'humour', though with a key difference. Vapours, unlike humours, are transitive. For instance, *Bartholomew Fair*'s horse-courser, Knockem, can vapour *at* fairgoers: 'I do vapor him the lie,' says Knockem, of anyone who calls him an ass (5.6.175). As Paster points out, this transitivity allows for positive models of social interaction, such as listening and turn-taking in the 'game of vapours' joined in by both fair folk and fairgoers.[35] However, vapours can also assume their own antagonistic agency, as in Kitely's soliloquy, where vapours such as jealousy are waiting to pounce upon an unwary fantasy and to so infect a vulnerable judgement. If Kitely's struggle reflects an internal combat between a pestilential jealousy and the houses of his brain, Matthew's lesson with Bobadil and Bobadil's encounter with Squire George Downright externalise the combativeness inherent in learning and exerting judgement.

Downright Prose, Downright Blows

the multitude commend writers as they do fencers or wrestlers, who if they come in robustiously, and put for it with a deal of violence, are received for the braver fellows

Ben Jonson, Timber, or Discoveries, 521

The friendship between the false fencing master and the rhymester represents one of many pairings between sword and pen Jonson makes throughout his career. In *Bartholomew Fair*, for instance, he will similarly pair a stagehand pining for sword-and-buckler fights with a scrivener and bookholder reading out a legal contract. In this play, he matches Bobadil the bragging soldier with Matthew the bad poet. Refusing to continue a fencing lesson, Bobadil criticises Matthew by saying, 'I have no spirit to play with you; your dearth of judgement renders you tedious' (1.5.125–6). As we have seen, this reference to Matthew's judgement indicates the commonly held understanding that fencing competitions could and should exercise judgement as well as demonstrate techniques. Bobadil's promise to 'learn' Matthew by 'the true judgement of the eye, hand, and foot, to control any enemy's point i' the world' (1.5.133–4) evokes the corporeality of the faculty of judgement, its proprioceptive characteristics.

The English were primed to think of fencing specifically as an exercise for judgement, as the lengthy title of the first fencing manual printed in that language suggests: *Di Grassi his true Arte of Defence . . . with a waie or meane by private Industrie to obtain Strength, Judgement, and Activitie* (1594).[36] Di Grassi gives a number of methods for training judgement, which he complains is neglected in the teaching of his contemporary fencing masters. He begins with a series of rules based in geometry and physics such as the 'right or straight line is of all other the shortest', meaning that you should make sure your arm is straight before you lunge. These abstract rules swiftly give way to an explanation of how 'every motion is accomplished in time' and to specific drills and exercises for students to practise recognising, seizing and generating *tempi* of opportunity. As fencers practise adapting to unexpected situations, judgement is written into the muscles of the body, informing psychosomatic capacities like boldness and courage. In this way, fencing not only reveals one's moral qualities, but also actively shapes values and personalities. Masters developed dynamic drills aimed at developing faster response time and encoding into muscle memory the right movements to make based on visual and tactile stimuli. Even more than reacting quickly to immediate stimuli, however, judgement is the capacity to interpret and defeat an adversary's strategy. In contrast, rote drills, which involve only the memorisation and repetition of predictable movements, are easy to teach to a large group, but not effective in training the kinaesthetic reasoning required in a match.

Given these ways in which Jonson's contemporaries understand judgement and its training, it is no surprise that he uses a pair of fencers to illustrate the literary values embodied by his staccato, Neo-Stoic prose style.[37] Bobadil and Squire Downright exemplify two postures of self-representation: affectation and plainness. Jonson's decision to change Giuliano's name so significantly to George Downright may, in part, be prompted by the notoriety occasioned by George Silver in his vocal defence of the 'downright blow' (and, by extension, the downright and honest native English spirit). Silver's own bitingly funny satirical polemic against Italian 'strangers' who, like Bobadil, promise to teach true judgement but actually teach bad habits was printed between *Every Man in His Humour*'s first quarto and folio editions. While it is not certain if Jonson personally read Silver's 1599 *Paradoxes of Defence*, Jonson at least draws on the same stories and incidents, which suggests that the conflicts between Silver and the Italians were such common knowledge as to make for good fodder for the playwright's inside jokes. For instance, Saviolo has already been widely acknowledged as the butt of Shakespeare's 'very butcher of a silk button' joke in *Romeo and Juliet*.[38] Silver records another incident of Saviolo's accessorising that was notorious in Elizabethan England but has been largely forgotten today. Like Shakespeare, Jonson mines Saviolo's boasts for comic material. *Every Man in His Humour* establishes early on Squire Downright's irascibility and Bobadil's bluster, as Bobadil casually insults Downright by calling him a 'scavenger', or street cleaner. Downright, to his continued vexation, keeps encountering Bobadil throughout the play but is unable to engage him in combat. Finally, Downright finds Bobadil on a London street accompanied only by the useless Matthew. When Bobadil refuses to draw his sword, Downright beats him with a stick instead as the Italian cowers and pleads. Rather than avenging himself in through single combat, Bobadil goes to Justice Clement to press a suit against Downright.

Bobadil's fate closely follows a similar sequence of bragging, beating and threatened litigation in *Paradoxes of Defence*. Silver claimed that Saviolo 'gave out speeches' that he had been 'thus manie years in *England*, and since the time of his first coming, there was not yet one Englishman, that could once touch him at the single Rapier or rapier and Dagger'.[39] An unnamed gentleman in London whose 'English hart did rise' to hear the boasts of Saviolo sent for Bartholomew Bramble, a 'verie tall man both of his hands and person, who kept a schoole of Defence in the towne' to take Saviolo down a peg.[40] At Saviolo's school and in front of the gentlemen he taught, Bramble first invited Saviolo to drink wine with him and then to play at rapier and dagger. Saviolo refused rudely, saying 'by God me scorne to play with thee'. Bramble, 'being more then halfe full of Beere', boxed Saviolo's ear and knocked him into a 'Butterie hatch'. All Bramble's abuse was not enough to provoke Saviolo to settle the question in a manner anticipated by the English. Instead, Saviolo threatened Bramble with legal action, saying 'I will cause to lie in the Gaile for this geare, 1. 2. 3. 4. years'.[41] Disgusted, Bramble threw his beer on Saviolo and called him a coward. Apparently, Saviolo never rose to the bait – Silver reports that, the next day, Saviolo met Bramble in the street and said, 'you remember how misused a me yesterday, you were to blame, me be an excellent man, me teach you how to thrust two foote further then anie Englishman, but first come you with me'.[42] Saviolo makes a show of offering mysterious Italian tricks to traditional English fencers. The lesson is only spoken of, however, as they step not into a fencing school but rather a nearby mercer's shop. Perhaps realising, as Bobadil does not, that his case will not fare well before an English judge, Saviolo attempts to buy off

Bramble with a dozen of the shop's 'best silken Pointes'.[43] This story shows how the influence between fencing manuals and drama was a two-way street. Silver reproduces a foreign accent with broken English as he writes Saviolo's dialogue, emphasising the distance between Saviolo's urbane claims to teach Englishmen to fight well and obey a strict code of honour, and his own hypocritical and deficient physical presence mediating Italian courtly ideology. Silver's phonetic imitation of Saviolo's accent in writing is strongly inflected by the oral medium of drama and verges on theatre itself.

Scholars from an English cultural tradition around fencing such as Aylward and Anglo are understandably inclined towards the perspective of George Silver, but the situations arising in *Every Man in His Humour*, *Paradoxes of Defence* and in Italian-authored sources like *His Practice* are more complicated than a simple story of boastful cowardice and condign punishment. The English believe in a rough-and-ready sort of accountability – a 'put up or shut up' mindset, which is reflected in the way fencing figured as a social practice and public spectacle in England. In contrast, the Italians tried to settle things through legal channels whenever possible. The duel over the point of honour frequently ended in death, and they were an aristocratic offshoot of the privilege nobles could invoke of saying 'no' to the sovereign in very limited cases.[44] Such meetings were, at least in theory, constrained to situations in which it was one man's word against another's. In such a context, a duel was supposed to show who was telling the truth, much like the point-of-honour duel's predecessors, the trial by ordeal and the trial by combat.[45] This cultural difference led to conflict, particularly given Bonetti's readiness to go to the Privy Council and his patron, Sir Walter Raleigh, for redress. For instance, in a letter to the Lord Mayor and Aldermen of London, we learn that:

> He is daylie vexed by the common fencers of that Cittie because he professethe the use of weapons, they are therefore required to call suche of them before them as the said Roche shall name unto them to have offered him violence, and thereupon as they shall fynde them culpable to see them effectuallie punished, and bandes to be taken of them for their good behaviours hereafter towards hym, that he be no furder molested by them, but that without impediment he maie teache the use of weapons within his howse to such gentlemen as shall like to resorte unto him.[46]

Bonetti's legal navigations disgusted contemporary Englishmen who thought of fencing matches as contests, which, in Silver's words, had the ideal of no harm being done to either fencer.

Bobadil's bragging, cowardice, and altercations with English fencers parallel Silver's account of Saviolo's behaviour.[47] In contrast to these Italianate affections, Jonson sets up Squire Downright. The *Cambridge Edition of the Works of Ben Jonson Online* cites the tune 'Downright Squire' as a source for the character's name.[48] While this song may have been on Jonson's mind as he penned the city comedy, Silver is a more direct and proximate source, though this connection has yet to be recognised. Silver was infamous for tangling with foreign Italian fencing masters and for promoting the 'downright blow' as opposed to their 'school tricks' or 'juggling gambols'. Silver wrote *Paradoxes of Defence* as a confutation of a new, Italianate system of fencing in vogue in London among the elite and would-be elite. He argues against taking up the 'vices and devices' (techniques and weapons) of Italian fencers.[49] He singles out the rapier for censure as an encroaching Italian device – for instance, Silver calls the longer, thinner and primarily thrust-oriented weapon specialised for civilian combat a 'bird-spit'.[50] As for vices, he denounces Italian footwork for attacks. Instead of the *passado*, a running attack that likely appeared suicidal to the English, whose footwork is more cautious, or the *stocatta*, a direct thrust delivered with a lunge, Silver recommends instead 'gathering', meaning pulling the body backwards to safety, and the 'down right blow'.[51]

The downright blow is proverbial in Jonson's time for a simple, direct way of striking, one that invalidates the pretensions of fencing 'experts' in favour of the common labourer. The Italian masters living in England may have judged downright blows to be simple, strong and lacking in cunning. In some instances, it even seems like Silver is in agreement with them, as he taps into a strain of fencing anti-intellectualism to see this assessment in positive terms. In his complaint against the Italian fencing masters, and the English fencing masters who follow their lead, Silver recounts: 'it grew to a common speech among the countrymen "Bring me to a fencer, I will bring him out of his fence tricks with down right blows. I will make him forget his fence tricks, I will warrant him."'[52] Downright means more than straightforward, however, as its use in the technical sections of fencing manuals shows. Florio's 1611 Italian–English dictionary glosses *mandritto* as 'a right-handed, or downe-right blow'. 'Forehand' and 'backhand' in tennis also refer to this biomechanic, but without the same emphasis on both the vertical and horizontal axes of movement. Silver and contemporary English treatise authors used 'downright' and 'reverse' instead.

English fencing of the 1590s had much in common with Italian fencing of the 1550s–70s: both schools emphasised cuts, used wards which were less point-forward, and employed shorter, broader swords than what we think of today as the rapier. Rather surprisingly, given Silver's polemical opinion, it was not uncommon for English fencers to look to Italian sources like di Grassi's 1570/1594 treatise to articulate favoured English techniques. For instance, Hale uses di Grassi's advice to describe proper preparation and execution of the downright blow. The illustration shows how to defend against the downright blow – or, in di Grassi's terms, the *mandritto* (Fig. 3.1).

These images show two potential attack trajectories. In the C-to-D and D-to-E trajectory, the fencer on the right lowers his sword for a thrust. In the A-to-B trajectory, he delivers a downright blow. Di Grassi makes clear from this image that the attack is direct and fast – the arc inscribes a more efficient path to the adversary's target than do the lines representing the thrust.

The technical dimension of 'downright' is usually eclipsed in glosses of *Every Man in His Humour*, with the term being generalised to its etymological cousin, forthright. For instance, Nicholson

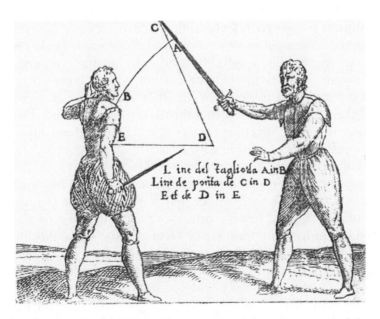

Figure 3.1 Giacomo Di Grassi. The downright blow. 'De i modi del difendere', *Ragione di adoprar sicuramente l'arme*, 1570. Engraving. Vienna, Österreichische Nationalbibliothek, digitised by Google Books.

suggests 'Downright, as his name implies, is a straightforward honest English gentleman, with as much idea of turning sharper or cheating a man as the north and south have of coming together, perhaps less'.[53] However, in Jonson's day, the term had a specialised meaning as the opposite of a *reverse*, or backhand blow. In *Arden of Faversham*, for instance, Michael questions 'Who would not venture upon house and land, / When he may have it for a right-down blow?' (1.174–5). As the synonymous substitution of right-down for downright suggests, the most important aspect of the cut is its directionality and force. A downright blow is a strong attack with the blade travelling from high to low, right to left. However, this passage is not simply about opposing the complex with the simple, but about correctly reading intention and calling bluffs. For instance, in the passage where he excoriates the techniques of Italian rapier fencers, Silver recommends downright blows as counterattacks. Rather than initiating an attack, in this case the 'countrymen' wait for 'fence tricks' – needless movements, flourishes and posturing. Then, they deploy a downright blow to interrupt the frivolous motions.

The use of 'downright' in the technical sections of fencing manuals shows other ways in which the term means more than straightforward. It was also popularly used as the first motion of a feint. Silver later cautions fencers to 'take heed that [the adversary] deceives you not with the downright blow at your head'.[54] Swetnam (1617) writes in his staff section that a useful 'falsifie' is to 'proffer a downe-right blow at your enemies head, fetching him with a great compasse, so that it may seeme to your enemie, that you meane to strike him downe' then change the blow to a thrust at the last second.[55] As this discussion suggests, Silver represents fencing throughout his books as mixing efficiency of motion with adaptability and cunning – qualities which seem on the surface to be at odds. His interest in the contraries of fencing theory and practice is, perhaps, why he names his book *Paradoxes of Defence* rather than *Simple Rules of Defence*. As this example suggests, fencing offers a crucible of at-speed training in embodied judgement. Swetnam's 'falsifie', what we could call now a feint (a simulated attack that so closely resembles a real attack that the adversary is forced to take a defensive action such as a parry or retreat), is an especially risky and sensitive action because it relies upon fine gradations in timing. For example, when the fencer sees the adversary extend as if to cut his or her head, the fencer must both decide what to do (that is, parry immediately if the fencer believes it is a real attack or counterattack into it if the fencer believes it is a feint) and put that decision into action. As the fencer improves, so does his or her reaction time – the *when* of judgement comes to the fore as a crucial skill. It is unsurprising, then, that fencing masters offer advice about assessing the adversary's probable reactions based on personality, nationalism, handedness and size as well as possible techniques in order to narrow down choices of action. For instance, Swetnam writes that 'it is the nature of an Englishman to strike with what weapon soever hee fighteth with all, and not one in twenty but in furie and anger will strike unto no other place but onely to the head'.[56] Because of this tendency, learning to defend cuts to the head takes an important role in Swetnam's system, and he downplays the 'falsifie', and 'false play' in general, as being dangerous against the kind of opponent his readers will most likely face.

Even when it is not the first movement of a feint, the downright blow can be a dangerous proposition if one is not reading the adversary accurately. To defend against the downright blow, di Grassi recommends the low ward because one may 'very easily withstand the downright blow, and the reverse by giving a thrust, for that he shall hit him first'.[57] By reading the opponent's timing correctly, the fencer can take advantage of, or even generate, a lapse in the adversary's judgement. In this case, the mistake would be if the opponent misjudges both the distance they are from the adversary and the preparedness of that adversary. In these conditions, drawing back the sword arm to deliver a downright blow leads to the fencer's action being interrupted by the speedier straight thrust of his or her waiting adversary.

The players' lessons in judgement are also lessons for the playgoers, as Jonson incites ridicule for what he sees as annoying and harmful social behaviours. Such pedagogical moments in *Every Man in His Humour* do more than reaffirm what we already know about the theatre and its potential to educate audiences through examples and ridicule. They also give us some of the mundane, embodied avenues through which exercises in judgement – whether through the art of poesy or the art of defence – develop literary judgement. Like the downright blow that can be a fully executed simple attack or a feint to the head with a change in target at the last second, a literary downrightness conceals within itself the potential for multiple meanings and dissimulation. This seeming plainness layered over deep tactical complexity was especially appealing to Jonson as he developed what Jonas Barish terms 'antirhetorical naturalness' as opposed to Shakespeare's school of 'rhetorical ornament'.[58] Jonson's comic prose may at first seem simplistic. However, upon closer inspection, it is actually quite complex: his orthographic representation of a wide array of English accents, his sentence structure, and the interruptions he inserts into character conversations all point to a kind of English *sprezzatura* (practised spontaneous grace) that is both crafty and crafted. We should look at Jonson's antecedents in the fencing school as well as the grammar school to develop a temporal, corporeal model of theatrical judgement. By doing so, the antagonistic and intersubjective nature of discernment becomes clearer, as do the 'mechanisms of enskilment' offered via the English stage.[59]

There is certainly much more to be said about the presence of duels in plays and their encoding of masculinity and other social norms. Plays like *A Faire Quarrel* and *Cynthia's Revels* give much more direct views of duels and prizefights, respectively. What I hope to have done in this chapter is to frame the conceptual apparatus for viewing fencing in more than thematic terms. Thus far, I have discussed the temporal, subjective and aesthetic kinds of knowledge generated through these antagonistic encounters. Now I will turn to a closer discussion of the formal influence of specific fencing techniques on the formal structure of plays: *contratempo* in Shakespeare's *Titus Andronicus* and the feint in *As You Like It*.

Notes

1. Thomas Wilson, *Rule of reason*, 36.
2. 'judgement | judgment, n.' *OED Online*. Oxford University Press.
3. The current model of judgement, which originates in the post-Enlightenment period defines judgement as a moment of decision informed by a baseline of shared understanding. In Kantian aesthetics, this backdrop incorporates a universal model of beauty, which makes it possible to determine artistic merit. Emmanuel Kant in his *Critique of Judgment* posits 'judgments of taste'. These judgements are rooted in subjectivity and universality. The subjectivity of judgement means that individual responses to beauty are not empirical but come from feelings of pleasure or displeasure. With the universality of judgement, in contrast to individual preference, the person passing judgement feels that others ought to share the same reaction to whatever it is he or she is judging. In Kant's view, these judgements of taste may be rooted in pure reason and therefore transcendental – what he terms a 'taste of reflection'. Or, the judgements of taste may instead be particular, embodied and based in sensation – the 'taste of sense'. In both these types of judgement, the role of skill is diminished or eclipsed altogether. For transcendental, reflective judgements, the appeal to a shared, universal frame of reference lessens the importance of individual ability. For the embodied judgements enabled by the taste of sense, the

durational aspect becomes less urgent – the speed of discrimination and response to aesthetic pleasure is not one of Kant's central concerns. However, in the early modern period, judgement was conceived of as a temporal process subject to training.

4. Hale, *The Private School of Defence*, 'Epistle Dedicatorie', n.p.
5. Ibid. 'Definition of the Science', n.p.
6. For more on the temporal dimensions of embodied skill as it pertains to the English theatre, see Tribble and Sutton, 'Minds in and out of Time'.
7. I treat judgement in a limited scope as a species of embodied cognition. For a broader treatment of judgement's significance in the early modern theatre, see Curran, ed., *Shakespeare and Judgement*, and Klotz, 'Ben Jonson's Legal Imagination in *Volpone*'.
8. All references to *The Comedy of Errors* are taken from the Norton Shakespeare, 2nd edition, and all references to *Every Man in His Humour* are taken from the Cambridge University Press edition. Quotations from both plays will be cited parenthetically by act, scene and line numbers.
9. Mazzio, 'Acting with Tact', 170.
10. Ibid. 168.
11. See Chapter 5 of Knecht, *Grammar Rules of Affection*.
12. Koslow, 'Humanist Schooling', 123.
13. Heller-Roazen, *The Inner Touch*, 295.
14. Crane, *Shakespeare's Brain*, 37.
15. See Mazzio, 'Acting with Tact'.
16. Shannon, 'Poor, Bare, Forked', 177.
17. Ibid. 191.
18. Competition would have occurred among adults as well as children. Mulcaster in his *Positions Concerning the Training Up of Children* explicitly addresses the pros and cons of football for children. Curiously, he opens his discussion of ball games with skin that is being desensitised. Mulcaster makes reference to Galen, who described a German practice of parents 'who used then to dippe their new borne children into extreme cold water over head and eares, so to trie their courage and to harden their skinne' (110). This method of training, Mulcaster hastens to say, is not what Galen had in mind, or what the English should imitate. Though Mulcaster concludes that people in his day have not retained the same games as the Greeks and Romans played, he argues that the contemporary English ball games 'worketh the same effects, which theirs did' (ibid.). Like the ancient German baby-dipping practice, football 'as it is now commonly used, with a thronging of a rude multitude, with bursting of shinnes, and breaking of legges', is not a healthy sport to train young bodies: 'it be neither civil, neither worthy the name of any traine to health' (111). However, with a proper training master to enforce the rules, the sport is useful because it strengthens the body and drives downwards unhealthy 'superfluities' (ibid.).
19. Enterline, *Shakespeare's Schoolroom*, 48.

20. Ibid. 53

21. Harvey, *Sensible Flesh*, 4.

22. Lyne, 'The Shakespearean Grasp', 49–52.

23. Foucault draws out the connection between timing, pedagogy and erotics in *The Use of Pleasure* (see, especially, 'Erotics', 187–203). He notes that the 'theme of the "right time" had always had considerable importance for the Greeks, not only as a moral problem, but also as a question of science and technique. The exercise of practical skills as in medicine, government, and navigation . . . implied that one was not content with knowing general principles but that one was also able to determine the moment when it was necessary to act and the precise manner in which to do so in terms of existing circumstances . . . in the use of pleasures, Morality was also an art of the "right time."'

24. Wagner, *Shakespeare, Theatre, and Time*, 46.

25. Ibid.

26. See Wagner, 'The Bodies of Time', ch. 3 in *Shakespeare, Theatre, and Time*, 34–68.

27. As Matthew Wagner argues, the depiction and description of clocks on stage became important in Shakespeare's theatre in part because of a larger cultural process of using small clocks in order to 'create a sense that time itself was *here* for humans to actively and reciprocally engage it' (*Shakespeare, Theatre, and Time*, 53). Personal clocks allow for the measurement and control of time on an individual level.

28. See Enterline's 'The Art of Loving Mastery: Venus, Adonis, and the Erotics of Early Modern Pedagogy', ch. 3 in her *Shakespeare's School-room*, 62–94, for a more detailed discussion of the erotics of school beatings.

29. Harris, *Untimely Matter*, 4.

30. While *Every Man in His Humour* was not entered into the Stationers' Register until 4 August 1600, a letter from September of 1598 references the play.

31. Donaldson, *Ben Jonson*, 129.

32. The quarto version was first performed in 1598 and it was published in 1601. The folio revision is difficult to date with certainty. The *Cambridge Edition of the Works of Ben Jonson* editors summarise ongoing discussion as favouring either sometime around 1605 or 1612. While some of the topical references I examine here support an earlier date of revision, it is not the intention of this chapter to treat or resolve this long-standing debate. Unless otherwise noted, all notations refer to the Cambridge Edition folio of the play.

33. For more on the embodied aspects of terms such as passions, spirits and humours, see Paster, *Humoring the Body*.

34. The 1598 version of the play included a defence on the part of the scholarly son, which is cut in the folio edition. David Bevington speculates that this move was made because Jonson now expounds upon his literary aesthetic in the new prologue attached to the folio.

35. On vapours and humours as forms of embodied emotion, see Paster, '*Bartholomew Fair* and the Humoral Body'.

36. The full title is *Di Grassi his true Arte of Defence, plainlie teaching by infallible Demonstrations, apt Figures and perfect Rules the manner and forme how a man without other Teacher or Master may safelie handle all sorts of Weapons as well offensive as defensive: With a Treatise Of Disceit or Falsing: And with a waie or meane by private Industrie to obtain Strength, Judgement, and Activitie* The book was translated by an anonymous 'I. G.' from the 1570 *Ragione di Adoprar Sicuramente l'Arme si da Offesa, Come da Difesa, Con un Trattato dell'inganno, & con un modo di essercitarsi da se stesso, per acquistare forza, giudicio, & prestezza.*

37. For more on Jonson's literary aesthetic, see Barish, *Ben Jonson*.

38. See Turner and Soper, *Methods and Practice*, 52.

39. Silver, *Paradoxes of Defence*, 68.

40. Ibid.

41. Ibid. 69.

42. Ibid. 70.

43. Ibid. 69.

44. See Quint, 'Dueling and Civility'.

45. See Bryson, *The Sixteenth-Century Italian Duel*.

46. *Acts of the Privy Council of England Volume 10, 1577–1578*. Ed. John Roche Dasent. London: Her Majesty's Stationery Office, 1895. 334 *British History Online*. Web. 24 March 2017. http://www.british-history.ac.uk/acts-privy-council/vol10.

47. J. D. Aylward has touched upon some of the correspondences between *Paradoxes of Defence* and *Every Man in His Humour* as they concern Rocco Bonetti in 'The Inimitable Bobadil'.

48. Jonson, *Every Man in His Humour*, 'Persons in the Play', notes.

49. Silver, *Paradoxes of Defence*, 2.

50. Ibid. 5.

51. See, for instance, Silver's discussion of gathering and the downright blow in ch. 5 of *Paradoxes of Defence*, 98–101.

52. Silver, *Paradoxes of Defence*, 2.

53. Nicholson, '"Rook"'.

54. Silver, *Brief Instructions*, 100.

55. Swetnam, *The Schoole of the Noble and Worthy Science of Defence*, 152.

56. Ibid. 96.

57. Di Grassi, *Di Grassi his true Arte of Defence*, 24. Di Grassi's translator renders *mandritto* and *riverso* as 'downright blow' and 'reverse', respectively.

58. Barish, *Ben Jonson*, 2.

59. On such mechanisms, see Tribble, 'Skill'.

Chapter 4

Killing Time in *Titus Andronicus*

As you can see, this discipline relies in great part on the ability to subtly deceive your opponent.

> Salvator Fabris, *Lo Schermo, overo Scienza d'Arme*, 18

Now is a time to storm. Why art thou still?

> Marcus Andronicus in *Titus Andronicus* 3.1.264

Introduction

Storming and stillness, movement and suspension, action and empty words: Marcus Andronicus, the politician and rhetorician, incorrectly understands these activities as opposites in *Titus Andronicus*.[1] He urges his brother towards immediate and public mourning and revenge. In contrast, Titus, a military leader and expert at hand-to-hand combat, understands that stillness is an integral part of storming. Modern literary scholarship has a stronger inheritance from the pedagogy of rhetoric than from the pedagogy of combat, and so it has become something of a critical commonplace to see waiting as the opposite of acting in Shakespearean revenge dramas like *Hamlet* and *Titus Andronicus*. In fact, strategic suspension of action in these plays can function to prompt mistakes in timing on the part of the avenger's adversary. The model of preparation and provocation set out in *Titus Andronicus* draws from the form of fencing *contratempo*. The structuring influence of fencing upon the plot and pace of *Titus Andronicus* is evident in the play's seeming moments of digression and hesitation. By elucidating the play's nuanced approach to waiting and action, I aim to recover a finely gradated approach to the exercise of timing.

Scholarship on *Titus Andronicus* is robust in its treatment of the tragedy's rich and complex usage of literal and figural actions and frequently maps the distinction between the two to a separation between sword and pen. However, as this chapter will demonstrate, leaving behind the idea of a unidirectional trajectory from figural to literal opens up new ways to see the playwright's formal adoptions and transpositions of structural elements from combat to drama such as the logic of *contratempo*. The forms of embodied, antagonistic movement and those of literary and dramatic representation combine to offer useful alternate models to conceptualising conflict.

Pen and Sword

In modern parlance, the 'pen is mightier than the sword' formula is often used to express the contrast of non-violent and violent means of resolving conflict. However, the phrase, in its many permutations, acknowledges the violence inherent in both words and arms: the pen is 'mightier', not 'nicer'. Writing tools and weapons exist on the same continuum because they are both instruments that exert power. Shakespeare, like Castiglione and other Renaissance authors, participates in this arms versus letters debate, but rarely with a simple hierarchy. Rather, pen and sword, word and flesh, are held in generative interaction as he continually muddies the division between the activities of wounding and writing.

Word and sword exist on a continuum, but not one which follows an intensifying progression from less to more violence. The relationship between sword and pen, dramatic violence and rhetorical tropes, in *Titus Andronicus* in particular has attracted a great deal of scholarly attention. These readings valuably explore questions of embodiment and violence (both linguistic and corporeal), but often understand pen and sword as analogous to word and body and posit a trajectory from one to the other. Indeed, the narrative of the metaphor becoming violently real has become a received idea. That the figural-to-literal trajectory has become commonplace is made apparent by its inclusion in Marjorie Garber's *Shakespeare after All*, a book based on her undergraduate lectures. She argues that in 'early points in the play [*Titus Andronicus*] words like "headless" and "unspeakable" are metaphors' but that later in the play 'these dead or sleeping metaphors will come to grisly life'.[2] Heather James describes *Titus Andronicus* as the Shakespeare play which 'cites the most Latin yet hacks up the most bodies', arguing that the play's 'perverse links between language and action, rhetoric and violence' are part of its Ovidian poetics.[3] Similarly, Albert Tricomi aligns the figurative with writing and the literal with wounding, contending that the way in which 'figurative language imitates the literal events of the plot' is what dignifies *Titus Andronicus*.[4] Mary Fawcett also focuses on the play's investment in the roles of violence and language, calling *Titus Andronicus* a 'luminous, beautiful meditation on the relationship between language and the body'.[5] She points to a trajectory in which as the Andronici 'become words, they reduce their enemies to bodies'.[6] Thomas Anderson, in his consideration of the play's 'promissory language and violence', maintains that oaths are 'virtually identified with the acts of violence that accompany them', that violence follows promise and that oath and violence intermingle.[7] These contentions that the play is structured around a shift from words to flesh presupposes the opposition of writing and wounding and align writing with *logos* and wounding with the body. These approaches importantly foreground the play's interest in rhetorical and dramatic violence, but there is more to the relationship between the two than a unidirectional progression, or an opposition. Fencing and rhetoric shared territory and had similar educational goals and pedagogical claims, especially around the teaching of timing and readiness.

Transmitting practical knowledge about time is clearly a goal of humanist rhetorical education, from the timing of hand gestures in an oration to the seven-part argument structure that insists upon establishing the timeliness and relevance of a claim. Fencing masters, too, stake a claim on this kind of embodied knowledge. As we saw in the Introduction, George Hale, in *The Private Schoole of Defence* (1614), defines the two parts of fencing practice both in terms of temporal skill, arguing that 'The science of defence is an Art Geometricall . . . the parts thereto required are Strength and Judgement. Under Strength are comprehended swiftness of motion and quicknesse of eye . . . Under Judgement fall the considerations of Time, Place, and Distance.'[8] Speed of execution and an ability to evaluate when (and if) one should act are both skills demanded and taught by fencing. On the Continent, the Italian fencing master Angelo Viggiani, in his three-volume *Lo Schermo* (1575), saw the competition between arms and letters as important enough to treat first (and at great length). Disarming many common lines of reasoning used to denigrate his occupation, Viggiani argues that the science of defence is devoted to the most important kinds of knowledge, movement and time, which are fundamental to all natural things. War, more than any other art or faculty, requires skill in movement and time.[9] Viggiani capaciously classifies manipulations of time and motion, along with any other sort of deceit, as under the purview of arms: 'I do not call war only that which one does with weapon in hand, but also that which is waged with cunning (*ingegno*)'.[10] Viggiani's use of *ingegno* in this context is grounded in a larger cultural movement. As Jessica Wolfe describes, attempts to translate terms such as *ingegno* and *engin* into English demonstrate the difficulty of navigating the relationship between two forms of power, force and fraud. Viggiani positions his *schermo*, or system of defence, to speak to obvious forms of physical domination as well as to the subtler exertion of power practiced through deceit.[11] Fencers and writers both lay claim to a mastery of the tactics of deception, but in doing so they appropriate one another's tools. Fencers like Viggiani defend their claim with words, and writers are frequently called upon to prove their own words through armed combat with the rise of the point-of-honour duel.

As I have argued, the ways in which fencing conceptualises tempo are a necessary supplement to rhetorical pedagogy on generating and seizing opportunity. Fencing tempo is crucial to our understanding of timing in *Titus Andronicus* because, while rhetoricians do theorise conflict, the fencing device is often more focused on disrupting the timing of the adversary than the rhetorical phrase. Though their influence has become less culturally legible to us, fighting disciplines figured importantly in the formation and interpretation of early modern plots. Elaborating on an aesthetic of interruption and anticipation, dramatists import the focus of fencing training on readiness.

Pragmatically, fencing masters develop readiness through a combination of imparting fencing theory to students and drilling actions repeatedly. The timing of an attack is frequently one of the first pieces of fencing theory presented to students. According to conventional wisdom, masters asserted that the best moment to attack someone was during the tempo of the adversary's movement. For example, as fencer A tries to engage the blade of fencer B, fencer B evades the attempted engagement and hits fencer A with a shorter, faster attack. In practice, this led to protracted encounters where neither fencer would initiate an action for fear they would be attacked in time. Such responses drew ridicule from contemporaries because of the naive view of good timing: the strategy allows the opponent essentially to dictate the moment of attack through his or her movement or stillness. Unsurprisingly, the chauvinistic Silver attributes the common Italian practice of waiting for the opponent to give up a tempo to cowardice:

For they verily thinke that he that first thrusteth is in great danger of his life, therefore with all speede do put themselves in ward, or Stocata, the surest gard of all other, as *Vincentio* [Saviolo] saith, and thereupon they stand sure, saying the one to the other, thrust and thou dare; and saith the other, thrust and thou dare, or strike or thrust and thou dare, saith the other: then saith the other, strike or thrust and thou dare for thy life. These two cunning gentlemen standing long time together, upon this worthie ward, they both depart in peace, according to the old proverbe: It is good sleeping in a whole skinne.[12]

Waiting on guard might have certain advantages when facing the faint-hearted or unskilful, but fencers cannot wait for opportunity to present itself when they face skilled opponents. Instead, they must be able to trick the opponent into a moment of vulnerability, often through a pretended weakness or mistake. On this more sophisticated level, making tempo becomes an elaborate game played between two fencers.

While there is broad consensus among fencing masters regarding the importance of generating, seizing and stealing tempo, not all masters agree on the best way to do this. Fabris and Capoferro resist the conventional wisdom of waiting for an opponent to give up a tempo in measure as too passive. Capoferro does so by classifying stillness as well as movement in measure as a tempo. He writes, 'it is important to note that all of the adversary's movements and rests are tempi, if he is in measure'.[13] Fabris teaches how to generate errors in timing on the part of the opponent through one's own constant movement. His book *Lo Schermo, overo Scienza d'Arme* (previously composed under the title *Scientia e prattica dell'arme*) contains two parts. The first, a beginners' section, details what all reasonably competent masters should be teaching their students already. The second, an advanced section, includes Fabris's more original contribution: creating promising tactical situations through one's own constant movement rather than waiting for the opponent to move. Fabris guides his own readers in how to 'astutely make a tempo' through movement of body and blade to tempt an opponent to attack, opening the opportunity to wound 'in contratempo'.[14] He notes that the discipline of fencing 'relies in great part on the ability to subtly deceive your opponent',[15] and this deception turns upon the skill of timing – recognising an opportune time and tricking the adversary into thinking that they have an opportunity when they do not. These theories of tempo enrich our understanding of the unusual dramatic structure of *Titus Andronicus* because they illuminate the movements of the plot and the flow of initiative among characters.

Tamora's Tempo

Titus Andronicus (1594) is the first of two revenge tragedies under-taken by Shakespeare, the other one being *Hamlet* (1600). Perhaps unsurprisingly, *Titus Andronicus* has a long history of being over-shadowed and sometimes dismissed as an early attempt at the genre that is later brought to perfection in the Danish tale. However, there is much to be said for Shakespeare's first revenge tragedy, especially in relationship to the intertwining themes of rhetorical and corporeal violence. *Titus Andronicus* riffs on Roman sources such as Ovid's *Metamorphoses* and Livy's *History of Rome* to create a story about a decaying empire that faces external threats from violent Goths and internal threats from a corrupt emperor. Titus, the Roman general-turned-avenger, and his antagonist, Tamora, the usurping Goth queen, stage their battle for control of Rome via their sacrifice, mur-der, rape, mutilation and baking of each other's children. Given that Titus and Tamora are both military leaders, it should come as no surprise that their encounters are grounded in the *kairos* of fencing. Tamora and Titus exemplify good timing, the ability to grasp oppor-tunity as well as generate vulnerability in the *duello* (war between two) that structures the play. The pedagogy of timing illuminates Titus's strategy and contextualises some of the characters' seemingly inexplicable decisions.

Tamora's exploitation of tempo is the driving force of Acts 1–3, though the play's first moments may lead its readers and viewers to expect a story about male sovereignty and inheritance. *Titus Androni-cus* begins with an argument over the temporal politics of succession: should the eldest son rule, or the man with superior merit? Saturninus, the first-born son of the late emperor of Rome, insists that primogeni-ture be observed. Bassianus, his younger brother, argues that his own virtue makes him a better candidate for the throne. To complicate the matter of succession even more, Titus's brother, Marcus Andronicus, offers the crown to Titus on behalf of the Roman people who elected him based his military prowess and honour. Titus is less interested in assuming a new position of political power and more interested in interring his sons who died in battle. When he decides to make the ritual sacrifice of Alarbus (the eldest son of the captured Goth queen, Tamora) part of the funeral ceremony, he makes it impossible for himself to remain apolitical, however. He refuses the honour of being emperor and instead recommends Saturninus rule as the eldest son. In gratitude (or perhaps in a fit of pique since she is currently betrothed to Bassianus), Saturninus declares his intention to marry Titus's only daughter, Lavinia. Lavinia promptly flees, deeply offending Saturninus and creating a rift between him and her father. Saturninus consoles himself by marrying Tamora, Titus's chief captive.

The play can be understood as three devices, or phrases of combat. Titus begins the play with the initiative when he returns from war to bury his dead sons and present Rome with treasure and captives. Tamora cannot stop Titus's ritual execution of her son, Alarbus. However, Titus stumbles: he helps to put the weak and corrupt Saturninus on the throne, whose favour he immediately loses. Tamora then seizes the initiative and puts Titus into obedience in a series of attacks that leave Lavinia severely injured and Titus without a hand and bereft of two more sons. In the third phrase, Titus regains the advantage but conceals it until the banquet scene in which he bakes Chiron and Demetrius into a pie and feeds them to their mother.

The play blurs the borders of rhetoric and combat from its opening moments when Saturninus urges his constituents to 'plead my successive title with your swords' (1.1.4). Saturninus rhetorically places swords, rather than plaintiffs, front and centre in the courtroom. However, as Saturninus demonstrates when he believes Titus has supplanted him, his supporters' swords, unlike people seeking legal redress, are not bound by law. The substitution of weapons for words in a legal sense is a continuing theme in the play: weapons and wounds are also called to 'witness' repeatedly. For example, Demetrius stabs Bassianus for Tamora, asserting '[t]his is a witness that I am thy son' (2.2.130). Echoing this legal language, in the final scene when Titus reveals that Chiron and Demetrius were baked into the pie fed to Tamora, he says, ''Tis true, 'tis true, witness my knife's sharp point' (5.3.58). The legal acts of pleading and witnessing still resonate with Elizabethans as shared domains of combat and speech due to England's legacy of the judicial duel (wager of battle) and trial by ordeal. In cases where truth cannot be determined through traditional channels of witness, accused and accuser face each other on the field of battle.[16]

Saturninus's first words reveal the play's interest in the intersection of swords and words, and Titus's first lines introduce the theme of timing that is key to understanding the relationship between rhetorical and physical violence. Titus's engagement with timing is initially focused on the belatedness of his sons' burial rites: 'Titus, unkind and careless of thine own, / Why suffer'st thou thy sons unburied yet / To hover on the dreadful shore of Styx?' (1.1.89–91). When Titus rejects the crown offered him by the people of Rome, it is for reasons of timing: his head is too old for Rome's body, a temporal mismatching inviting disaster. He refuses Marcus's invitation to 'set a head on headless Rome', saying, 'A better head her glorious body fits / Than his that shakes for age and feebleness' (1.1.189–91). Titus, like a more famous example of early retirement in Shakespeare's oeuvre, Lear, comes to regret the decision.

Tamora exploits Titus's missed opportunity, showing her skill at generating and seizing tempo. When begging Titus to spare Alarbus's life does not change his mind, she is silent until Saturninus unexpectedly places her in a position of political power as his wife. Then she cautions Saturninus to take a similar strategy and to hide his fury at losing his claim on Lavinia, instead waiting until she provokes the Andronici into giving up a tempo that she may seize in retaliation: 'You are but newly planted in your throne' (1.1.449), she warns him, 'Yield at entreats – and then let me alone: / I will find a day to massacre them all' (1.1.454–5). Timeliness significantly cuts across word and deed: Saturninus's unwise public anger at Titus does nothing to 'dissemble' Saturninus's 'griefs and discontents' (1.1.448), a necessary part of a strategy to position the Andronici advantageously for Tamora's revenge.

Aaron, Tamora's Moorish lover and fellow captive, demonstrates strategic skill at generating and seizing opportunity, from his opening lines, where he resolves to 'mount aloft' (2.1.512) with Tamora in her unexpected elevation, to his forest entrapment of Quintus and Martius in Act 2, scene 2. He shows his skill at exploiting the spatial as well as the temporal dimensions of tempo by suggesting the woods, a space that creates opportunity, as a site for revenge: '[t]he forest walks are wide and spacious, / And many unfrequented plots there are, / Fitted by kind for rape and villainy' (1.1.614–16). Aaron uses place and event, woods and the hunt, to create a kairotic situation for revenge. He then ties himself explicitly to time and death during his encounter with Tamora in the woods. Aaron checks her amorous enthusiasm, saying 'Madam, though Venus govern your desires, / Saturn is dominator over mine' (2.2.30–1). Jonathan Bate glosses 'Saturn' here as referring to the god's role as revenger, and this is certainly consonant with the themes of the play.[17] However, Saturn (Kronos) is also the god of time and grandfather of the god Kairos. Tamora and Aaron seize the tempo they need for revenge stealthily through proper timing under Saturn's influence.

The kinds of swordplay taking place in early modern England further illuminate the correspondences between the theory and practice of fencing, on the one hand, and the theme of timing in *Titus Andronicus*, on the other. Tamora's surviving sons, Chiron and Demetrius, both declare their desire for Lavinia and fall out with each other at the end of Act 1 in a reprise of the birth order argument that begins the play. Swaggering onto the stage in the middle of a heated conflict, the brothers' lines tie them to the Italianate courtly culture of duelling, and Aaron's subsequent concern evokes the public spaces of the London streets. Chiron swears that, despite the small difference in age between the brothers, he is just as worthy as Demetrius to possess Lavinia. He threatens Demetrius: 'my sword upon thee shall approve, / And plead my passions for Lavinia's love' (1.1.534–5). The language here reflects the underlying judicial structure of the duel: both the private duel over the point of honour that was beginning to flourish in England as well as the Continent, and the duel as trial by ordeal. The kind of proof that the sword offers was a last resort and was only sought when the question under arbitration was not one that could be proved through witnesses. Though England's jury system had long displaced the trial by combat as the typical method of settling disputes, the trial by combat persisted through the sixteenth century and lived on in cultural memory, as we can see in the abortive duel at the beginning of *Richard II* between Thomas Mowbray and Henry Bolingbroke. Shakespeare invokes these associations in the brawl scene of *Titus Andronicus* as part of his comic and gruesome juxtaposition of high and low: love and rape, the gentleman's duel and the street brawl join together with later pairings of pathetic flies and cannibal feasts.

Chiron's invocation of the trial by ordeal foreshadows the emptiness and failure of the judicial system. Chiron's use of legal language is hardly more responsible than Saturninus's corrupt and foolish rule. Demetrius brushes aside Chiron's reference to judicial duelling conventions and taunts him for his youth:

> Why, boy, although our mother, unadvised,
> Gave you a dancing-rapier by your side,
> Are you so desperate grown to threat your friends?
> Go to, have your lath glued within your sheath
> Till you know better how to handle it.   (1.1.537–41)

These lines evoke dance and theatre, two arts that require cooperative timing between partners.[18] Demetrius patronisingly dismisses Chiron, describing his weapon as purely ornamental, or wooden and fake altogether. Demetrius also uses the rhetoric of duelling when he refuses to put away his rapier until: 'I have sheathed / My rapier in his bosom, and withal / Thrust those reproachful speeches down his throat / That he hath breathed in my dishonour here' (1.1.552–5).

When Aaron emerges with his plan, it redirects the competition of Chiron and Demetrius into cooperation against the Andronici. Aaron bathetically calls for 'clubs' in an aside that reduces the courtly rhetoric of the duel over the point of honour to a street brawl that needs the intervention of the watch to curtail. What the brothers imagine in terms of the aristocratic privilege of the point-of-honour duel, Aaron reduces to the petty misdeeds of London delinquents.

The initial argument over Lavinia between Chiron and Demetrius casts them as the dangerous youth of London infected with foreign practices. A generational as well as a national approach to the threat that Chiron and Demetrius pose to Roman social order here is useful. In a play where sons are systematically murdered and executed, Chiron and Demetrius are among the last of their generation still standing. Their 'braving' entrée into the play resonates with Elizabethan anxieties over gang violence from idle and bellicose young men who earned the titles of 'roaring boy' and 'swashbuckler' as they took to the streets, sliding their swords against the inside of their bucklers to indicate they were spoiling for a fight.[19] This association is further cemented when Aaron calls for clubs to separate them. The roaring boys in Elizabethan England signal a failure of humanist goals to replace violence with writing. Placed inside a scriptive order that trains him to read, Chiron (Χείρων, literally 'hand') becomes the decorporealised hand dismembered from the social body through a process of discipline that ultimately does not replace material violence with immaterial writing, but rather continues to implicate the scene of writing with the scene of violence.[20]

Aaron's usage of the term 'device' further underscores the mingling of rhetoric and combat. The device is a linguistic crossover between the two domains of knowledge, rhetoric and the science of defence. Though the *Oxford English Dictionary* focuses on the form of 'device' referring to a scheme, an intention or a heraldic emblem, as we have seen, the word is also a specialised term in fencing, denoting a phrase of combat or a technique. Silver cautions his fellow countrymen to shun the 'vices and devices' of foreign fencing masters,[21] and he has choice words to say about 'those Imprfyt Italyon Devyses wt rapyor & poniard'.[22] When Aaron sees Chiron and Demetrius brawling with their swords, he cautions them: 'you do but plot your deaths / By this device' (1.1.577–8). Aaron puns on both senses of the word – a device as something that is plotted, a stratagem or instrument, and device as a phrase of combat, the duel or brawl that he interrupts. The pun foreshadows Titus's own combination of words and weapons in Act 4.

Titus's Turn

The first three acts of the tragedy are dominated by Tamora's skill at seizing tempo, but in Act 4 Titus succeeds in regaining the initiative. Act 4 occurs at an unspecified point in time after Act 3, curiously flattening to simultaneity Lavinia's explication of Ovid and Tamora's gestation and delivery. Due to its temporal tactics, this part of the play can be as puzzling to its audience as it is to the characters within it. It is often read as a digression in the revenge plot. For example, according to Bate's analysis, Titus demonstrates his madness when he 'spends the fourth act sending jokey messages, first to Chiron and Demetrius, then to Saturninus via arrows and Clown'.[23] Bate sees Titus's actions in the fourth act as working more to engage the audience's sympathy rather than to accomplish anything in the plot. In contrast, I would argue that the act represents Titus's skilful deployment of both the waiting and acting elements of tempo.

Act 4 contains three scenes that Titus supposedly instigates due to his madness, each one involving a letter wrapped around a weapon: the weapons from his armoury delivered with a verse from *Lilly's Grammar*, the arrows bound in notes that plead for divine justice fired inside Rome's walls, and the knife folded into a note to Saturninus and delivered by the unfortunate Clown. The instances represent different deployments of *contratempo*. The first is a feigned weakness designed to make the Goths overconfident and to free Titus to pursue revenge. The second and third are attacks that purposefully fall short in order to prepare the people of Rome for a new leader and engage their sympathies, while making Saturninus jumpy and eager to conciliate Lucius and Titus. The beginning of the play sees Tamora's seizure of tempo with the forest murder. The remaining acts involve Titus's retaliation, which models both the intentional waiting and the decisive activity necessary to seize tempo.

Fencing pedagogy employing the principle of tempo holds that a fencer can place the opponent into obedience without actually making attacks. The temporal position refers to an index of initiative and opportunity rather than to specific actions. Parries performed to lull the adversary into a false sense of security, or to gain a more advantageous positioning of body and blade can be performed by the fencer who takes the initiative, without the adversary knowing that they have been put into obedience. In such a move, Titus stealthily regains the initiative in the scene where he sends a letter to Chiron and Demetrius, and the bloody four lines that accompany three

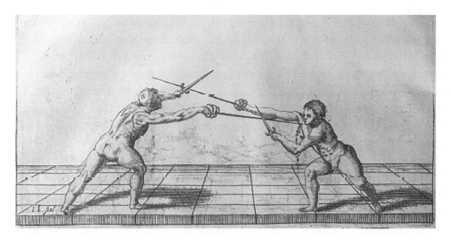

Figure 4.1 Salvator Fabris. Contratempo. Plate 73, *Sienza e Pratica d'Arme di Salvator Fabris*, 1606. Engraving. Courtesy of Guy Windsor.

deaths in the banquet scene represent Titus's final stroke, emerging from the device victorious over Tamora. Tamora fatally initiates the contact that Titus exploits when she dresses as Revenge and brings Chiron and Demetrius to Titus's door (Fig. 4.1).

Critical attempts to deal with the 4.2 letter scene tend to dramatically abstract its action in order to maintain the thrust of some greater argument. This moment has been read variously as a strike at Horace and classical authority, a moment for Aaron to revel in his superior historical and literary knowledge over Chiron and Demetrius, and a demonstration of bad pedagogy and reading practices that involve emulation without discretion.[24] However, when read in dialogue with the discourses of fencing and tempo, the scene quite literally speaks to the play of time as Titus creates opportunity for himself by feigning madness.

Following Lavinia's explication of Ovid and the vows of the Andronici to revenge her, Young Lucius understandably wants to deliver a dagger-message to the bosoms of the perpetrators. Titus, instead, promises to 'teach [him] another course' (4.1.119). Deferring immediate revenge, Titus sets the stage for a more condign and satisfying revenge. Titus's next move is to gather up a gift basket of weapons from his armoury and to wrap a citation from Horace around them: *Integer vitae, scelerisque purus, / Non eget Mauri iaculis, nec arcu*, 'The man of upright life and free of crime does not need the javelins or bows of the Moor.' Heather James reads the *integer* of *integer vitae* as 'physically whole', referring to the maimed Titus who no longer intends to stay free of crime.[25] While these resonances are certainly in play, *integer* also reads as 'morally upright', and as such the letter works to lull his future victims into inaction rather than threatening them. The gift bewilders Titus's family and inspires his enemies with a feeling of safety. In the end, however, Titus's promise to Young Lucius to teach him another course is fulfilled not by the letter but by the play's final feast when he kills the Goth boys and feeds them to their mother.

When the young Goths receive this scrap of Latin poetry from Titus, Chiron, preening himself on noticing its classical allusion, fails to attach any greater significance to it. Aaron, on the contrary, seems smugly assured that he has correctly read Titus's wounding lines. But what does Aaron know (or think he knows) and what is the significance of Chiron's interpretation of the note? The initial exchange around the letter is remarkable, not least for the often noted fact that the characters apparently have some knowledge of Latin and Roman literature, 'a common ability to "speak the language of Empire"'.[26] Demetrius seizes the letter first and exclaims:

> DEMETRIUS: What's here? A scroll, and written round about?
> Let's see:
> [*Reads.*] *Integer vitae, scelerisque purus,*
> *Non eget Mauri iaculis, nec arcu.*
> CHIRON: O, 'tis a verse in Horace, I know it well:
> I read it in the grammar long ago.   (4.2.18–23)

Chiron seems to agree with Demetrius's reading of Titus's gesture as an overture of friendship in a pathetic bid for favour from the politically ascendant Goths. In fact, the receipt of the letter initiates a scene of pedagogy, but in a different, more darkly comic register than is usually suspected. The interactions of the three recipients with the letter are those of a patronising schoolmaster who thinks he understands more than he does, and his two dense pupils over whom he enjoys intellectual superiority a little too much. In Aaron's aside, he snickers:

> Ay, just – A verse in Horace, right, you have it.
> [*aside*] Now what a thing it is to be an ass.
> Here's no sound jest! The old man hath found their guilt,
> And sends them weapons wrapped about with lines
> That wound beyond their feeling to the quick.
> But were our witty empress well afoot
> She would applaud Andronicus' conceit.   (4.2.24–30)

Made overconfident by his intelligence in relation to Chiron and Demetrius, Aaron ultimately underestimates the other adults of the play. Of Aaron's pupils, the older brother, Demetrius, reacts first to the delivery of the letter, seizing it and reading out loud the lines of poetry. Chiron's subsequent recognition and citation of Horace's ode is done in direct speech. He recognises it not as part of the longer ode, but rather as an aphorism learned in his school grammar book. *Lilly's Grammar* and Shakespeare's plays appropriate and redeploy stories and aphorisms from multiple cultural and temporal contexts. This eclecticism contributes to a disorientation and difficulty in fixing and organising time and space. Aaron's response to Chiron is straightforward and humorously emphatic. Aaron condescendingly flanks Chiron's observation, 'a verse in Horace', with two affirmations, 'Ay, just' and 'right, you have it.' In his aside, however, Aaron's rhetoric becomes more complex.

Aaron offers his own interpretation of the letter. His first thought is of what the gift reveals about its sender. The 'sound' of 'no sound jest' describes most obviously what Aaron views as Titus's mental state, 'sound' in the sense of health and wholeness. Aaron believes that Titus is not making a jest from a state of mental soundness, and thus the jest reveals his insanity. 'Sound' for Aaron clearly functions as an adjective modifying the noun 'jest'. However, the internal rhyme of 'sound' with 'found' in this line also evokes the verbal form of the word. Shakespeare ironically positions Aaron to think he is doing one thing with language (questioning Titus's sanity), while revealing to the audience that Aaron is perhaps not in as full control of his rhetoric as he believes he is. Aaron unintentionally gestures to what Titus is really doing: sinking in, penetrating and discovering, sounding them out with a test and creating opportunity for himself. In his arrogance, Aaron becomes the victim of Titus's scheme and reads the letter the way that Titus assumes that all three of them will – as 'some mad message from [Lucius's] mad grandfather' (4.2.3), evidence of Titus's harmlessness. Once Titus has revealed his knowledge of Demetrius and Chiron's crime, he has only to wait for their reactions to see if he is safe in moving forward with the rest of his plan. If they are so convinced of his insanity that they do not feel the need to retaliate, then Titus has more freedom in pursuing his vengeance.

Chiron and Demetrius do not understand the allusion, much less that they are being sounded out. Here Titus, as well as Aaron, experiences rhetorical failure as his message goes amiss to two-thirds of his audience. Neither Titus nor Aaron are exemplary tutors: both either fail to communicate or fail to apprehend their text. Though Titus's message is misunderstood by Aaron and the Goth brothers, the letter serves a practical purpose in the plot to advance Titus's ends. While it is common for critics to read this scene as Titus sending a threat that Aaron understands but that Chiron and Demetrius do not, in fact the letter reveals Titus's calculating intelligence and his ability to generate and seize tempi of opportunity.[27]

The letter indicates that Titus considers Chiron and Demetrius as being under the tutelage of Aaron, and that this instruction is in something criminal and savage. Additionally, the message suggests that Chiron and Demetrius are not men of upright lives and free from crime – they need javelins and bows (thus the weapons from Titus's armoury). Ostensibly following the advice of humanist educators like Vives, Titus renounces the barbarous tools of warfare (the javelins and bows of the Moor) and delivers his own weapons to a Moor's students, while seemingly taking up the writers' quill as his weapon. Titus opposes the realms of rhetoric and combat to imply that he has given up a physical mode of violence for something subtler. He manipulates this expectation to his advantage, ignoring the expected linear trajectory from brutal bloodshed to peaceful writing.

The letter's valence of new pacifism overshadows the threat of the message, explaining Aaron's amused indifference to Demetrius and Chiron's lack of perception. The letter can be read as an exposure of the brothers, but in the same breath, as indicative of Titus's intentions not to pursue the matter any further. Practically, this strategy means that, because Titus is able to dissimulate and encrypt his true intention, which is to pursue violent revenge, he is left free to work out his plans, which include having arrows fired into Saturninus's court wrapped in pleas for divine justice. Titus incites revolt within Rome's walls, as his son Lucius approaches from the outside with his new Goth army. Titus's careful planning explains why Tamora leaves her sons at his house without fear. Tamora and her sons' conviction that Titus is mad, which leads to their renunciation of violent means, is their only reason for putting themselves into Titus's grasp. The letter heightens the effect of Titus's return to violence – after an entire act where Titus writes letters and intertwines them with weapons, wounding beyond feeling but not wounding bodies, his murder of Chiron and Demetrius becomes all the more spectacular to the audience, who may or may not have been persuaded by Titus's apparent turn to non-violence. In Fabris's sense, Titus seizes tempo by feigning weakness to trigger an attack he is ready to counter.

The antagonistic and interruptive timing taught by the 'art and science of defence' provides an alternative to the timing of the narrative arc. Often, where Shakespeare and his contemporaries seem to unexpectedly digress from an expected plot trajectory, they are in fact drawing from this and other models of timing in circulation in early modern England. Reading *Titus Andronicus* from this perspective sheds light on the structure of the play by contextualising Titus's strategic moments of madness. Shakespeare's use of the letter device works tactically to manoeuvre his audience into obedience by crafting an unpredictable narrative and avenger. The uncertainty around Titus's sanity creates the conditions for surprise in the audience, just as it sets Tamora up within the play.

Another Course

Suspense and surprise are more pleasurable experiences in a dramatic spectacle than in feasts with one's enemies, and it may seem out of place to try to relate the cultural work that the notoriously gory *Titus Andronicus* accomplishes to our own social and civic contexts. But Titus's *contratempo* strategic moves, excessive and historically particular as they are, connect in deep ways to contemporary concerns and conversations around ethics. Linda Woodbridge explores one important axis of these connections in her *English Revenge Drama: Money, Resistance, Equality*, where she argues that a widespread perception of systematic economic unfairness is at the root of the popularity of the revenge drama genre: 'revenge plays obliquely respond to inflation and failed economic regulation'.[28] For Woodbridge, eroding belief in the capability of the justice system to be fair spurs the popularity of revenge dramas like *Titus Andronicus*. The connection between a commonly held public distrust in the fairness of the judicial system and the popularity of vigilantism in entertainment has compelling force in today's popular cultural landscape as well, dominated as it is by superhero film and television. Woodbridge's analysis calls into question the critical assumption that early moderns would have condemned private revenge and watched revenge drama as a guilty pleasure. In this same vein, this chapter has nuanced the view that pen and sword exist in opposition to each other, with the pen's application of power seen as peaceful and positive while the sword's application of power is seen as violent and destructive.

Fairness, as Woodbridge describes it, turns on the issue of likeness and unlikeness. The popularity of revenge tropes, both in

Shakespeare's time and our own, is driven by an urgent interest in the ethical question of sameness and difference. Humanist rhetorical education stresses an understanding of sameness on the way to the development of ethical relationships and communities. Children are powerfully socialised to imagine and attempt to understand the internal states of others in order to predict their likely actions, or to interpret past behaviour. For instance, *Sesame Street*'s prime-time special 'The Magic Wand Chase' is described as 'deeply connected to the season's respect and understanding curriculum' by Sesame Street Workshop.[29] The show aims to teach children the admirable lessons that 'kindness is universal and new friends can be found anywhere'. While there is certainly a good deal to be said in favour of a respect and understanding curriculum, the hunger of contemporary viewers for vigilantes and superheroes suggests a deep-felt desire for alternate scenarios as well, those that stress difference and punish injustice instead.

The syntax of fencing I have described in this chapter focuses on difference rather than sameness. This syntax speaks to urgent questions such as the responsibility of each member of the community to dis-identify with powerful people exercising unethical behaviour especially, to recognise their difference from an acceptable social order, and to acknowledge that it is unethical to build rapport with those whose actions and rhetoric encourage violence. Titus's 'another course' (of the feast, of action) is so much more emotionally satisfying than the 'course' Marcus thinks Titus is choosing because sometimes interruption is a better response than identification. The rhythms of response to conflict offered to us by the embodied expressions of fencing and drama, then, are useful on a formal level: emptying the grotesque content specifics of baking scenes and the technical jargon of fencing, we are left with powerful forms for understanding conflict. In these examples, one does not identify with an enemy in order to predict their next action and engage in conversation or resistance. The model of conflict demonstrated in *contratempo* moves away from empathy (looking for the good in each person and shaping one's own feelings in response) to projection and anticipation.

Notes

1. All references to *Titus Andronicus* are taken from the Arden Shakespeare Third Series. Other references to Shakespeare's plays are taken from the Norton Shakespeare, 2nd edition. Hereafter, Shakespeare quotations will be cited parenthetically by act, scene and line numbers.

2. Garber, *Shakespeare after All*, 76.
3. James, 'Cultural Disintegration', 124.
4. Tricomi, 'The Aesthetics of Mutilation', 11.
5. Fawcett, 'Arms/Words/Tears', 272.
6. Ibid.
7. Anderson, '"What is written shall be executed"', 303.
8. Hale, *Private Schoole of Defence*, n.p.
9. Facsimiles of all sixteenth- and seventeenth-century fencing manuals, including the 1575 edition of *Lo Schermo*, are taken from the Raymond J. Lord collection hosted by the Massachusetts Center for Renaissance Studies. Viggiani argues, through the historical figure Aluigi Gonzaga, that 'Il moto, e il tempo mi paiono due grandissimi fondamenti, e due basi di tutte le cose naturali. Quale è quella arte, o facultà, a cui facciano bisogno il tempo, e il moto, piu della Guerra?' (*Lo Schermo*, 11r).
10. Viggiani, *Lo Schermo*, 13r.
11. See Wolfe, *Humanism*, 10–11.
12. Silver, *Paradoxes*, 7–8.
13. 'si vuol sapere che tutti i movimenti e tutti i riposi dell'avversario sieno tempi, però a misura' (Capoferro, *Gran Simulacro*, 33).
14. Fabris, *Lo Schermo*, 17–18.
15. Ibid.
16. Though fallen into disuse, the wager of battle was revived during the reign of Elizabeth I for the last time in September of 1583. The trial by combat took place in Ireland between members of the O'Conor clan. Thomas Cooke and William Cooke wrote that 'a dispute between two chiefs of the O'Conors of Offaley' was 'decided at the castle of Dublin in September 1583, in a trial by single combat or wager of battle, before Sir Henry Wallop, and Adam Loftus Archbishop of Dublin, the Lords Justices' (254). Conor MacCormac O'Conor accused Teige MacGillpatrick O'Conor of killing men under his (Conor's) protection. Teige responded that they were rebels because they worked for a rebel. Teige offered to prove this assertion with combat, and Conor accepted the challenge. They fought with sword and target (a small, light shield). Teige emerged victorious, and 'he, with Conor's own sword, cut his head off, and presented it to the Lords Justices' (255). The combat took place only a decade or so before the first performances of *Titus Andronicus*.
17. See Bate's notes on p. 170 of the Arden Shakespeare Third Series' *Titus Andronicus*.
18. These taunts mirror the kinds of insults offered by native Englishmen like George Silver, who calls the favoured weapon of the Italians 'birdspits' (*Paradoxes of Defence*, v). Silver bemoans the transformation of 'men into boyes' (57) that Italian teachers and rapiers effect, and Demetrius's language similarly stresses inexperience, incompetence and youthfulness.

19. Thomas Cooper uses *swash* in his 1565 *Thesaurus linguae Romanae & Britannicae* to define the Latin word *concrepare*: 'to swashe, or make a noyse with swoordes agaynst tergattes'. Cooper's 'target' is a term often used interchangeably with 'buckler' to denote a small, light shield. Sword and buckler formed a traditional weapon combination for the English. In contrast, Italian teachers called the single sword (meaning rapier) the 'Queen of Weapons' and advocated for teaching its use to beginners before allowing an offhand offensive or defensive item such as a dagger, second sword, buckler or cloak.

20. See Goldberg, *Writing Matter*, on the disciplinary properties of handwriting education. By allying Chiron and Demetrius with foreign bravado, Shakespeare engages with audience anxieties about the disintegration of traditional methods of knowledge transfer. At the heart of the contentions over foreign teachers was the question of bad influence and infection from foreign vice. From Saviolo's text *His Practice*, published in 1595, and from the criticism the Italians as a group drew from English contemporaries like Silver, we can gather that their lessons focused on duelling and individual self-defence more than military preparation.

21. Silver, *Paradoxes*, 'Dedicatorie', n.p.

22. Silver, *Instructions*, 74.

23. Bate, 'Introduction' to the Arden *Titus Andronicus*, 12–13.

24. Heather James in *Shakespeare's Troy* argues that Titus's letter attacks classical authority because it 'hardly seems worth the trouble to humiliate Tamora's foolish and villainous sons in a literary contest' (72). Titus does not intend for his barbaric audience to understand the poetry of their colonisers, or to use it as a common medium of communication. She suggests that, when Titus turns the literature of Rome into a weapon, he subverts the capacity to instil and encourage Roman virtues. Dickson also assumes that Titus means for the note to be incomprehensible to its recipients. He argues that the letter scene functions as part of the play's questioning of the model of emulation, wherein England attempts to imitate and improve upon Rome: 'the judgments, beliefs, and precedents that the play enacts undercuts any sense of proper closure and satisfaction in emulating the examples of Rome' ('"A pattern, precedent, and lively warrant"', 406). Carolyn Sale ('Black Aeneas') enlists the letter scene as part of her argument about the interplay between violence and rhetoric in the play's moments of writing to comment on colonial relationships, and is more interested in Aaron's 'scornful amusement' than Titus's motivations. Bate, in his introduction to the Arden *Titus Andronicus*, considers how this scene contributes to the morbid humour of the play, and how the registers of grief and comedy intermingle in a reflection of the disintegrating decorums of Roman honour and dramatic expectation.

25. James, 'Cultural Disintegration', 132.

26. Antonucci, 'Romans versus Barbarians', 121.
27. Dickson, for example, assumes that we, like Aaron, apprehend the true meaning of the letter. He writes that Demetrius and Chiron's 'specific disregard for education [is] exhibited through their inability to read Titus's warning, so clearly apparent to Aaron' ('"A pattern, precedent, and lively warrant"', 389). Bate, in his introduction to *Titus Andronicus*, also suggests that Chiron and Demetrius 'misinterpret [the letter's] meaning (though that cunning reader, Aaron, does not)' (35). However, these readings of the letter-as-warning are problematic, because Aaron wishes in his next breath for Tamora to be there to share the joke with him, and he dismissively calls Titus an 'old man' (4.2.25) and his message a 'conceit' (4.2.30). It seems unlikely that Aaron, given his position as Tamora's favourite and his knowledge of Tamora's affection for her sons, would risk the sons' lives or their mother's goodwill. It seems even less likely that he would imagine that Tamora would be amused by a serious threat to her sons.
28. Woodbridge, *English Revenge Drama*, 8.
29. 'The Magical Wand Chase: A Sesame Street Special', *Sesame Street Workshop*, n.d., Web, Accessed 3 March 2021, www.sesameworkshop. org/press-room/press-kits/sesame-street-season-48/about-show-s48

Chapter 5

Taking Time for Love in *As You Like It*

Introduction

As You Like It is notorious for its aimlessness. As Maura Kuhn observed in 1977, the play's 'lack of plot after Act I has been observed by critics through the centuries'.[1] More recently, James Shapiro calls the play 'relatively plotless' in his work on the year 1599.[2] The play's dramatic structure reflects a knot of temporality and genre, with the time-fleeting *otium* of the pastoral contrasted to the ordered *negotium* of the court. Scholars have convincingly argued that this pastoral-romance experiments with plot structure to create an effect of suspended time in the ludic space of Arden forest. Fencing tempo, seen through the more expansive view of the art of defence that I have been describing, contributes to our understanding of the play's narrative time. As of yet, discussions of fencing in *As You Like It* have been mostly limited to the penultimate scene, Touchstone's extended comic explanation of duelling codes. Serious, deadly duels are antithetical to the fleeting time of Arden forest, and so Touchstone unpacks the ways in which duels are slowed and ultimately suspended through the verbal games of lies and responses to lies. This scene is important but is a culmination of less obvious moments of fencing's formal influence throughout the play. The absence of a linear, driving plot in *As You Like It* does not denote the play's aimlessness. Shakespeare drew from both the conventions of the pastoral and from the structure of the feint: a simulated menace to one target to draw a parry that is then eluded, and the sword directed at a different target. In contrast to *contratempo*, feigning relies not on pretended weakness to lure the adversary to attack but on distraction. Like the conditional 'if' for which *As You Like It* is famous, feints posit in their first movement a hypothetical.[3] The subsequent movements hold in suspense many possibilities at one time until the action is concluded with a touch to the open line. Seemingly plotless scenes in fact enact the back and forth of the play's narrative structure. Shakespeare uses both linguistic and non-linguistic methods to explore the theme of courtly dissimulation and to craft a suspended sense of theatrical time.

The play begins with intense sibling rivalry in the court of the late Rowland du Bois, as the eldest son, Oliver, denies his younger brother, Orlando, the education of a gentleman. Driven by jealousy of his well-liked younger brother, Oliver arranges for the wrestler, Charles, to murder or maim Orlando when they meet in the wrestling ring for a competition. This plan failing, Oliver decides to set fire to Orlando's house, with his brother still inside. Catching wind of the plot, the loyal elderly servant Adam escapes with Orlando into the exile of Arden forest. Meanwhile, in a neighbouring court, Duke Frederick has usurped the role of his older brother, Duke Senior, who has fled to Arden to live with a few of his devoted courtiers. His daughter, Rosalind, stays behind with her cousin, Celia, for a time. The women observe Orlando's wrestling match, and Rosalind falls in love with him. Soon thereafter, Frederick's paranoia prompts him to banish Rosalind. Celia and the court fool, Touchstone, decide to leave with Rosalind and head for Arden. Rosalind disguises herself as a shepherd boy, Ganymede, and Celia disguises herself as a shepherdess, Aliena. In the forest, Orlando is subjected to a number of tests to prove his love and to develop his courtly skills. Rosalind/Ganymede must both fend off the attentions of the besotted shepherdess Phoebe and teach Orlando how to woo properly. That the forest is a suitable environment for the inculcation of valuable character traits and abilities is confirmed when Oliver, cast off into the forest by Frederick, has a change of heart and reconciles with his younger brother. Oliver and Touchstone decide to marry local shepherdesses – Aliena, who pleasantly surprises the courtiers by being a noblewoman in disguise, and Audrey, who does not. The play concludes with a four-way wedding.

I have already touched on the ways in which fencing signifies as a mode of *poiesis* in Jonson's comedy. Shakespeare, too, draws a close relationship between the fictions of fencing and those of aesthetic representation. Three scenes of feigning exemplify the play's debt to fencing tactics and techniques, which culminate in Touchstone's final disquisition on giving the lie. The first scene, Orlando's wrestling match, introduces the play's interest in sports and body language as a supplement to the love language of poetry he practises later in the play. Later, as Rosalind and Orlando disguise themselves, the play explores the generative potential of dissimulation via their fictions of selfhood. In a second scene of commingled fictions, Orlando bursts threateningly into Duke Senior's banquet to demand food. Though seeming to display ineptness, Orlando actually shows again his keen sense of tempo as he adapts to the unexpected situation. The rhythm of his movement – threat, perception, adaptation – reflects the structure of the feint, as English and German fencing theory understand it. Finally, Orlando's seeming shift to verbal methods of displaying and developing courtiership through his love poetry is telling. Rosalind, disguised as Ganymede, tutors Orlando on a lover's dilated and experiential sense of time while Jaques, Touchstone and Celia/Aliena comment on the tempo of his poetry. Orlando's feet, both metrical and physical, become the locus of the play's interest in embodied models of time. The play's unusual four-way stichomythic exchange in the final act formally reflects the sideways movement of the feint and the preparatory footwork for launching an effective attack.

The art of defence in *As You Like It* brings with it a digressive timing that dilates the pace of the plot. There are certainly several ways to account for the play's odd pacing. For instance, Jay Halio argues that Arden's sprawling forest pace is a necessary tempo foil to the tempo of city and court life – Arden's timelessness 'links life in Arden with the ideal of an older, more gracious way of life that helps regenerate a corrupt present'.[4] Maurice Hunt suggests that classical and religious senses of *kairos* motivate sequences in the play, as characters mature and learn to seize opportunity at its ripest moment.[5] To these, I would add that the shift in timing occurs as a formal reflection of the play's interest in the sporting elements of deception: when fencing makes its way into the literary it is often in relation to the discipline's techniques of dissimulation. Changes in tempo (in this case, the narrative timing of the plot) are crucial to crafting an effective feint. In the wrestling scene at the beginning of *As You Like It*, Oliver uses the modality of playful performance common in English prizefighting to cover up a more profound form of 'wiles and new deceits' with his attempt on Orlando's life. The play does not simply divide court and country into scenes of deception and sincerity, however. Throughout the play Orlando is introduced to the ways in which being a courtier is about practised, timely feigning – Castiglione's *sprezzatura*. The movements of the characters, their entrances and exits, as well as their words, exemplify feints on a non-linguistic level, while their wordplay on themes of time and dissimulation verbally mimic the delivery of the feint.

Poiesis, Genre, Feints

The poetic register associated with the activity of swordplay has a long literary history, particularly as lovers and competing rhetoricians appropriate the figurative landscape of a fencing match. Lovers may be pierced with the cold steel of their beloved's indifference and ripostes to arguments may be delivered skilfully, but these examples represent only a small portion of the whole family of fencing tropes. Appropriately for the playfully and romantically antagonistic context of *As You Like It*, the same linguistic element, *lac*, or play, modifies the activities of fighting in battle (*beadu-lac*) and getting married (*wedlac*) – what we now know as wedlock. However, as we have seen, Florio's expansion of the definition of *finta* illustrates the alliance between these two modes of creative expression, both verbal and non-verbal. In his shift from the 1598 definition of *finta* as 'a faigning, an offer, a proffer to do any thing' to the 1611 inclusion of 'a fiction', Florio illuminates the connection between the feints of fencing and those of fiction. As we have seen, however, Florio recognises, rather than invents, this common ground.[6] Fencing authors such as Viggiani, Giganti and Alfieri and literary authors such as Castiglione both extensively use the feint to articulate the connection between deception and aesthetics. Alfieri, too, admires the skilful use of feints. Like Castiglione's Federico, who defends courtly dissimulation by citing dissimulation in fencing, Alfieri sees deception as something to be celebrated in this context. While 'deception in itself is an odious word,' he argues, 'no one will deny that military conventions allow for stratagems of war . . . war is nothing but a duel between two kings, in which deception is permitted and is a virtue'.[7] Specifically, Alfieri goes on to write, 'the deception of which I speak offends neither justice nor the faith, but is a precept of the art used to defeat your enemy without difficulty called the feint'.[8]

Alfieri gives a rare illustration of a feint in action in Figure 6 of *L'arte di ben maneggiare la spada*. Plates often depict the fencer either before or after the feint is executed. Here, Alfieri uses letters to demarcate potential lines of attack. The feint represents two of the four ways in which the fencer on the right can hit after allowing the fencer on the left to gain his sword and come into measure. Alfieri writes that the fencer can feint to A, then lower the hand to B to wound in the chest, or feint to A and cut the leg in C with a retreat (Fig. 5.1).

That fencing masters still felt the need to defend the ethics of the feint well into the seventeenth century is suggestive of the

Figure 5.1 Francesco Alfieri. The feint. 'Del ferire di seconda e di Piè fermo', *La Scherma*, 1640. Engraving. Vienna, Österreichische Nationalbibliothek, digitised by Google Books.

technique's cultural freight. On the practical rather than the moral side of the issue, Capoferro, who focuses more on the duelling field and less on a student's performative ability, warns against using the feint except in very restricted situations because it gives up a tempo and exposes the fencer to being hit with a counterattack in a serious encounter: 'Feints are not good because they lose tempo and measure . . . if you feint outside of measure, it does not convince me to move, but if you feint in measure I will hit you while you are feinting'.[9] The feint's riskiness is part of its elegance, but its successful execution calls for a careful reading of the context and its stakes – the genre of the match.

Scholars have long recognised the importance of feigning to *As You Like It*, but often assume negative connotations. Kuhn, for example, writes that 'Feigning, poesy, and lying are all in league with flattery, that staple of court life and courtly love which is exposed in the play'.[10] While this association is certainly present, it does not represent the full spectrum of the play's engagement with what Castiglione terms 'comely dissimulation'. Orlando's education, in large part, involves learning to more artfully deceive and to allow himself to be deceived.

'Swashing and a martial outside': Disguise and Self Performance

Shakespeare collapses verbal and non-verbal modes of interaction throughout *As You Like It*, especially around love and play. One of Rosalind's first lines involves the sport of falling in love. Her conversation with Celia about the figurative sport of amorous conquest is immediately followed by an invitation to see a wrestling match. The sport metaphors continue throughout her courtship, with Orlando first 'throwing' Rosalind's heart by throwing Charles, then Rosalind's beauty turning Orlando into a jousting target. Rosalind laments: 'Sir, you have wrestled well, and overthrown / More than your enemies' (1.2.219–29). Orlando remonstrates with himself after Rosalind's greeting and departure, saying: Can I not say 'I thank you'? My better parts / Are all thrown down, and that which here stands up / Is but a quintain, a mere lifeless block' (12.215–17). This interaction reveals the extent to which the non-verbal expression of sports and combat is linked with the verbal expression of love and love poetry in the play. That Rosalind and Orlando are rendered speechless reflects the play's larger engagement in body language. Orlando goes from boasting about 'not being yet breathed', or out of breath from strenuous exercise, to losing all of his verbal ability. Charles cannot speak after he is thrown, foreshadowing the figurative throwing of Orlando's heart a few lines later. Duke Frederick cites Rosalind's reticence as evidence for her untrustworthiness. Given no reason to exile Rosalind due to her behaviour, he construes her silence as deceptive, telling Celia '[s]he is too subtle for thee, and her smoothness, her very silence, and her patience speak to the people, and they pity her' (1.3.71–3). The non-verbal language of sports comes to fill the lacunae left by these silencings.

The formal properties of the wrestling match reflect the play's central concerns around courts, courtiership and the true meaning of nobility.[11] As early as 1606, Fabris deprecates physical contact in a fencing match because touching the opponent leads to wrestling, and wrestling is a degeneration of true fencing. However, he treats it himself in a number of plays (sequences of attack), and he admits that it has its place as part of a long tradition of foundational combat training. In earlier Italian manuals and in contemporary English and German-language manuals, wrestling was often taught first as part of the art of defence rather than a lower-class alternative to it. Pietro Monte, for instance, places wrestling first in his fighting treatise, arguing that 'No other skill . . . teaches us to temper and control our bodies like wrestling'.[12] Castiglione recommends wrestling, though for more pragmatic than artful reasons, saying that 'it will serve his turne greatly, to know the feate of wrestling, because it goeth much together with all weapon on foote'.[13] Orlando, like the sport of wrestling in which he excels, occupies a somewhat uncomfortable position. Noble, martial and manly? Or peasant-like, brutal and uncouth?

Rosalind, at least, is filled with admiration for Orlando's youth and skill. As she wishes Orlando good luck, fully expecting him to be disabled or killed in his wrestling match with Charles, she alters a common conversational formula to Orlando's situation: 'Hercules be thy speed' (1.2.175). Rosalind's transformation of the more common 'God speed thee' is significant. 'Speed' denotes success and good fortune as well as velocity, and 'godspeed' was a common way to 'express a wish for the success of a person who is setting out on some journey or enterprise'.[14] Rosalind's unconventional appropriation of the formula draws attention to the multiple senses of 'speed' as noun and verb. While today the term has undergone significant semantic narrowing to refer mostly to a measure of the quickness of movement, in Shakespeare's day 'speed' encompassed fortune, skill, context and timing.[15] In this adapted formula, Rosalind links together the sportive qualities of the wrestling match and the play's later concerns around speed in poetry, love and social interaction.[16]

Both Rosalind and Orlando treat dissimulation as a generative process rather than a vice responsible for the downfall of a golden age. They react to their banishments by strategising how they will survive, setting up an elaborate game of make-believe before they even leave their courts. In this way, they reflect the ideal courtiership as they learn to project the fiction of selfhood across various contexts.[17] Rosalind's fiction centres on constructing a 'swashing and a martial outside' through props and performance. She plans to place a 'gallant curtal-axe' upon her thigh and a 'boar-spear' in her hand to hide the 'woman's fear' in her heart (1.3.111–14). She renames herself Ganymede, which, as has been commonly noted, emphasises the indeterminacy of her gender and her availability as a love object. However, Jove's cupbearer is also a displaced participant in the court of Olympus. Kidnapped from his task of sheep-tending on Mount Ida, Ganymede is the inverse of Rosalind. Where Rosalind is forced to move from the court to the pastoral, Ganymede travels under duress from the serene pastoral to the dangerous court of the gods. Meanwhile, Orlando contemplates whether he should beg for food or 'with a base and boisterous sword enforce / A thievish living on the common road' (2.3.33–4). Orlando's words foreshadow his actions at the forest banquet, sketching out the two paths he sees as available to survive. Ultimately, Orlando takes neither of these routes, but adapts to the circumstances he finds in the forest by beginning his training as a courtier.

'The countenance of stern commandment': Orlando's Feint

In Act 2 of *As You Like It*, Orlando displays his skill at reading and adapting to situations in a different social context than the wrestling ring when he crashes a forest banquet of exiled noblemen. Simulating a threat, Orlando approaches with a commanding countenance and a drawn sword, ordering 'Forbear, and eat no more!' (2.7.88). His victims, far from exhibiting fearful compliance, calmly critique his feast etiquette. Duke Senior speculates as to whether the interloper is a 'rude despiser of good manners' or someone made desperate by circumstances (2.7.92). Orlando immediately recognises that his initial tactic will not work under these circumstances, and he quickly shifts to verbal methods as he explains that he is 'inland bred' and not generally given to such uncouth behaviour (2.7.96). Ultimately, however, Duke Senior's dignified insistence that he will only share his meal if Orlando asks nicely for it prompts Orlando to put away his sword in embarrassment and apologise, saying:

> I thought that all things had been savage here,
> And therefore put I on the countenance
> Of stern commandment. But whate'er you are
> That in this desert inaccessible,
> Under the shade of melancholy boughs,
> Lose and neglect the creeping hours of time
> If ever you have looked on better days,
> If ever been where bells have knolled to church,
> If ever sat at any good man's feast,
> If ever from your eyelids wiped a tear,
> And know what 'tis to pity, and be pitied,
> Let gentleness my strong enforcement be,
> In the which hope I blush, and hide my sword.   (2.7.106–17)

Orlando's interruption and apology encapsulate the larger themes of timing and feigning fundamental to the comedy's treatment of courtiership. Shakespeare imagines social awkwardness as a species of untimeliness – an integral part of the education of a gentleman being to know how to read context and decide when to speak as much as what to say. Just as important, however, is the ability to adapt midway through a course of action based on the new information acquired. Orlando initially bungles the tempo of this forest interaction when he attempts to intimidate at an inappropriate time. When Orlando realises his mistake, his new tactic is to use an apology to deliver an implicit critique, reversing his out-of-placeness at the banquet feast and replacing it with the exiled noblemen's temporal and spatial dislocation.

Orlando identifies the forest courtiers by their temporal mismanagement. They intentionally neglect time's 'creeping hours' rather than seizing or making time. Whereas in *Titus Andronicus* Titus uses deception to generate tempi of opportunity from his opponents, the passive forest court of exiled noblemen seems content to be suspended in time. Orlando's 'If evers' highlight this sense of temporal dilation. The hypotheticals roll out, sonorously mimicking the knolling of the church bells he invokes. However, where church bells mark the passage of time, in this speech Orlando co-opts their rhythm to formally reinforce the sense of suspension he crafts. Not coincidentally, these themes of timing – poor social timing, indifference to opportunity and the 'if's' pausing of time – are caught up with questions of disguise and misdirection, as Orlando assumes the wrong countenance for the occasion. This scene demonstrates how dissimulation is not confined to either the court or the forest. In the wrestling match, Orlando disguises himself as well, as a person of lower class. Charles sees through the deception, but the disguise does allow Orlando to enter the context in the first place. In the scene of the forest banquet, he continues to disguise himself, this time as a fearless and violent bandit. Later, the fiction of selfhood he projects will shift again as he defines his courtly identity through his love for Rosalind.

Orlando's intrusion enacts the structure and timing of the feint in addition to highlighting time as a theme. With sword drawn, he offers an initial threat. However, based on his adversary's reaction, he quickly adapts to the situation. In this way, he follows the advice of masters like Meyer and Silver who advocate 'eyes-open' feints. The initial attack is as much of a probing action as it is the first part of a compound attack because it attempts to provoke a response that Orlando is prepared to counter. This kind of feint stands in contrast to the one described by Johann Georg Pascha in his 1661 *Short Though Clear Description Treating of Fencing on the Thrust and*

Cut: 'The feint must also be made swiftly, and thereon you must thrust however possible . . . when you make a feint, you must not wait on whether the adversary parries or not, but thrust in the weak, as you have already decided'.[18] Both models of feinting have their own appropriate contexts based upon the conditions of the match and the opponent. Orlando's feint, while still more showy and dangerous than non-feinting attacks, is of a more conservative variety of feint. Because the situation is, for him, a life-or-death encounter – he must get food to keep his elderly servant from starving – he uses the feint with adaptation. However, the kind of feint Pascha advises is a better display of virtuosic *sprezzatura* because it is made with full speed and commitment. Having already timed the adversary's parries and predicted the likely response, the fencer barrels through at full speed. If the attacker has guessed correctly about the adversary's response, they an advantage because the momentum of the feint is not checked midway through to perceive the enemy's reaction. If the prediction is wrong, then the attack ends in spectacular failure. It is this second variety of feint Rosalind employs.

The play's movement from Orlando's skilful footwork in the wrestling ring to the stumbling feet of his poetic meter represents his overextension as he attempts to adapt to the expectations of the forest court. Orlando's inept versifying occupies much of Act 3 scene 2, as Rosalind and Touchstone read and comment upon the poetry Orlando has carved into trees. Touchstone describes Orlando's poetry as 'the right butterwomen's rank to market' – that is, the insubstantial chatter of a group of women. He follows it up by describing the next poem as 'the very false gallop of verses' (3.2.85–6, 101). Touchstone's criticism equates speed-as-swiftness to superficiality and ineptness. Mistakes in metrical timing – what Rosalind describes to Celia as verses which 'had in them more feet than the verses would bear' – come from an overcrowding and artificial acceleration (3.2.151–2). Her poetic critique reflects a contemporary debate in fencing about the role of the feet during the feint. Some masters taught students to strike the floor with the lead foot in order to accentuate a feint. Others criticised this extra beat – the technique places in the phrase of combat more feet than it can safely bear. For instance, Fabris writes:

Some tend to feint more with the feet rather than the sword: they stomp their foot on the ground in order to make as big a noise as possible, startle the opponent and wound him in the tempo of his jolt. This may be successful indoors, especially on a wood-paneled floor, where the 'boom' may be great enough to indeed upset the opponent; but certainly not outdoors where the ground does not make noise. Besides, an experienced fencer will get the better of this feint no matter what the surface is: if you stomp your foot while out of measure, he will know that your sword is too far; if you do so in the measure, he will use your movement as a tempo to wound you *or trick you with a feint of his own*, in which case your stomping the ground will get you wounded, since you cannot defend an opening without creating another.[19]

Indeed, Rosalind does take the tempo Orlando gives up as he overextends himself through his poetry in order to instigate her own playful feint of her own – the giant 'if' of the Ganymede love game, where Orlando acts as if the shepherd boy is his beloved. Orlando and Rosalind/Ganymede's first discussion is about the different modalities of a lover's time, and she/he draws him into the competition of her love game. However, Rosalind is not in full command of the footwork of love either. When Celia informs Rosalind of the verse's author, Rosalind's amusement quickly turns to the irrational and impatient behaviour of a too-eager lover as well. She continually interrupts Celia's account of having seen Orlando, until Celia remonstrates, 'I would sing my song without a burden; thou bringest / me out of tune' (3.2.225). Musical timing joins the meter of poetry and the antagonistic timing of the court as instances of tempo in Arden forest. Good tempo in poetry, as in the art of defence, is not so much a fast pace but rather the ability to recognise a quality of time, to seize the opportune moment.

Where Touchstone critiques the speed of Orlando's poetry, the normally censorious Jaques unexpectedly finds something to admire in Orlando's verbal celerity. Jaques describes Orlando's wit as 'made of Atalanta's heels' (3.2.253). Reinforcing the verbal and non-verbal aspects of courtly fictions of selfhood, these heels resonate with both Orlando's poetic (and physical) feet as well as 'the swift foot of time' Ganymede later evokes (3.2.27). While current discussions of theatrical gesture and embodied cognition often focus on the hands, for early moderns the feet were also key in both the reception and delivery of sensory information. As Natasha Korda points out, 'The epithet "treading the boards" (or the stage), which has long been synonymous with the actor's art, suggests the reliance of that art upon footwork and footwear'.[20] Orlando's fast feet centrally feature in how others define him via his poetry as well as his athletic skill. Jaques's, for instance, alters Rosalind's invocation of Hercules' speed with that of Atalanta's, and the sport of wrestling with that of racing.

Hercules' wrestling match with Antaeus is decidedly martial, consonant with the courtly atmosphere that made a competitive sport into an assassination attempt. Atalanta's open challenge to marry any man who can beat her in a race follows the later thematics of the play, with love cast as competition rather than life-or-death struggle disguised as sport.

'If this be so': Feints and Stichomythia

The final act of *As You Like It* contains a scene that has often been read as a variety stichomythia, the Greek dramatic technique of witty one-line sallies and rejoinders. Four characters on the stage echo one another in sighing after someone else until Rosalind, disguised as Ganymede, ends each exchange in an inside joke with the audience. After Ganymede shows Phoebe's love letter to Silvius, Phoebe comes storming back on stage with Silvius trailing behind her. When Ganymede tells Phoebe to look at Silvius and love him, Phoebe orders the shepherd to explain what it is like to be in love.

> SILVIUS: It is to be all made of sighs and tears,
> And so am I for Phoebe
> PHOEBE: And I for Ganymede
> ORLANDO: And I for Rosalind
> ROSALIND: And I for no woman.   (5.2.74–9)

This pattern is repeated twice more in response to Silvius's different propositions. The effect is an incantatory rhythm. Rather than a traditional stichomythic exchange of parry and riposte, this one seems strangely slippery and circular. Characters are not given a clear adversary to defend and rebut, but instead are each sighing in displaced attention from their lovers. None of the characters directly confront each other and debate until this repetition:

> PHOEBE [to Rosalind]: If this be so, why blame you me to love you?
> SILVIUS [to Phoebe]: If this be so, why blame you me to love you?
> ORLANDO: If this be so, why blame you me to love you?
> ROSALIND: Why do you speak too, 'Why blame you me to love you?'
> ORLANDO: To her that is not here nor doth not hear.   (5.2.93–100)

Even here, rather than responding to the pointed question of each lover, the characters redirect their inquiries to someone else. These repetitions at first seem to be far away from the witty parry and riposte banter that is stichomythia's primary definition. However, there are two ways in which the exchange does evoke a logic of combat. The first is the sideways movement of the feint, as the characters ignore their lovers and address their beloveds. The second is the rhythmic nature of the scene. Skilful combat requires extensive reading and preparation before the moment of the attack to ensure the adversary is taken by surprise and to make an accurate prediction of what the adversary is likely to do. Thus, it would be a familiar pattern to the audience to see a long back-and-forth (or, in this case, round-and-round) sequence of probing intention and setting a pattern before launching an attack. The attack then breaks the tempo set previously and catches the adversary off guard. If this exchange is the preparatory pattern-setting phase of making an attack (in this case a feint), the next lines show the first movement of the compound attack:

> Rosalind: [to Silvius] I will help you if I can. [To Phoebe] I would love you if I could. – tomorrow meet me all together. [To Phoebe] I will marry you if ever I marry woman, and I'll be married tomorrow. [To Orlando]: I will satisfy you if ever I satisfy man, and you shall be married tomorrow. [To Silvius] I will content you if what pleases you contents you, and you shall be married tomorrow.   (5.2.101–5)

These hypothetical statements act as the first movement of a feint with each person she addresses. She makes a proposition that, given what they know, seems agreeable. In the second movement of the feint, Rosalind reveals herself at the four-way wedding.

Before the wedding, Touchstone mirrors Rosalind's interplay between verbal and physical modes of posturing and deception as he initiates a long discussion on duelling conventions. In many productions, his speech is cut because it seems tangential to the action of the wedding plots. However, it is actually directing the audience to that intersection of verbal play and swordplay in the courtier's context. Touchstone is given over thirty lines to showcase his understanding of the degrees of a lie, during which a legalistic quibbling overtakes and derails any real feat at arms. He describes these degrees progressively as:

> The first, the Retort Courteous; the second, the Quip Modest; the third, the Reply Churlish; the fourth, the Reproof Valiant; the fifth, the Countercheck Quarrelsome; the sixth, the Lie with Circumstance; the seventh, the Lie Direct . . . all of these you may avoid but the Lie Direct; and you may avoid that, too, with an 'if' . . . Your 'if' is the only peace maker; much virtue in 'if.' (5.4.83–92)

This list shows an escalating sequence in response to a continued provocation (in this case, a badly cut beard). Touchstone picks up on the play's investment in the hypothetical 'if' as a means of holding time suspended, but he applies it to the complex etiquette governing the point-of-honour duel, which included written *cartelli* of challenge posted in public places as well as verbal gymnastics such as Touchstone ridicules. While the intersection between verbal and non-verbal expression in Orlando and Rosalind's courtship moves from Orlando's wrestling to his poetry, in this list the verbal never quite makes its way into the non-verbal expression of aggression. Written challenges like the *cartelli* worked frequently to endlessly displace the actual moment of combat. In this way, Touchstone's disquisition on the lie seven times removed evokes the kind of courtiership Rosalind calls upon earlier in the play – the cowardly man who pretends to be brave by strapping on weapons and using a bragging voice, hoping to 'outface it with their semblances' (1.3.114). Self-construction is laudable, but also open to ridicule. Castiglione's ideal courtier and Touchstone share many points of similarity. They both are driven by the need to project their best attributes and to perform in social situations according to their scripted roles, and they both need to have an acute sense of timing and judgement. For Touchstone, to know when to back down from a verbal sparring contest, for Castiglione to show oneself to best advantage in order to be better placed to advise one's prince.

Duke Senior's reaction to Touchstone in the play's final scene reinforces the sportive, dissimulatory logic of the play with a reference to hunting. The Duke remarks approvingly that Touchstone 'uses his folly like a stalking horse, and under the presentation of that he shoots his wit' (5.4.95–6). That is, Touchstone's foolishness serves as an instrument of misdirection and distraction meant to lull unwary game into complacency while the fowler creeps into measure. The tactic is intended to be seen through by those who, like Duke Senior, are really in the know. In this sense, Touchstone is *As You Like It*'s unlikely model of *sprezzatura*. The combination of the role of courtier and the role of fool in their common ground of virtuosic dissimulation resonates with the strategies of the commercial theatre. Early modern drama finds itself facing charges which range from the profaning of sacred things through their representation on stage to the cultivation of the audience's lewd and idle propensities in its representation of the non-sacred. Timing as a mode creating and managing opportunity and finding an appropriate moment is a religiously and politically charged challenge. When viewed in terms of the play's timing rather than its role in furthering a linear plot, Touchstone's seemingly digressive disquisition gains new significance. The indirection discussed in this monologue reflects the timing of the feint, with its deceleration and sideways movement. The relationship between theatre, fencing and courtiership goes back to the play function of *poiesis*. However, the court of Arden forest does more than contrast artificial and complicated court life to the authentic and simple pastoral life. Instead, the pastoral works to train potential courtiers in the right kind of deception.

Given the patterns set by the rest of the play, the wedding should be the triumphant touch to the line opened by the feint's misdirection. However, Rosalind keeps up her verbal feinting long after there seems to be any plot-motivated reason for it. As Rosalind solves the paradox of satisfying Silvius, Phoebe, Orlando and her father, she still uses conditional language: 'I'll have no husband if you be not he' (5.4.112). Even after the conclusion of the play, when the player playing Rosalind speaks the epilogue, she continues: 'If I were a woman I would kiss as many of you as had beards that pleased me' (14–16). Why the continued insistence upon the conditional? If we add fencing to our analysis of the play's *poiesis*, an answer comes from the aesthetic values of English fencing. As Silver articulates: 'men may with short swords both strike, thrust, false and double . . . when two fight with short swords, having true fight, there is no hurt done'.[21] That is, in the ideal fight between skilful opponents, misdirection, interception, defensive and offensive measures are perfectly matched and so continue endlessly, to the pleasure of those watching. *As You Like It* is as reluctant as a good fencing performance with long phrases of action to end its play as spectators watch and listen to the clash of weapons.

Conclusion

As You Like It, read alongside the work of Renaissance fencing masters, demonstrates the ways in which social timing was imagined in a courtly context. The logic of the feint and of the conditional 'if' inform the games of *As You Like It*, from the opening wrestling match to the wooing game to the verbal games of the *cartelli* described by Touchstone. Read in terms of fencing tempo, *As You Like It*'s well-recognised central themes of tardiness and haste take new meaning. Theories of social timing, unlike other theories of time as measurement, occasion or theme, introduce the performative element of bodies arranged in space and the strong cues of how those bodies interact to suspend, manage and generate tempo. In turn, this allows for a better understanding of the verbal play of timing which reflects this structuring property and adds to the generative interaction of words and bodies on stage via Touchstone's digression, Rosalind's diction, and the games played by all the characters.

Shakespeare enacts cunning on stage in genre-sensitive ways. For Titus, dissembling madness poises him to attack Tamora when she overextends. Rosalind, in contrast, signifies cunning as a crossdressing heroine. Crossdressing is closely tied to fencing as Rosalind straps on a sword to project a threatening countenance. The sword does not signify just another piece of costuming but is one of an array of cues to represent deception in non-verbal as well as verbal ways. The structure of the hypothetical 'if' linguistically follows the pattern of the feint, but the costuming reinforces the playful misdirection visually. Shakespeare uses similar cues in another famous crossdressing comedy, *Twelfth Night*. Swords and swordplay here, too, are intimately tied with questions of dissimulation and comic cunning in Viola's comic near duel as well as Rosalind's disguise.

Rhythms of words and gestures carried with them ethical, pragmatic and social nuances that deeply informed the early modern stage. In this chapter and the previous one, we have seen two recommended methods for managing the opponent's time: the *contratempo* tactic of feigned weakness that is prominent in revenge drama versus the playful and digressive structure of the feint. While it is true that we do not need fencing theory to talk about general properties of deception and types of dissimulation such as feigned weakness versus active misdirection, what fencing brings us is a specific context complete with embodied timing and games in which to situate these considerations. These particularities significantly impact our reading of dramatic pacing across an entire play, and even across whole genres. The context also gives us the tools to understand individual scenes that to modern critics appear unmotivated and digressive. If *As You Like It* is one of Shakespeare's most genre-bending plays, *Bartholomew Fair* is one of Jonson's most experimental comedies. Both draw from fencing form, but where *As You Like It* formally reflects the feint, *Bartholomew Fair* has more in common with the counterattack, a traditional opposition to the feint.

Notes

All references to *As You Like It* are taken from the Norton Shakespeare, 2nd edition, and will be cited parenthetically by act, scene and line numbers.

1. Kuhn, 'Much Virtue in *If*', 46.
2. Shapiro, *A Year in the Life*, 204.
3. Maura Kuhn notes that '*As You Like It* has 138 *If*'s . . . for a relative frequency of 0.647, significantly higher than the relative frequency of *If* in all of Shakespeare's works, 0.4256' ('Much Virtue in *If*', 44).
4. Halio, '"No Clock in the Forest"', 197.
5. Hunt, '*Kairos* and the Ripeness of Time'.
6. In fact, an underlying tropology of combat runs through many early modern literary works, as authors such as Castiglione, Tasso, Sidney and Shakespeare co-opt the vocabulary and dissimulatory techniques of fencing.
7. Alfieri, *L'arte di ben maneggiare la spada*, 31.
8. Ibid.
9. Capoferro, *Gran Simulacro*, 29.
10. Kuhn, 'Much Virtue in *If*', 8.
11. As Gina Bloom emphasises, the formal qualities of specific games matter because 'different games call for unique competencies in players and in spectators of games' ('Spatial Mastery', 6).
12. Forgeng, *Pietro Monte's Collectanea*, 99.
13. Castiglione, *Book of the Courtier*, trans. Hoby, 53.
14. See 'godspeed, n.1'. *OED Online*. Oxford University Press.
15. Most commonly at the turn of the seventeenth century, to speed is to succeed or prosper. However, Shakespeare also uses the term to refer to 'an evil plight or awkward situation' in *The Taming of the Shrew* (see 'godspeed n.7'. *OED Online*. Oxford University Press). Further, the term can refer to one being prepared or equipped – 'skilled or versed in something'. Together with skill, fortune, and social context, the word has the more familiar modern connotations of velocity or swiftness, as well as that of timing – bringing an early end to a matter.
16. Donn Taylor's work on time and occasion ('Try in Time in Despite of a Fall') approaches the question of time in terms of growth to maturity. He argues that Shakespeare envisions time as 'a phenomenon which exists objectively' (122), but one which is perceived differently by different characters in varying stages of personal development. He discusses *kairos* and the gradual merger of the imagery of Fortune with that of Occasio to argue that the play uses the metaphor of growth to ripeness to reflect the proximity of Occasion. I agree that this background of character development is important for reading how time operates in *As You Like It*, but I would like to discuss the seizure of ripe times in terms of the social landscape of the play as well.

17. As Cynthia Marshall points out, Rosalind later falls into an error deprecated by the courtiers. Princes should not undermine their authority through participating in masquerades as themselves because it confuses their political authority with the fiction of play. 'When Rosalind, disguised as Ganymede, masquerades her own role with Orlando, the flexible, contiguous, and collapsible boundaries of play and reality are displayed' ('Wrestling as Play and Game', 282).
18. Pascha, *Short Though Clear Description*, 4.
19. Fabris, *Lo Schermo*, 6 (emphasis mine).
20. Korda, 'How to Do Things with Shoes', 86.
21. Silver, *Paradoxes of Defence*, 19.

Chapter 6

Wasting Time with Puritans in *Bartholomew Fair*

Introduction

> When't comes to the *Fair* once, you were e'en as good go to *Virginia*, for any thing there is of *Smith-field*. He has not hit the Humours, he do's not know 'em; he has not convers'd with the *Bartholmew*-birds, as they say; he has ne'er a Sword and Buckler Man in his *Fair*.[1]

Bartholomew Fair famously begins with an extended metatheatrical commentary. A stage-keeper, or stagehand, emerges to inform the audience that the play is running late and to advise them not to waste their time with this new subpar comedy. Among a litany of complaints about the quality of *Bartholomew Fair* recited by this stage-keeper, the play's sad lack of displays of fencing prowess heads the list. The stage-keeper's expectation is a fair one, and probably one shared with the audience at large who had come to know Jonson as a playwright who frequently incorporated fencing into his plays. In *Epicoene*, for instance, a long comic anti-duel sequence pillories social climbers and the noise of drums animates the soundscape as a parade of fencers march through London to attract an audience for a prizefight. *Cynthia's Revels* satirises the worst excesses of court flattery by following the conventions of a fencing prizefight but changing the weapons to courtly affectations and the combatants to vain courtiers.[2] In *Every Man out of His Humour*, Fastidious Brisk illustrates his foolishness by recounting, blow by blow, a duel that shredded his expensive clothes. Given all these explicit invocations of fencing as a social practice, one might echo Jonson's stage-keeper and wonder where the Smith-field sword-and-buckler fights are in *Bartholomew Fair*. Perhaps more to the point for *Fencing, Form and Cognition on the Early Modern*

Stage why use this play, where direct allusions to fencing are so sparse, to learn about Jonsonian judgement through an exploration of fencing and stagecraft? While *Bartholomew Fair* admittedly evidences a deficit of sword-and-buckler men, it makes a less obvious but equally important contribution to work at the intersection of cognitive science and historical phenomenology as it touches on questions of perception and learning. As the apotheosis of Jonson's experimentation with busy, agonistic character interactions, the play most clearly shows the ways in which Jonson's interest in fencing and fencing theory allowed him to import creative ways to think about the training of judgement as an embodied skill. Drawing from the English fencing theory of his contemporaries, Jonson saw fencing, like theatre, in its role as a training ground for individual judgement.

Thinking and feeling, as I hope to have demonstrated already, are conceived of as congruent activities in the early modern playhouse. A humoral framework undergirds the fluidity between the two, as has been well documented.[3] By extension, linguistic and physical modes of expression exist on a continuum rather than in a binary: pen and sword are both instruments of power to self-discipline and to inflict violence. Prior chapters have explored the expression of certain fencing tactics and techniques such as *contratempo* and the feint as they are translated into narrative form. This chapter will return to the epistemological questions posed in the introduction and third chapter: what counts as temporal knowledge? How was this knowledge disseminated? How can something as abstract as judgement be trained through physical activity? To address these questions, I build on the concept of kinesic intelligence as articulated by Ellen Spolsky and elaborated in relationship to the early modern stage by Evelyn Tribble. Kinesic intelligence is an interdisciplinary construct with roots in anthropology and cognitive science. Where kinesics is the study of non-verbal communication, kinesic intelligence focuses specifically on bodily modes of knowing and thinking. As Spolsky defines it, kinesic intelligence is 'our sense of the relationship of the parts of the human body to the whole, and of the patterns of bodily tension and relaxation as they are related to movement'.[4] Trained, instinctive bodily responses are joined with the active interpretation of and reflection on these responses.[5] That is, kinesic knowledge is also 'our sense of the muscular forces that produce bodily movement and of the effect of that movement on other parts of the body and on objects within the environment'.[6] In the medium of performance, Tribble applies the construct of kinesic intelligence to the activities of early modern actors who trained in a range of mental and physical skills. She writes that the 'concept of kinesic intelligence, built upon a foundation of training and practice in demanding practices such as fencing and dance, helps to explain how early modern players could produce plays despite a minimum of group rehearsal time'.[7] Kinesic intelligence has proved a rich lens through which to examine early modern performance. I propose a further distinction in this mode of embodied knowledge: kinesic judgement, a temporally charged form of kinesic intelligence.

Kinesic judgement is the ability to apply the right skills at the right moment. Tribble includes timing as a subset of kinesic intelligence when she proposes early modern players practised not only specific skills such as dance and swordplay but also 'an entire way of being in the world, including wit, timing, grace, and skilful coordination with others'.[8] The formulation of kinesic judgement combines the insights of cognitive science and anthropology with the historical vocabulary and pedagogical frameworks of early moderns. Where the term 'intelligence' emphasises a holistic picture incorporating a range of abilities, the term 'judgement' focuses on an agenda that is particularly salient for Jonson: teaching timing thought antagonistic moments of emotional and literal contact across playwright, players and playgoers. Jonson uses metatheatrical techniques to pull his audience out of the story's immediate framing and so to encourage conscious reflection on these moments of contact. This chapter will specifically focus on what the German fencing master Joachim Meyer terms *Fühlen*, a species of antagonistic feeling indicating temporal initiative.

In *Fühlen*, the relationship of the fencer's body to the adversary's as well as the sensation of pressure yielded from the contact of blades combine to give powerful cues to the fencer. Through this antagonistic feeling, a fencer can predict the adversary's reaction and adapt. *Fühlen* exemplifies the middle path described by Tribble between that of conscious mastery (for example, Malcolm Gladwell's famous 10,000 hours) and romanticised flow states. As Castiglione and modern skill experts might agree, hours of practice and mastery allow for the dedication of attentional resources in expert ways – judging what to pay attention to. The records left by sixteenth-century teachers of embodied skill yield a rich vocabulary and conceptual apparatus for theorising such mastery. The experimental plot structure of *Bartholomew Fair* shows formal indebtedness to the rhythms of the fencing device and the technique of *Fühlen*. Metatheatricality is part of Jonson's pedagogical strategy to develop kinesic judgement in playgoers and players. Through a reading of the play's metatheatrical commentary and moments of *Fühlen*, I will explore the ways in which Jonson models inept and skilful applications of kinesic judgement in the intersubjective antagonistic environments he creates in order to train his audience.

Form, Feeling and Fencing in *Bartholomew Fair*

If there was ever a play that Jonson dashed off at the last minute, it was not *Bartholomew Fair*. The day after the play premiered at The Hope in front of a popular audience and before it was a confirmed commercial success, it was performed (with the Induction replaced by a Prologue to the King's Majesty) before James I. The comedy is exceptional both for the number of speaking parts (thirty-six) and the length of the play text (over 4,000 lines).[9] The dizzying profusion of people, motives and activities on stage in *Bartholomew Fair* stands in tension with its underlying careful construction. The comedy involves several groupings of citizens and fair workers enjoying the atmosphere (and navigating the perils) of Bartholomew Fair. John Littlewit, his wife, Win-the-Fight, and her mother, Dame Purecraft, make up one family group. They are accompanied by Zeal-of-the-Land Busy, a hypocritical Puritan and suitor of the widow Purecraft. Another group is comprised of a country simpleton, Cokes, his illiterate and belligerent tutor, Wasp, and Cokes's intellectually superior fiancée, Grace. In a smaller grouping, Quarlous and Winwife are widow-hunters, young men trading on their charm and appearance to marry a wealthy widow. The fair centres on two structures and movement between them, a booth with roast pig and beer and a puppetry show tent. The former is presided over by the corpulent and obscene Ursula, called the pig-woman, and the latter by the puppeteer, Lantern Leatherhead. Adam Overdo, a justice of the peace intent on rooting out 'enormities', seems to think he is in a play like *Measure for Measure* as he self-importantly disguises himself as a commoner to catch evildoers. Throughout, characters get lost, get in fights, play games and split off in groups of different configurations for various dubious purposes. The play ends with all the characters gathered at Leatherhead's booth to enjoy the final puppet show. Busy is converted to a be a 'beholder' of the puppet show (5.5.101), and Justice Overdo realises he has been too harsh, 'overdoing' the prosecution of trivial offenses, and invites everyone back to his house for a feast.

As my summary suggests, the play's plot can come across as sporadic and episodic. Jonson shows more interest in following places and groupings of people than in developing a single line of action. Commentators from T. S. Eliot and Ian Donaldson to David Bevington and R. Levin have been drawn to Jonson's experimental comedy and would agree that *Bartholomew Fair* is highly self-conscious rather than a casual endeavour. Critics have disagreed, however, about whether Jonson's genius was in leaving behind or doubling down on plot structure. Weighing in on the former viewpoint, T. S. Eliot comments on Jonson's skill in 'doing without a plot' in *Bartholomew Fair*,[10] and Donaldson notes the play's dramatic action is 'replaced by *activity*: urgent, random, uncoordinated, digressive'.[11] From the latter perspective, Bevington argues that the comedy's structure is elegant as well as busy, with each act containing six scenes and the stage only cleared at the end of a distinct arc of action. As fencing masters and Jonson knew well, there is more than one way to have a beginning, middle and an end in devices. Freytag's pyramid – the plot structure consisting of exposition, rising action, climax, falling action and denouement – is only one way to look at dramatic structure, and it is not particularly compelling one for *Bartholomew Fair*, which consists of a series of flowing movements together and apart. *Bartholomew Fair* has few moments when the stage is clear, as clearing the stage provides a sort of punctuation frequently used by Shakespeare and other dramatists. Such theatrical punctuation breaks into clean phrases a number of action sequences. By avoiding this strategy of structuring plays, Jonson offers an alternate model of plot and rhythm, one which recommends adapting in response to chaos, sensed via antagonistic moments of contact. Exits and entrances – the breakdown and reconstitution of various assemblages of fairgoers and fair workers – are more important to Jonson's dramatic experiment than a unified plot. Instead of a singular story, Jonson uses the chaotic energy of the play to explore the spaces between groups, both on and off the stage. In addition to mimicking the real-life flow of crowds to add to the comic realism of the comedy, the moments of contact challenge the bounds of the autonomous individual and of spectators and players. Individual identity is subsumed in an intersubjective 'between' and reconfigured via physical and emotional contact.

Jonson's formal exploration of in-betweenness allows him to accentuate the role of feeling in judgement. Early moderns understood feeling as an active, corporeal process, in the sense we still retain in phrases such as 'I am feeling out my options'. More than internal state or mood, feeling in this framework retains a strong connection between the work of the hand and that of the emotions.

As Hobgood persuasively argues, 'Early modern playgoers did not accept feeling but rather enabled and created it' via their collaborative cultivation of passions.[12] Theatrical feeling, then, is a process through which 'selves' are constituted via emotional encounters played out in the theatre.[13] The tangible form of feeling encountered in theatre is contagious and as emotions operate like diseases jumping from person to person. Eric Langley similarly explores this corporeal understanding of feelings like sympathy and compassion in his work on compassionate communication (of sympathy, of diseases).[14] This corporeal understanding of feeling expresses the riskiness as well as the more positive communal aspects of the theatre. The education of judgement via feeling is addressed in fencing discourse where feeling circulates as a technical term referring to a bodily skill of perception and prediction. This conversation brings an antagonistic framework that resonates with Jonson's own understanding of adversarial competition as a component of developing judgement.

Suspending judgement, taking time to make the right call, and being comfortable with uncertainty, are all themes that Jonson explores throughout his career. As the editors of the Cambridge edition note, *Bartholomew Fair* demands:

> [A] double vision, leaving us bereft of the characters' sense of certainty, but also without their blinkers. The induction requires and trusts us to respond flexibly . . . the play also encourages us to hold the 'discordant qualities' of incompatible meanings not in synthesis but in suspension, and it is exhilarating as well as disturbing to have our expectations and our judgement so disrupted. (266)

Much of the comedy's action takes place in this place of suspended judgement and uncertainty. Jonson goes beyond verbal means to express and visualise the suspended moment of doubt and/or certainty. To translate to a fencing idiom, Meyer would call the moment of suspension as one gathers information before taking action the 'handwork'. Hands are conceptually central for Jonson, both as a way to physically find information through feeling and as a symbol of agency. The comedy asks the audience to suspend judgement as they see the characters feel out for information in the chaotic setting of the fair, as in Quarlous's opportunistic and successful pivot from despising widow-hunting to seizing the opportunity to try his own hand at it. Or, in an example of ineptitude, when Overdo feels for his opportune moment but is gulled and framed, failing spectacularly. The hasty and harsh judgements of

Zeal-of-the-Land Busy and Justice Overdo are punished, while the ability to adapt is rewarded. Jonson highlights the importance of flexibility, seizing the moment more than making elaborate plans. The phrase of combat and the structure of *Bartholomew Fair* both promote flexible behaviour and are built on a logic of disruptive and often antagonistic intersubjectivity. Knowledge is developed in Jonson's drama verbally and contemplatively, as characters speak with each other or wrestle with ideas out loud. Knowledge is also developed kinetically, through touch, movement and interaction with the environment and others.

In-between states and transformations are reflected formally most clearly by the way in which characters move and interact with each other. Joel Kaplan notes the importance of timing of character interactions in his analysis of the comedy's underlying organisation as the 'elaborate regularity in the play's handling of pacing and tempo'.[15] The unity of *Bartholomew Fair*'s action as it pertains to the tempo of character interaction is not only a question of form, however, but also a link to an embodied theatrical history. As Tribble argues, Jonson's emphasis on motion reveals a different 'kinesic style' from that of Shakespeare because 'Shakespeare's large-scale scenes are generally synoptic – attention is focused on the speaker and secondary players throw attention on the main action. But Jonson's are distributed, atomistic – his comedies are distinguished by their relentless busyness; characters are in constant motion all at once'.[16] Often, the motion that the characters engage in are activities of assessment and perception. *Bartholomew Fair* stages examples of both inept and skilful feeling throughout, as in Cokes's and Wasp's obliviousness to theft or Lantern Leatherhead's virtuosic prodding of Busy.

The recurrence of *feeling* in contexts of theft, learning and perception signal the play's interest in this antagonistic mode of perception. Feeling, coupled with conventions of metatheatricality, allow Jonson to persuasively stage and explore antagonistic intersubjective movement in many scenes such as the extended 'game of vapours' in which a group of characters loudly and chaotically contract each other. Jonson translates this same model of intersubjective antagonism, taken from the world of game and sport, to the theatrical experience of the puppet show. This final show posits productive antagonistic interactions that work to bring pleasure and train judgement. The interactions do not stop at the borders of the stage, but blur into the audience as well through Jonson's use of metatheatrical techniques to inculcate judgement.

Contracts and Custodians: Jonson's Metatheatrical Methods

Processes of discernment fascinated Jonson throughout his career, perhaps in part because of his own frequent and public lapses in judgement. However, it is the judgement of playgoers, Jonson implies, that is in desperate need of training. His insistence on this point is far subtler than in prior comic drama. *Bartholomew Fair* shows an evolution in his strategies for educating tasteful audiences. In the prologue to *Every Man in His Humour*, Jonson comes out swinging against playwrights who 'purchase' the audience's delight by catering to whatever the fashion of the day is, even if it is something as ridiculous as recreating large historical battles 'with three rusty swords / And help of some few foot-and-a-half words' (Prologue, 9–10). In contrast, Jonson promises to show realistic actions and every-day speech, 'deeds, and language, such as men do use' (21). By bringing the action of his play into a socially immediate setting, Jonson makes it easier for audiences to learn to avoid common errors by laughing at familiar examples of problematic behaviour. In a departure from the harsher lessons of *Every Man in His Humour*, the Induction to *Bartholomew Fair* shows a more light-handed and relaxed approach to audience engagement. A book-holder and scrivener emerge to interrupt the stage-keeper's complaining and offer a contract. These 'articles of agreement' between Jonson and his audience include clauses both humorous and practical: he expects them to only judge up to the price of their admission tickets, and he also asks them to judge the play themselves rather than looking around to see others' reactions. Like in *Every Man in His Humour*, Jonson here pairs pen and sword suggestively. Matthew the bad poet and Bobadil the cowardly fencing master are the bookends for his earlier humours comedy. The sword-loving stage-keeper and the contract-toting book-holder and scrivener do similar work in *Bartholomew Fair* of conflating verbal and combative expression as it relates to training and aesthetic judgement.

Jonson's sometimes adversarial relationship with his audience is well known. Unpleasant characters such as the judgmental Crites from *Cynthia's Revels* and the venomous Asper from *Every Man out of His Humour* are frequently read as mouthpieces for the playwright. Because these characters act as doctors administering medicine to the sick judgement of their patients (the audience), a condescending and judgemental air predominates Jonson's public image.[17] However, as Ross Knecht argues, the status of Jonson's plays as either Juvenalian (rigid, didactic and judgemental) or Horatian (lenient, tolerant, self-parodic) satire can miss the ways in which the comedies are both: 'Consistent with the Horatian tendency towards self-parody, the plays rebuke their own often vituperative style: they are in part Horatian satires on the Juvenalian mode, self-conscious critiques of the satirist's moralistic fervor.'[18] While Knecht makes this point specifically in reference to the humours comedies, arguing that the plays allow no 'outside' position from which a character free from humours can accurately judge the foolishness of others, the point that embodiment is 'a condition of social existence' rather than an error is also pertinent to *Bartholomew Fair*.[19] This comedy is conspicuous for its lack of an arbiter of taste, but the concept of an aesthetic judgement tied to embodied experience infuses the play throughout with its relentless corporeality. Jonson's closing is also indeterminate, as the fairgoers leave the fair to join Justice Overdo at a feast in his home and Cokes takes the puppets with him, suggesting they finish the puppet show there. This indistinctness both pulls the audience in by addressing them as if they were also in the action of the play and it also distances them by reminding playgoers of the playwright's control and connection.

The transaction expressed in the articles of agreement, Jonson intimates, is not a one-way street. With these articles of agreement, Jonson acknowledges the theatre as a space of collaborative knowledge-making. Where *Every Man in His Humour* explores realism and downrightness as a literary and fencing aesthetic, *Bartholomew Fair* shows an interest in the role of feeling in cognition and aesthetic taste and reflects Jonson's growing interest in the role of drama in developing community. As Donaldson notes, 'For Jonson, humorous behaviour provides much more than entertainment value; it builds into a critical reflection on current social modes, thereby both registering and responding to his audience's sense of its own make-up as a community rather than a crowd.'[20] In his fair, while there are plenty of morally questionable characters like pickpockets and pimps, the only real villain is Zeal-of-the-Land Busy, an individualistic baker-turned-Puritan-leader intent on quashing the communal interactions of the fair – at least, if he can do so after he has himself partaken of whatever parts of the fair he enjoys. The crowd at the end of the play during the final puppet show mirrors the real-life crowd and provides a space for recognition, reflection and interpretation.

In the shifting boundaries among audience, player and playwright, Jonson feels out the theatrical participants and disrupts the expected temporality of the playhouse. In the real world, he puts on a play that was twice as long as the audience was accustomed to. The play does not have a clear starting point and is deferred and interrupted multiple times as the sword-loving stagehand fights with the bookkeeper and scrivener for the audience's attention. In the fictional space of the play, Jonson stages scenes of attack and counterattack between judges (of both civic and religious varieties) and fairgoers as well as authors, puppet players and spectators. In these counterattacks, Jonson shuttles between the play world and his audience's social world, metatheatrically blurring the distinctions between the two. Jonson scales the underlying logic and syntax of individual adversarial encounters to the larger interactions among players, playgoers and playwrights in *Bartholomew Fair*. The comedy showcases the logic and the timing of the counterattack as Busy and Overdo make a sequence of poorly executed attacks against the fun of the fair. In the same way, audiences are trained to read textual and performative attacks and counterattacks when it comes to matters of aesthetic taste.

The sprawling action of *Bartholomew Fair* reflects Jonson's experimentation with the theatre as a site of collaborative and often antagonistic knowledge production. Jonson's model of embodied judgement, both kinesic and aesthetic, takes place not only in the space of one-on-one character encounters as in *Every Man in His Humour*, but also in group interactions. Stage plays and 'playing at fence' come together in this comedy to enact a theory of movement – of groups' bodies, of their emotions. Jonson's interest in processes of judgement is informed by his understanding of fencing theory and practice, which he applies to his own dramaturgy as he blurs the distinction between the literal and figurative touching of others.

Aesthetic Judgement and Fencing Feeling

Previously, as we have seen, Jonson found in the *sprezzatura* of a well-delivered downright blow a useful analogy for his own downright Neo-Stoic prose. Based on the discipline's frequent inclusions in *Timber, or Discoveries*, it is apparent that Jonson also finds in fencing a useful analytical lens for combative writing and rhetoric. In this compilation of others' writings along with Jonson's own musings, he frequently copies down passages that use fencing as an analogy for other activities. For example, he quotes and paraphrases

Quintilian both in *Timber* and *The Alchemist* in his discussion on skill and judgement:

> Indeed the multitude commend writers as they do fencers or wrestlers, who if they come in robustiously, and put for it with a deal of violence, are received for the braver fellows; when many times their own rudeness is cause of their disgrace, and a slight touch of their adversary gives all that boisterous force the foil. But in these things, the unskillful are naturally deceived, and judging wholly by the bulk, think rude things greater than polished, and scattered more numerous than composed.[21]

Novelty replaces quality across physical and verbal disciplines. It takes skilled spectator vision or an education in rhetoric to understand truly effective fencing or writing attacks. Those in the know, however, can exploit this 'boisterous force' through a seemingly effortless counterattack, the 'slight touch' of the skilful adversary. Jonson quotes the Elder Seneca in his own conceptualisation of the value of antagonistic, competitive environments for truly testing knowledge: 'There is a difference between mooting and pleading; between fencing and fighting. To make arguments in my study and confute them is easy, where I answer myself, not an adversary.'[22] In a distinction that could have been made by the irascible George Silver, fencing here is aligned with more complex and artificial movements that are closed off from real contexts for application, while fighting stands for reactions to real opponents in real time.

Jonson is matched in recognising the shared ground between these verbal and non-verbal arts by his near-contemporary Joachim Meyer. The two-way influence between the disciplines is seen both in Jonson's adoption of the logic of combat and Meyer's use of metaphors from writing in his own pedagogy. In his discussion on the importance of repeatedly drilling techniques, for instance, Meyer explains the role of iterative training through a comparison to literacy:

> For if you wish to write a full proper word, you must hold in your mind and memory all the letters, and also know thoroughly what the nature and property of each one is, so that the useful and appropriate letters will fly into the pen one after another in order; so likewise in combat you shall hold and conceive the previously explained elements in your mind, so that whenever you come to fight with an opponent, the ones you need at that moment will come to you at once.[23]

Just like a debater cannot follow the thread of an argument when they are carefully deciding which letters to use to spell the words, fencers who are fixated on how to execute the basics of their techniques will be at a loss during an at-speed encounter. In this analogy, fencing actions, like letters, each have their own definitive essence and contextual meaning – their nature and property. A downward cut to the head, for example, has a certain technical ideal nature and it has a contingent context of tactical application, or property. A fencer would not aim a descending cut at an adversary who has already assumed a guard position protecting the head because there is no opening to hit. Alternately, a fencer who has protected their chest but not their head will move instinctively to block an incoming cut. Arguments, whether by verbal or combative means, are built upon core memories that have been internalised to the extent that they cause nearly instinctive behaviours.

As these analogies suggest, Jonson and Meyer share a pedagogical disposition. *Bartholomew Fair*'s elaborate planning paradoxically works to produce an effect of openness and improvisation, just as Meyer and other fencing masters seek to instil complicated patterns and reactions into muscle memory to create artful and opportune reactions to the opponent's stimuli. All competitive fencing incorporates an element of improvisation, but German and English fencing treatise authors such as Meyer and Silver embrace the necessity of deciding on the spur of the moment while Italian authors such as Capoferro, Fabris, Giganti and Alfieri tend to idealise planning and predicting an opponent's responses several movements in advance. For example, Capoferro's plays generally end in the observant fencer (*persona accorta*) eliciting an anticipated reaction from the adversary, which the observant fencer is then prepared to counter. Alfieri similarly explains: 'Experienced fencers will also consider a maneuver called *contratempo*, which is simply a ploy whereby you lure your enemy into creating a *tempo* (by attacking you) and then land your blow before his'.[24] Meyer and Silver tend to be leerier of predicting likely actions: they stress the suspension of judgement until the opponent reveals his final intention. However, this is not to say that they have no advice for fencing with an opponent who does not easily reveal a final intention. As we have seen, Silver recommends adaptable tactics in the 'two-fold mind' (being prepared to fly in or out as soon as one perceives what the adversary is doing in response to one's movement). Meyer's advice is to take what the opponent offers rather than looking for an ideal scenario. If Shakespeare's *Titus Andronicus* and *As You Like It* are better understood alongside texts from Italian fencing traditions, *Bartholomew Fair* shows best in conversation with German and English pedagogical models.

Drawing from the English fencing theory of his contemporaries, Jonson saw fencing, like theatre, in its role as a training ground for individual judgement. More specifically, like Meyer, Jonson imagines *feeling* as a key mechanism for training judgement. To flesh out a model of theatrical feeling that is both cooperative and antagonistic, Jonson could draw on the already well-explained tenets of Meyer's Germanic tradition with its goals of training judgement via feeling, or *Fühlen*. This tradition of fencing holds perception via blade contact as paramount for reading and deceiving the adversary. As Meyer will detail, perceiving the amount of pressure exerted by the adversary in an engagement of blades provides a window into future intention and clues as to whether one is ahead or behind the adversary in terms of initiative. Feeling in this technical sense differs considerably from an interior emotional state. Instead, as a bodily skill of reaching out and perceiving, feeling can be trained and managed. Jonson co-opts the forms and figurative language of fencing both in his exploration of the aesthetics of downrightness, and in his conceptualisation of the theatre as a risky and quasi-adversarial space.

Fencing masters across traditions saw blade contact as a crucial moment of a fencing match, one that generates its own knowledge about time. Training oneself to parse the meaning of the feeling of the adversary's blade against one's own educates temporal judgement: *when* to take an action as well as *what* action to take. Approaches to the risk and potential of educating judgement via feeling differ across national traditions and personal preference of fencing masters. The Italian master Salvator Fabris, for instance, suggests that the knowledge gleaned from blade contact is more of a liability than an asset. As he explains:

> [Do] not touch your opponent's sword with your own when you find his blade[25] . . . usually, if you do not molest the enemy's sword, he will not even notice that you have gotten into an advantageous position. If you touch it, he has more of an opportunity to disengage, retreat, or change his guard to free his weapon in such a way that you will lose the advantageesides, when you touch his sword you end up disordering your own guard.[26]

In contrast, Marco Docciolini, a Florentine contemporary of Fabris's, is enthusiastic about the possibilities of blade contact and recommends using the weapon to dominate and deviate the opponent's:

'Your true edge should slide along your opponent's sword, thus moving his sword away from the *punto*, with your sword moving to strike the point of his right shoulder'.[27] Blade contact is crucial to the Spanish tradition as well. Carranza advises his students in the use of *atajo*, a preparatory defensive action that constrains the opponent and opens opportunities via blade contact. He describes the *atajo* as the position in which one weapon is placed over the other, subjecting the enemy's blade so as to 'make it so that the technique that can be performed must be done with more movements and the participation of more angles than those that nature requires'.[28] While these authors see the dangers and potentials of blade contact in limiting options, predicting the future and gaining information about the opponent's intentions, nowhere is this moment of contact as explicitly linked to timing and cognition as in Meyer's 1570 *Thorough Descriptions of the Art of Combat*.

Meyer's deep connection to the medieval manuscript tradition is evident in his pedagogical orientation towards the particular and contingent.[29] He remarks, 'only the Market can instruct the Buyer' – since fencing occurs in context between two people, it is crucial to be able to respond appropriately and instantly to the situation as it unfolds.[30] Meyer gives a profusion of examples of techniques employed in different situations. The temporal terms he emphasises in his discussion of initiative and timing are particularly salient: the before (*vor*), the after (*nach*) and instantly (*indes*). These time terms are linked to the concept of *Fühlen*, or feeling, central to Meyer's thought. Via the sense of touch, the fencer predicts the adversary's intentions and adapts to them. In his discussion of *Fühlen*, Meyer describes two kinds of sustained blade contact, contact used to probe and contact used as part of an attack:

> [T]he first is when the swords are held against one another to see what the opponent will execute and where he intends to attack his adversary. The other happens with striking . . . note here the word 'feeling', which means testing or perceiving, to find out whether he is hard or soft on your sword with his bind.[31]

Touching the adversary's blade, the fencer initiates *Fühlen* and is able to sense the strength of resistance met, to predict the opponent's next movement and to react accordingly. The sword acts as a cognitive prosthesis in this scenario, mediating timing and judgement. Meyer, following Aristotle, uses change between states as a way to think of time. Meyer's conceptualisation of this mutation between states (before and after) is non-linear and can flow both ways – before and after can bleed together because they are temporal terms that measure initiative as well as change. Meyer's treatment of time/timing illustrates the ways in which fencing time is conceptualised as an index of opportunity and initiative rather than only as a unit of measurement. He begins his discussion of time by laying out an orderly beginning, middle and an end to each *Stück* (sequence of actions). However, within this apparent order is a knot of coexisting potentialities: for Meyer, the 'now' of the bout is non-linear; before and after blend together and must be pried apart. The beginning of a device comprises the initial guard and cut. The middle is when the fencer responds to what the adversary does in response to the cut. The end is when the fencer withdraws safely without being hit. However, within this seemingly linear sequence, fencers can inhabit either the before or the after. Fencers are in the after when they are solely reacting to the opponent's manoeuvres, for example wildly parrying a series of feints, or simulated attacks. Alternately, when the fencer has the initiative and can force the adversary to react, the adversary is now the one in the 'after'.

A shifting and multifaceted initiative is part of the theatrical experience when we view playgoers as essential co-creators of meaning rather than as passive spectators. If, as Hobgood argues, 'Early modern playgoers did not accept feeling but rather enabled and created it . . . playgoers collaborated in the cultivation of "anxiety" – or other more distinctly early modern passions – and that collaboration *itself* brought pleasure', the mechanism by which feeling circulates and the critical work it accomplishes is of paramount importance.[32] *Bartholomew Fair* in its layering of spectators, participants and creators shows a model of theatrical initiative that can be illuminated by its cousin in fencing discourse. Rather than building to a climax and a resolution, Jonson's play represents the interactions between the fair and its visitors (and the real-life playgoers, players and playwright) in Meyer's sense. That is, they approach one another in the onset, meet in the middle and spring back apart at the end (or end the *Stück* with a touch). There are many examples of this formal movement. Take, for instance, one of the earlier instances of antagonistic 'feeling' we are presented with at the end of Act 2. Overdo, in disguise, attempts to identify the cutpurses he knows are working with Ursula to fleece the fairgoers. Loudly preaching against tobacco, he distracts Cokes and Wasp and inadvertently helps the real cutpurses steal Cokes's purse. The culprits snicker at Cokes, 'nor you feel', as he complains about his tutor's lack of understanding. Wasp blames Overdo and beats him.

The stage is cleared at the antagonistic culmination of this scene and Act 3's focus shifts to a conversation among Haggis and Bristle (constables) and White (a pimp) about the earlier commotion.

As Meyer articulates, the balance between being ready to react to whatever your adversary does in the middle of the device's sequence and being able to force your adversary to react to you is delicate. Fencers, then, 'struggle over the Before with their simultaneous devices and strive for mastery'.[33] Meyer terms the middle the handwork and writes that here there is

> [a] constant changing and transformation between the Before and After, for now your opponent gets it, now you in return. But he who has the After, that is, is so crowded upon that he must always parry, shall be well mindful of the word Instantly, and not forget it; for through it he must rush back to the Before, if he wishes to withdraw without harm.[34]

Timing in the handwork becomes spatialised, a contested battlefield. Moreover, during the same time unit, fencers inhabit different temporal positions based on their relationship to each other rather than an external measurement. All this is not to say that Meyer does not believe in planning ahead. He affirms the importance of being able to generate kairotic moments as well as seize them through such measures as the 'provoker, taker, hitter' attack combination. In this combination, the fencer throws an intentionally short attack at an opponent's open line, acting 'as if you had overcommitted to your cut'.[35] If the opponent is fooled and moves quickly to attack that opening, the fencer essentially parries and ripostes: 'recover for the stroke, and cut out his incoming cut or thrust with your forte . . . As soon as you have thus taken his stroke or thrust, then rush to the nearest opening with cutting or thrusting.'[36] This sort of sequence is what modern fencing terms a 'second-intention' action, as the failed attacks of *Arden of Faversham*. That is, the fencer does not necessarily expect the initial attack to hit, but rather to provoke a reaction the fencer is ready to counter. While it does rely on looking ahead, the present orientation is still noticeable. Context is crucial – the opening one makes depends on the circumstances, the defence used against the incoming attack differs based on the opponent's reaction. Meyer emphasises that the fencer must judge 'depending on the situation' in each instance.

Single combat, particularly the point-of-honour duel, is frequently made to represent a model of autonomous subjectivity: two individuals square off to try their relative worth and prove false-hood or truth. In the same way, readings of the theatrical situation can often assume a more monolithic encounter between playwright and spectator. However, though less familiar to us today, a systems-level approach to the fencing match was a customary configuration to early moderns. Terrain, time of day, length and type of weapon, and the opponent's disposition as choleric or timid combine to form a complex and dynamic environment.[37] Silver, for example, advises fencers to examine the field prior to a duel: 'observe well the scope, evenness and unevenness of your ground, put yourself in readiness with your weapon, before your enemy comes within distances, set the sun in his face traverse if possible you can'.[38] The theatre, like the duelling field, incorporated a good deal of uncertainty in its distrib-uted mechanisms for feeling and cognition. The model of cognition described in fencing manuals illuminates the training of timing and judgement at the level of practice in a way that is transferrable to the theatrical context. *Fühlen*, an antagonistic mode of perception, translates to the emotional and cognitive system of the playhouse among playgoers, players and playwrights.

At the intersection of emotion and cognition, feeling and *Fühlen* complement recent work on embodied and extended cognition and extend it into antagonistic contexts that are crucial for understand-ing the contagious and contentious playhouse. As cognitive work is performed across the body and the environment, both tool use and social coordination blur the boundaries between areas of the brain as well as between the brain and the body and the body and its environ-ment.[39] In Meyer's *Fühlen*, the sword extends the body by allowing the fencer to gather temporal information based on the softness or the hardness of the bind (blade contact). The future is brought into the present via the sense of touch. Trained through numerous drills to respond in certain ways to certain types of pressure, the body carries memories built and deployed across time. In this sense, touch brings together both two fencers, and two temporalities, with the fencer in the before and the fencer in the after meeting during this connection. Jonson also plays with antagonistic connection in his comedy, using *feel* or *feeling* eight times, all in contexts which highlight the congru-ence of cognition, emotion and sensation. Littlewit enthuses: 'I do feel conceits coming upon me' (1.1.25) as he admires his wife and her clothing. Quarlous uses the word in a distinctly sexual register in his outline of the downside of widow-hunting: 'thou must visit them as thou wouldst do a tomb, with a torch or three handfuls of link, flaming hot, and so thou may'st hap to make them feel thee and after come to inherit according to thy inches' (1.1.57–60). Ursula worries about her own purported malnutrition and fatigue: 'I feel myself dropping already as fast as I can' (2.2.65–6). And Overdo sententiously opines, 'I do not feel it', as he endures the stocks, quoting Stoic philosophers to comfort himself while stubbornly refusing to learn from the experience (4.5.76). After his release, he continues to judge others harshly until the final puppet show scene where he is left without a leg to stand on.

Overdo echoes his brother-in-law's inability to learn via feeling. Most of the usages of *feel* and *feeling* in *Bartholomew Fair* occur in relationship to Cokes and his stubborn lack of perception. As a representation of a naive theatregoer, a connection made explicit in the final puppet show where he cannot tell apart reality from fiction, Cokes is ripe for exploitation. As we have seen, almost as soon as he arrives at the fair he is preyed upon while he is distracted by an argument with his tutor. Wasp ('Numps') is dismissive of Overdo's lengthy diatribe about the evils of tobacco. Cokes complains that Wasp 'does not understand', and the pickpocket Edgeworth snickers 'nor you feel' as he picks Cokes's pocket. Cognition – understanding an argument – and feeling – physically perceiving a threat – intertwine. Rather than learning, Cokes simply pulls out a second purse and makes the same mistakes again. Wasp will unconsciously echo Edgworth's words when Cokes realises that his purse is missing: 'Why so, there's all the feeling he has!' In this register, however, feeling means sensitivity, understanding and willingness to change and learn – a capacity Cokes and Overdo do not exhibit. Moments of failed or successful judgement are mediated by feeling at key points in the play like these. These brothers exemplify failures of feeling, but in the game of vapours and the final puppet show the audience is given models of successful antagonistic feeling. The 'game of vapours' showcases the antagonistic use of a literal and metaphorical feeling out, while the final puppet show transposes this antagonistic model of feeling overtly to a theatrical context.

Every Pig-Woman in Her Vapour

Throughout *Bartholomew Fair*, Jonson trades his customary framework of humours for that of vapours. Vapours are like humours in that they are a representation of the physiological make-up of each individual – their aggression, melancholy, apathy and optimism. Vapours, like the steam of Ursula's roasting pig, are distinct from humours because of the way in which heat (whether from sources such as lust or gluttony or from the smouldering bowl of a pipe) makes them rise. As Robinson notes, when the characters of the play are introduced to the heated pleasures of the fair, their follies gain ascendancy.[40] *Bartholomew Fair*'s engagement with vapours begins with the horse-courser Knockem's request that Ursula, whose pig- and beer-selling booth is the centre of the fair's vice, bring him a beer. Knockem uses 'vapours' nominally as a synonym for bad temper, reproaches, or an expression of reluctance: 'let's drink it out, Urs, and no vapours!' Later, Knockem expands the semantic range of the word by using it as a transitive verb – 'Any man that does vapour me the Ass . . . I do vapour him the lie' – when the citizens and fair-folk come together to participate in a 'game of vapours'. With this semantic flexibility, the term can allow players to vapour *at* each other, an important distinction from the work of the humours in other comedies.[41] Vapours, more than humours, extend Jonson's work in *Bartholomew Fair* with antagonistic intersubjective contact. Since the game relies on skilled timing, it also showcases the kinesic judgement of its participants.

Scholarship on *Bartholomew Fair* has long recognised the importance of vapours to Jonsonian poetics, but so far critics have read them primarily in terms of classical literary heritage or as a game to facilitate turn-taking, cooperation and listening. Robinson, for instance, argues that 'the center of structure and meaning of *Bartholomew Fair* lies in the symbolism of vapours that pervades the play's imagery, characterization, and action'.[42] Paster also finds in the vapours of *Bartholomew Fair* a social commentary on civic life and the humoral body: 'it is in his brilliant invention of the 'game of vapours' – in which contradiction is the outer expression of the inward self's most fundamental need to declare itself separate and unique – that Jonson hits the humors indeed'.[43] I agree with Robinson that Jonson draws from a strain of Aristotelian thought which understands the gradual growth of diverse parts into one whole as a mode of dramatic unity. The play's chaotic structure is integral, not incidental, to its mission and thematics. I also agree with Paster that Jonson uses vapours, and particularly the vapour game, in *Bartholomew Fair* in the same way in which he uses humours in other comedies – that is, to symbolise embodied emotion. However, I would like to add that Jonson's poetics were influenced by contemporary structures of thought as well as classical theory and that he works in antagonism as much or more than cooperation. For Jonson, feeling trains judgement in the antagonistic space of the in-between.

The symbolic activity of 'vapour' reaches its peak in the 'game of vapours' in which Knockem engages a group of fair patrons: Nordern, Puppy, Cutting, White, Mistress Overdo and Wasp. As Ursula's booth opens, spectators see a tableau of characters 'talking noisily' and argumentatively. Jonson glosses the game in a stage direction: 'Here they continue their game of vapours, which is nonsense: every man to oppose the last man that spoke, whether it concerned him or no.' Edgworth and Quarlous, intent upon stealing the special licence Wasp carries, enter and stand to the side, joining the theatre audience as spectators. This show-within-a-show foreshadows the culminating puppet act, as all of the characters assume Edgworth and Quarlous's positions looking down at the puppet play's action. Wasp ventures a non sequitur, 'Why I say nay to't' (4.4.22), which ignites the following argument.

KNOCKEM: To what do you say nay, sir?
WASP: To anything, whatsoever it is, so long as I do not like it.
WHIT: Pardon me, little man, dou musht like it a little.
CUTTING: No, he must not like it at all, sir: there you are i'the wrong.
WHIT: I tink I be: he musht not like it, indeed.
CUTTING: Nay, then he both must and will like it, sir, for all you.
KNOCKEM: If he have reason, he may like it, sir.
WHIT: By no meansh, Captain, upon reason, he may like nothing
       upon reason.
WASP: I have no reason, nor will I hear of no reason, nor I will look
       for no reason, and he is an ass that either knows any, or looks
       for't from me.   (4.4.25–35)

The vapours game is a game of counterattacks: the only rule is that one must immediately and vehemently oppose whatever was said before. It feeds Wasp's craving for competition as much as Ursula's pig purportedly satisfies the pregnant Win's craving. The game also makes Wasp as ridiculous as his charge, Cokes, by having him loudly declare that he has no reason. The linguistic free-for-all, as characters jump in on one another's behalf or to offer unprovoked insults, is reminiscent of the academic disputation.[44] Jonson cues that there are sportive as well as academic themes at work, however, by having the characters move in and out of verbal and non-verbal modes of aggressive expression.

The multiple aggressors in this scene evoke the brawls characteristic of the English streets between English and Italian masters of fence. This connotation is fully realised as the characters resort to physical exchanges, first when they 'fall by the ears' – presumably, scuffling without drawn weapons – and later when they draw their weapons to fight. To facilitate the theft of the marriage licence, Quarlous and Edgworth first exploit and then generate a tempo of opportunity. In the first instance, Knockem urges Whit to strike Wasp in retaliation for an insult. In the ensuing altercation, Edgworth steals the licence. In a separate exchange, Knockem and Whit, too, are able to seize opportunity when Quarlous defends his beard and instigates further conflict as they 'draw all, and fight'. The game of vapours into which the play descends is socially antagonistic as well as constructive, seamlessly blending into the physical fight and back out, using competition to educate kinesic judgement. Ultimately, these combat-inflected reading strategies reveal the workings of Jonson's theory of judgement and its inculcation. This game shows in action the modes of temporal, embodied, judgement marked by the intersubjective antagonism of fencing. By using the competitive game of vapours to set up an adversarial use of feeling in one group encounter, he prepares the audience to see this same intersubjective antagonism incorporated into theatrical experience in the final puppet show. In this final scene, Leatherhead, the puppeteer, sweeps up both Cokes and Busy in the tempo of his own performance.

The puppet show, written by John Littlewit, is a burlesque mash-up of the popular friendship tale Damon and Pythias and the romance of Hero and Leander. Jonson's use of stichomythia in the puppet show and the pervasive duelling imagery throughout suggest that the scene is meant to be read with modes of combat in mind. The show exemplifies a rhythm of theatrical expression in the temporality of its plot and the antagonistic, intersubjective interactions of Busy and Leatherhead. Leatherhead displays his skill as a master adaptor – a seizer of the before – as he confutes Busy and accommodates Cokes. Through Busy, Jonson delivers a critique of Puritan understandings of the theatre's relationship to the sacred, offering instead his own view of the ways in which drama can touch its audience's feelings.

The puppeteer works his audience's criticism and enjoyment into the fabric of the puppet show, as he takes Cokes's interjections up into the rhythm and details of the play. For instance, after Cupid sends the puppet Hero a pint of sherry, purportedly from Leander, she falls in love with Leander. In the next lines, Puppet Jonas narrates 'a pint of sack, score a pint of sack i'the Coney' (5.4.164). Cokes responds 'Sack? You said but e'en now it should be sherry', and Jonas responds 'why so it is: sherry, sherry, sherry' (5.4.164–5). In this and other moments of the puppet show, Cokes engages in a dialogue with the puppets, which Lantern Leatherhead works into the performance. Sometimes this adaptation also works at the level of the show's rhyme scheme, as when Cokes's interruptions are co-opted into the puppet play's poetry:

> LANTERN: 'Tis well, you can now go to breakfast to Hero;
>   You have given me my breakfast, with a 'hone and 'honero.
> COKES: How is't, friend? Ha' they hurt thee?
> LANTERN: Oh, no!
>   Between you and I, sir, we do but make show.   (5.4.220–4)

This slippage between puppet and puppeteer certainly showcases Cokes's naivety as a consumer of theatre. However, it also displays Leatherhead's compound subjectivity, an assemblage of human and non-human materiality that evokes the players and props of the larger theatre. Similarly showing his flexible abilities, Lantern adapts to Busy's presence through a quick-witted co-option of his interference, ultimately heightening the humour of the show by using inflated rhetorical tropes and the language of aristocratic duelling to contest Busy, making the Puritan himself antagonist in the puppet show.

Busy's initial onslaught on the puppet show ultimately rebounds upon him, as he loses control of his bellicose allusions. He storms 'Down with Dagon, down with Dagon; 'tis I, will no longer endure your profanations' (5.5.1–2). To Leatherhead's response, 'What mean you, sir?' Busy continues:

> I will remove Dagon there I say, that idol, that heathenish idol, that remains (as I may say) a beam, a very beam, not a beam of the sun, nor a beam of the moon, nor a beam of a balance, neither a house-beam, nor a weaver's beam, but a beam in the eye, in the eye of the brethren; a very great beam, an exceeding great beam; such as are your stage-players, rhymers, and morris-dancers, who have walked hand in hand, in contempt of the brethren, and the cause; and been borne out by instruments of no mean countenance.   (5.5.4–10)

The tempo of Busy's speech allies him with the foolish Italian fencing master of *Every Man in His Humour*, Bobadil. Both use voluble and self-contradictory language to project authority. In contrast to Bobadil, Busy's speech uses a rolling, repetitive rhythm to build momentum. Bobadil trades in the jargon of everyday language, but Busy assumes a more poetic preacher's mode of expression. Seizing on the notion of a beam, Busy loses track of his allusion's context, in which the beam denotes not idolatry but hypocrisy. The beam to which Busy refers is an ironic allusion to Jesus' famous injunction against hypocrisy, to 'cast out first the beam out of thine own eye' before attempting to 'pull out the mote' in someone else's (Luke 6.41). Because of this fundamental error in reading – perhaps he confuses the beam with the stumbling block – the point Busy hammers home is the opposite of what was intended: the puppets' eventual victory and Busy's conversion to a consumer of theatre is foreshadowed in his tirade. Jonson's reference serves as a reminder of the play's larger message, to pay attention to your own perception and discernment before critiquing others'. As Jonson puts it in the contract, the play-goers are to agree that 'every man here exercise his own judgement and not censure by contagion' (Induction 86). Judgement should be deliberately exercised rather than passively infected. However, it is the active versus passive ways of enjoying the theatre that Jonson contrasts, rather than rejecting the potential of emotional contagion altogether. The theatre is specifically a venue for developing robust judgement in audience members because of its vulnerability to such affective infection. Otherwise, his goal of using humour to induce laughter and therefore change – a playgoer would not wish to imag-ine that a neighbour in the next seat is laughing at them, after all – would be ineffective.

Jonson's investment in the commercial theatre as a venue for exer-cising judgement is also evident in the specific idol to which Busy alludes. When Busy figures Leatherhead as Dagon, and, by exten-sion, the commercial theatre as a heathen temple, he exhibits the ways in which Jonson understands Puritans as the intellectual heirs of the Philistines. Busy conflates dancing, poetry and stage plays with puppet theatre, all as hindrances to proper vision and obedience. The word choice 'idol' at first seems a strange one, since it seems that Busy objects more to the sexual immorality induced by such cultural production rather than observing the Second Commandment. How-ever, the allusion fits with a Puritan view of the future of the theatre. Dagon the idol was known for miraculously falling and breaking its hands and head off:

> When the Philistines took the ark of God, they brought it into the house of Dagon, and set it by Dagon. And when they of Ashdod arose early on the morrow, behold, Dagon was fallen upon his face to the earth before the ark of the Lord. And they took Dagon and set him in his place again. And when they arose early on the mor-row morning, behold, Dagon was fallen upon his face to the ground before the ark of the Lord; and the head of Dagon and both the palms of his hands were cut off upon the threshold; only the stump of Dagon was left to him. (1 Sam 5:2–5)

Referring to Leatherhead as Dagon evokes his hand puppets' eventual fall and destruction in the face of God's Ark. The 'handless' Dagon puppets walk 'hand in hand' with other performers, as both are symbolically linked to the hand's ability to touch and feel out. Busy sees the materiality of theatrical production, with its props and costumes, to be a species of blasphemy as well as a hotbed of immoral crossdressing as he later argues. This view is perhaps influenced by the theatrical nature of Anglo-Catholic liturgy. On a metatheatrical level, Busy's biblical allusions also reinforce the vibrant materiality of the fair. Just as the idol, Dagon, moves of its own volition to fall down and worship the Ark, so the puppets assume their own agency throughout the show. Dagon's hands are broken in the fall – for Busy, a vision of theatre's loss of social agency. Jonson, through the hand puppets' eventual victory, instead suggests the theatre's ability to feel out its audience, to touch emotions, and to change behaviour.

Jonson's development of the Dagon allusion, like the beam allusion, is ironic. Busy may think that he is making the point that the glory of God will overcome the pretensions of a blasphemous theatre. However, Busy actually enacts what Jonson sees as the Puritan's inheritance of the Philistine's obtuseness. If Leatherhead is Dagon, then his puppet theatre is the 'house of Dagon'. However, in this story it is not the idol itself that is at fault. Rather, it is the Philistines who assume that the Israelites' god is as collectible as an idol. Juxtaposing the truly sacred (the Ark) and the falsely sacred (the Dagon statue), the Philistines violate a central decorum and draw down God's wrath (God later afflicts whichever town hosts the Ark with tumours). Thus, it is the confusing of the sacred and the non-sacred that is at issue. Anti-theatricalists, by reading the theatre as a medium of blasphemy, place secular drama in the context of the sacred. In this sense, it is the Puritans' preoccupation, rather than any intention on the part of playwrights and players, which shifts God's presence into a commercial playhouse. Busy, and the Puritans for whom he stands in, show a fundamental error in judgement precipitated by their inability or disinclination to allow theatrical feelings to educate judgement.

In contrast to stichomythic tradition and in keeping with the rhythm established by the 'game of vapours', the exchange between Puppet Dionysius and Busy is marked by juvenile assertion and contradiction rather than sophisticated one-liners. Lantern engages in a mock stichomythic exchange which resembles an infantile tug-of-war more than a staccato, witty thrust-and-parry sequence. When Busy says of Puppet Dionysius's work, 'it is profane, idol', Dionysius answers back, 'it is not profane!', which is relayed by Lantern to Busy: 'it is not profane, he says.' Puppet Dionysius and Busy go back and forth twice more – 'It is not profane', 'it is profane' – until they give up. The underlying tactics of combat, specifically of the counter-attack, are still apparent despite the simplification of the exchange, however. Jonson pairs academic disputation with the complex eti-quette of the point-of-honour duel in order to craft the antagonistic temporality of the exchange. Using reiterations of giving the lie and the inflated rhetoric of bravos, the angry puppets repeatedly call each other to the duelling field. Upon Busy's arrival, the Puppet Diony-sius challenges him as well: 'You lie, you lie, you lie abominably' (5.5.80). Finally, Dionysius takes the battle to Busy by questioning typical Puritan occupations (5.5.57–60). Anticipating Busy's clichéd response concerning the moral dangers of the theatre, Leatherhead/ Dionysius sets Busy up as the victim of a well-executed counterattack. At this instigation, Busy is forced into his famous chief contention, that theatre involves crossdressing and is therefore an abomination, to which the puppet 'takes up his garment' to reveal his sexlessness.

In the exchange, Busy slips between addressing Leatherhead and the puppets as idols. This confusion reflects a seamless extension of Leatherhead into his puppets. More than simply another example of Busy's naivety, the indeterminacy expresses Jonson's vision of the theatre as a venue for joint perception and distributed cognition. The identity of character and player, puppeteer/author and interpreter are mingled. Leatherhead's hands do his arguing and thinking for him – or at least create the illusion of doing so. The puppet show's role as a microcosm of the theatrical experience as a whole has been discussed, and explanations of this analogy tend towards the cyni-cal. For instance, Scott Shershow argues that Jonson's motivation for ending his play with a puppet show was part of a larger project to 'transcend and transform popular performance by embracing it with a self-conscious irony'.[45] In this view, the importation of pup-pets marks Jonson's attempt to contrastively define literary theatre against the puppetry arts, or popular lowbrow theatre. However, this view of Jonson's creative project must either ignore the other instances of popular entertainment he introduces in his plays, or say that he uses all of them ironically. As I hope to have demonstrated throughout this chapter, Jonson's relationship with the popular entertainment of public prizefighting is more complex. I agree that Jonson uses the puppet show as a way to comment on the theatrical experience, and probably even to level critiques at his audience and at other playwrights. However, I do not think that this is the only, or even the primary, takeaway from the show. Instead, Leatherhead and Littlewit's collaborative venture showcases the theatre's capacity to break down barriers using a competitive and adaptive aesthetic logic.

While Jonson eschews the kind of emotional contagion that leads his audience to accept someone else's judgement rather than forming their own, this is not the only form of joint perception he addresses. He also draws attention to the generative potential of the 'middle', the 'handwork' or the 'suspension' as a locus of judgement inculcation. Moments of emotional contact among audience members, between self and other, player and puppet, audience and actor, offer arenas of growth through conflict. Jonson's antecedents in the fencing school as well as the grammar school are crucial to understanding his temporal, corporeal model of theatrical judgement. Discernment, for Jonson, is both antagonistic and intersubjective, which makes the 'mechanisms of enskilment' offered via the English stage a particularly appropriate vehicle for its training.[46] Judgement, a mode of knowing-when and a skill of selfhood, features prominently in Jonson's oeuvre, but its dimensions of embodied practice are often overlooked. The shared methodologies of fencing masters and playwrights are a rich vein of material for understanding how time inflects models of literary judgement.

Notes

1. Jonson, *Bartholomew Fair*, Induction 7–11. All references to *Bartholomew Fair* are taken from the Cambridge University Press edition. All quotations from the play will be cited parenthetically by act, scene and line numbers.
2. See Tribble, *Early Modern Actors* for an in-depth analysis of the prize-fight in *Cynthia's Revels*.
3. See Paster, *Humoring the Body*; Smith, 'Pre-modern Sexualities'; Barker, *Tremulous Private Body*.
4. Spolsky, 'Elaborated Knowledge', 159.
5. For recent work building on the concept of kinesic intelligence in literature, see Bolens, *Style of Gestures* and Banks and Chester, eds, *Movement in Renaissance Literature*.
6. Spolsky, 'Elaborated Knowledge', 159.
7. Tribble, *Early Modern Actors*, 11.
8. Ibid.
9. As David Bevington points out, '*Bartholomew Fair* requires an exceptionally, although not uniquely, large cast for the professional theatre of the time. Shakespeare generally wrote for a cast of 12 men and

4 boys, but *Bartholomew Fair* has speaking roles for at least 22 actors, and there are so many minor roles and supernumeraries that even with doubling the cast in 1614 probably approached 30' (*The Cambridge Edition of the Works of Ben Jonson Online*, introduction to *Bartholomew Fair*, n.p.)

10. Eliot, 'Ben Jonson', 155.
11. Donaldson, *Ben Jonson*, 333.
12. Hopgood, *Passionate Playgoing*, 183.
13. Hobgood, *Passionate Playgoing*.
14. Langley, *Shakespeare's Contagious Sympathies*.
15. Kaplan, 'Dramatic and Moral Energy', 141.
16. Tribble, *Early Modern Actors*, 65.
17. Readings of Jonson's relationship with his audience tend to emphasise fragility and anxiety on the part of Jonson. See Rowe, *Distinguishing Jonson*; Sweeney, *Jonson and the Psychology of Public Theater*; R. Dutton, Ben Jonson, Authority, Criticism (Houndmills ; New York: Macmillan Press ; St. Martin's Press, 1996); Hobgood, *Passionate Playgoing*.
18. Knecht, *Grammar Rules of Affection*, 182.
19. Ibid. 183.
20. *The Cambridge Edition of the Works of Ben Jonson Online*, introduction to *Every Man in His Humour* quarto, n.p.
21. Jonson, *Timber*, 90.
22. Ibid., 515.
23. Meyer, *Art of Combat*, 71.
24. Alfieri, *L'arte di ben maneggiare la spada*, 18.
25. 'Find' is a technical term in fencing meaning that you have gained mechanical positional advantage over the enemy's weapon.
26. Fabris, *Lo Schermo*, 12.
27. Docciolini, *Treatise on the Subject of Fencing*, 27.
28. For the translation of this passage from Pacheco's *New Science*, see Mary and Puck Curtis's 'From the Page to the Practice,' 42.
29. See Jeffrey Forgeng's introduction to *Art of Combat* for an analysis of Meyer's relationship to modernity and to the medieval manuscript tradition.
30. Meyer, *Art of Combat*, 44.
31. Ibid.
32. Hobgood, *Passionate Playgoing*, 183.
33. Meyer, *Art of Combat*, 44.
34. Ibid. 69.
35. Ibid. 189.
36. Ibid.
37. Tribble argues that actors and playwrights used a systems-level approach to the cognitive demands of memorising line and performing plays. This approach encompassed both physical environment and

the use of language, such as rhymed couplets, to promote memory and channel attention.

38. Silver, *Brief Instructions*, 84.
39. Teske, 'From Embodied to Extended Cognition', 759.
40. Robinson, '*Bartholomew Fair:* Comedy of Vapors'.
41. See Robinson, '*Bartholomew Fair:* Comedy of Vapors', for a full account of the Fair's capacity to melt its patrons and release their basest vapours. Paster argues that vapours and humours are synonymous, and I agree that this is mostly the case. However, as vapours are more mobile than humours and as the play uses vapours in a transitive sense, vapours lend themselves better to the intersubjective antagonism thematic of *Bartholomew Fair* than humours do. See Paster, '*Bartholomew Fair* and the Humoral Body'.
42. Robinson, '*Bartholomew Fair:* Comedy of Vapors', 66.
43. Paster, '*Bartholomew Fair* and the Humoral Body', 268.
44. On the academic disputation's role in *Bartholomew Fair*, see Beaurline, *Jonson and Elizabethan Comedy*.
45. Shershow, *Puppets and 'Popular' Culture*, 99
46. On such mechanisms, see Tribble, 'Skill'.

Coda

When James Burbage took possession of the Blackfriars Theatre he retrofitted the facility with galleries and dressing rooms, repurposing the fencing school to be an indoor theatre. Players trod the boards in the instructional spaces where the Ancient Master of Defence William Joyner had previously taught English footwork and Rocco Bonetti later taught the Italian rapier fight.[1] The story of Blackfriars – a fencing school adapted to create a theatrical environment – in many ways parallels the conditions of the early commercial theatre. Literally, fencing prize displays continued to lose stage space and participants to the commercial theatre. Boxing, originally a subset of fencing training, gradually came to dominate public displays of 'the noble science of defence'. As boxing grew in popularity during the following centuries, it eventually largely replaced English swordplay as a public sport and performance. It is not until the late nineteenth century that amateur historians and recreationists such as Alfred Hutton and Egerton Castle sought to revive England's native fencing style. Conceptually, dramatists and players repurpose ideas and approaches from fencing in the service of their own profession. What Burbage did with boards and nails in his remodel, dramatists accomplished on the level of narrative: they drew from useful elements in fencing discourse and redeployed them to create compelling visual cues to complement and extend the verbal elements of their plays. That is, playwrights captured and managed the trained attention of early modern spectators by using familiar sights to represent ideas as abstract as having good taste (aesthetic judgement) and applying cunning based on antagonistic timing – the 'artful devices' of feints, *contratempo* and second-intention actions.

The history of rhetoric and its place in the grammar school and on the public stage has proved a generative line of inquiry, but the potential of fencing pedagogy and practice also influenced early modern drama to an extent and in ways that have been largely overlooked. Literary scholars tend to have a stronger inheritance from rhetoric than from combat and are perhaps predisposed to oppose pen to sword, emphasising the former. Through its investigation of the intersections of fencing and drama, this book has re-envisioned theatrical form by identifying aspects of plot structure that are intentionally experimental rather than flawed and digressive as playwrights adapted the visual logic of fencing. More significantly, though, I have outlined the ways in which drama and fencing come together to train the tempo and judgement of its participants. By recasting the relationship between sword and pen to emphasise the shared territory and educational goals of fencing and rhetoric, I have reintroduced a historically contingent understanding of the generative interactions between these two power-exerting instruments. As I intimate in my last chapter, this has implications for our understanding of cognition.

As Tribble persuasively articulates, applying the insights of philosophy of mind and cognitive science research to literary texts contributes to a 'two-directional communication between the sciences and the humanities'.[2] Her systems-level approach to the question of how environments, audiences and players together form a system through which cognitive processes take place illuminates questions around how players were able to deal with the demands of their tasks. She argues that this 'playing system' has been 'consistently distorted by a tendency to view cognition as individual rather than social'.[3] Tribble's analysis, like others linking literary criticism to cognitive science, draws from the influential work of David Chalmers and Andy Clark on 'extended cognition'. They advanced their model of *active externalism*, which holds that thinking is distributed across agent and environment rather than being confined to an individual brain: 'the human organism is linked with an external entity in a two-way interaction, creating a *coupled system* that can be seen as a cognitive system in its own right'.[4] Where Clark and Chalmers use the example of a neural implant to discuss active externalism, a less technologically complex example is available as well: the cognitive prosthesis of the sword is similarly a version of the 'general tendency of human reasoners to lean heavily on environmental supports'. In the words of Capoferro, 'the sword should be thought of as forming one limb with the arm'.[5] Masters' writings on the role of touch in fencing demonstrate how thinking happens across environments as well as within an individual.

Recent work in historical phenomenology and cognitive science has done much to foreground the important embodied congruence between thinking and feeling. As of yet, however, it has primary focused on the implications of this shared ground for cooperation and sympathy. For example, Teske suggests that questioning the autonomous, bounded individual leads to new possibilities for integration and extension. The most important of these for the 'symbolic symbionts' are found 'in diachronic relationalities with other human beings'.[6] This interest in the more cooperative aspects of intersubjective experience is shared by the authors of *The Embodied Mind*, who explore the implications of Buddhist practices of mindfulness on contemporary ethical engagements, navigating the 'extremes of absolutism and nihilism'.[7] Rosi Braidotti, too, maps out the potentialities that arise with 'the decline of the unitary subject position' as it pertains to deeper connections to non-human configurations of matter.[8] The choice need not be between autonomous subjects cut off from their environments and cognitive agents who are embedded in the world and working synergistically, however. Early modern drama shows us an alternative to both: antagonistic as well as cooperative cognitive agents who think with and across environments.

With my focus on antagonistic intersubjective perception, I hope to have furthered our understanding of the volatile, knowledge-producing context of the playhouse in ways that are extractable to contemporary conversations in education and disability studies. For instance, as Margaret Price highlights in her influential work on classroom *kairos*, kairotic spaces are 'the less formal, often unnoticed, areas of academe where knowledge is produced and power is exchanged' with the defining characteristic of pairing 'spontaneity with high levels of professional/academic impact'.[9] As Price explores, the real-time unfolding of events along with the impromptu nature of the communication that is required or expected creates institutional challenges faced by students with disabilities. I do not mean to suggest a pedagogical praxis in which educators deliberately pit students against each other in antagonistic encounters. Rather, by recognising the complexity of interpersonal classroom timing, the ways in which the classroom is already inherently adversarial for some students comes to the fore, which ultimately helps instructors to craft effective learning environments. My research, by conceptualising judgement as a trainable, temporal process rather than a binary decision, offers tools for thinking about how to train student timing intentionally and fairly rather than unthinkingly replicating learning environments that disadvantage neurologically diverse students. Integrating activities that ask students to read other learners as well as reading texts – for example, predicting their likely responses, preparing counterpoints or agreements ahead of time, controlling the flow of a discussion, and so on – can help students navigate the demands of the classroom. Students learn to critically evaluate the space of the classroom and their role within it when instructors emphasise that classroom timing is a skill to be cultivated rather than an innate talent.

The early commercial theatre came under fire from anti-theatricalist and proto-capitalist rhetoric alike. Both strands of criticism complained that stage plays wasted the time of their patrons. In fact, playwrights, players and audiences came together to cultivate the embodied skill of timing through a wide array of practices and pedagogies. The model of projective (but not necessarily empathetic) attention to the other that is expressed by fencing and drama's intersection is especially useful in today's social and political contexts, as these artful devices bring to the fore the imbrications of timing and ethical decision-making. Entering into the timing of another person or system is a key skill. Cooperatively, the skill of critical timing allows for people to contribute to larger enterprises by building on prior research to create new knowledge or by participating in activities designed to create a more just society. Antagonistically, timing the opposing individual or system prepares people to puncture unjust ideas and plans at the most opportune moment. These skills become increasingly essential in our interactions with our own communities and those on the other side of the globe as well as the Globe.

Notes

1. Aylward records that 'Rocco removed to the Blackfriars in 1584/85, for there is a lease preserved among the Loseley manuscripts which shows that, in that year, he took from Sir William More premises which formed part of the former convent of the Blackfriars. They consisted of 'a hall, a chamber above the hall, a little room under the said hall, a yard, a little chamber or vault within the said yard, a cellar under the fence-school under the south end of the same' ('The Inimitable Bobadill', 29). This site had been in use as a fencing school since 1563/64 by William Joyner.
2. Tribble, *Cognition*, 7
3. Ibid. 135.
4. Clark and Chalmers, 'The Extended Mind', 222.
5. Capoferro, *Gran Simulacro*, 19.
6. Teske, 'From Embodied to Extended Cognition', 775.
7. Varela, Thomson and Rosch, *The Embodied Mind*, 235.
8. Braidotti, *The Posthuman*, 54.
9. Kairos.technorhetoric.net, n.p.

Bibliography

Agnew, Jean-Christophe. *Worlds Apart: The Market and the Theater in Anglo-American Thought, 1550–1750*. Cambridge: Cambridge University Press, 1986.

Agrippa, Camillo. *Trattato Di Scientia d'Arme, con un Dialogo di Filosofia*. Rome, 1553.

Albury, W. R. *Castiglione's Allegory: Veiled Policy in* The Book of the Courtier. Ashgate Surrey, 2014.

Alfieri, Francesco. *L'arte di ben maneggiare la spada*. Padua, 1653.

Anderson, Thomas. *Shakespeare's Fugitive Politics*. Edinburgh: Edinburgh University Press, 2016.

Anderson, Thomas. '"What is written shall be executed": "Nude Contracts" and "Lively Warrants" in *Titus Andronicus*', *Criticism* 45.3 (2003): 30–121.

Anglin, Jay. 'The Schools of Defense in Elizabethan London', *Renaissance Quarterly* 37.3 (1984): 393–410.

Anglo, Sydney. *The Martial Arts of Renaissance Europe*. New Haven: Yale University Press, 2000.

Anon. *Arden of Faversham*, ed. Martin White. London: New Mermaids, 2013.

Antonucci, Barbara. 'Romans versus Barbarians: Speaking the Language of the Empire in *Titus Andronicus*', in *Identity, Otherness and Empire in Shakespeare's Rome*, ed. Maria Del Sapio Garbero. Surrey, England, and Burlington, VT: Ashgate, 2009. 119–30.

Ascham, Roger. *The Scholemaster* in *The Whole Works of Roger Ascham, Now First Collected and Revised with a Life of the Author*, vol I. II, ed. Rev. Dr Giles. London: 1865.

Ascoli, A. 'Wrestling with Orlando: Chivalric Pastoral in Shakespeare's Arden', *Renaissance Drama*: 'Italy in the Drama of Europe', v. 36/37. Chicago: Northwestern University Press, 2010.

Aylward, J. D. 'The Inimitable Bobadill', *Notes and Queries* 195 (1950): 2–4, 28–31.

Bakhtin, M. *The Dialogic Imagination*, trans. Caryl Emerson and Michael Holquist. Austin: University of Texas Press, 1981.

Banks, Kathryn and Timothy Chesters, eds. *Movement in Renaissance Literature: Exploring Kinesic Intelligence*. Palgrave, 2018.

Barbasetti, Luigi. *The Art of the Foil*. New York: Barnes & Noble Books, 1998.

Barish, Jonas. *Ben Jonson and the Language of Prose Comedy*. New York: Norton, 1960.

Barker, Francis. *The Tremulous Private Body: Essays on Subjection*. Ann Arbor: University of Michigan Press, 1995.

Barker, Simon and Hilary Hinds, eds. *The Routledge Anthology of Renaissance Drama*. London: Routledge, 2003.

Bartels, Emily C. 'Making More of the Moor: Aaron, Othello, and Renaissance Refashionings of Race', *Shakespeare Quarterly* 41.4 (1990): 433–54.

Baumlin, James and Tina French Baumlin. 'Chronos, Kairos, Aion: Failures of Decorum, Right-Timing, and Revenge in Shakespeare's *Hamlet*', in *Rhetoric and Kairos: Essays in History, Theory, and Praxis*, ed. Philip Sipiora and James Baumlin. Albany: State University of New York Press, 2002. 165–86.

Beaurline, L. A. *Jonson and Elizabethan Comedy: Essays in Dramatic Rhetoric*. San Marino, CA: Huntington Library Press, 1978.

Beehler, Sharon. '"Confederate Season": Shakespeare and the Elizabethan Understanding of *Kairos*', in *Shakespeare Matters*, ed. Lloyd Davis. Newark: University of Delaware Press, 2003. 74–88.

Belsey, Catherine. 'Alice Arden's Crime', in *The Subject of Tragedy: Identity and Difference in Renaissance Drama*. London: Methuen, 1985.

Beltrami, Pietro and Simone Fornara. 'Italian Historical Dictionaries: From the Accademia della Crusca to the Web', *International Journal of Lexicography* 17 (2004): 357–84.

Bennett, Jane. *Vibrant Matter: A Political Ecology of Things*. Durham, NC: Duke University Press, 2010.

Berger, Harry. *The Absence of Grace: Sprezzatura and Suspicion in Two Renaissance Courtesy Books*. Stanford: Stanford University Press, 2000.

Berry, Herbert. *The Noble Science: A Study and Transcription of the Sloane Ms. 2530, Papers of the Masters of Defence of London, Temp. Henry VIII to 1590*. Delaware: University of Delaware Press, 1991.

Bevington, David et al. *The Cambridge Edition of the Works of Ben Jonson*. Cambridge: Cambridge University Press, 2014.

Bloom, Gina. '"My Feet See Better than my Eyes": Spatial Mastery and the Game of Masculinity in *Arden of Faversham*', *Theatre Survey* 53.1 (April 2012): 5–28.

Borden, Ian. 'The Blackfriars Gladiators: Masters of Fence, Playing a Price, and the Elizabethan and Stuart Theater', in *Inside Shakespeare. Essays on the Blackfriars Stage*, ed. Paul Menzer. Slinsgrove: Susquehanna University Press, 2006.

Bolens, Guillamette. *The Style of Gestures: Embodiment and Cognition in Literary Narrative*. Baltimore: Johns Hopkins University Press, 2012.

Bourdieu, Pierre. *Outline of a Theory of Practice*, trans. R. Nice. Cambridge: Cambridge University Press, 1977.

Bourne, Claire. *Typographies of Performance in Early Modern England*. Oxford: Oxford University Press, 2020.

Boyd, Brian. 'Laughter and Literature: A Play Theory of Humor', *Philosophy and Literature* 28.1 (April 2004): 1–22.

Braidotti, Rosi. *The Posthuman*. Cambridge: Polity Press, 2013.

Brown, Eric. '"Many a Civil Monster": Shakespeare's Idea of the Centaur', in *Shakespeare Survey 51: Shakespeare in the Eighteenth Century*, ed. Stanley Wells. Cambridge: Cambridge University Press, 1998. 175–92.

Bryson, Frederick. *The Sixteenth Century Italian Duel: A Study in Renaissance Social History*. Chicago: University of Chicago Press, 1938.

Burke, Peter. *The Fortunes of the Courtier: The European Reception of Castiglione's Cortegiano*. University Park: Pennsylvania State University Press, 1995.

Bushnell, Rebecca. *Tragic Time in Drama, Film and Videogames: The Future in the Instant*. New York: Palgrave, 2016.

Cahill, Patricia. *Unto the Breach: Martial Formations, Historical Trauma, and the Early Modern Stage*. Oxford: Oxford University Press, 2008.

Capoferro, Ridolfo. *Gran Simulacro dell'Arte e dell'Uso della Scherma*. Siena, 1610.

Castiglione, Baldassare. *Il Cortegiano*. Venice, 1528.

——. *The Book of the Courtier From the Italian of Count Baldessare Castiglione: Done Into English by Sir Thomas Hoby*, ed. W. E. Henley. New York: AMS Press, Inc., 1967.

——. *The Book of the Courtier*, ed. and trans. George Bull. New York: Penguin, 2003.

Castle, Egerton. *Schools and Masters of Fence, from the Middle Ages to the Eighteenth Century*. London, 1884.

Carranza, Jerónimo. *De la Filosofia de las Armas y de su Destreza y la Aggression y Defensa Cristiana*. Madrid, 1582.

Chapman, Alison. 'Lucrece's Time', *Shakespeare Quarterly* 65.2 (2013): 139–64.

Clark, Andy and David Chalmers. 'The Extended Mind', *Supersizing the Mind: Embodiment, Action, and Cognitive Extension*. Oxford: Oxford University Press, 2008.

Clark, Ira. *Comedy, Youth, Manhood in Early Modern England*. Delaware: University of Delaware Press, 2003.

Clubb, Louise George, *Italian Drama in Shakespeare's Time*. New Haven: Yale University Press, 1989.

Cohen, Richard. *By the Sword: A History of Gladiators, Musketeers, Samurai, Swashbucklers, and Olympic Champions*. New York: Random House, 2002.

Collington, Philip. 'Stuffed with All Honourable Virtue: *Much Ado about Nothing* and *The Book of the Courtier*', *Studies in Philology* 103.3 (2006): 281–312.

Cooke, Thomas Lalor and William Antisell. *The Early History of the Town of Birr, or Parsontown with the Particulars of Remarkable Events there in More Recent Times. Also the towns of Nenagh, Roscrea, Banagher, Tullamore, Philipstown, Frankford, Shinrone, Kinnetty and Ballyboy and the Ancient Septs, Princes, and Celebrated Places of the Surrounding Country.* Dublin, 1875.

Crane, Mary Thomas. *Shakespeare's Brain: Reading with Cognitive Theory.* Princeton: Princeton University Press, 2001.

Curran, Kevin, ed. *Shakespeare and Judgement.* Oxford: Oxford University Press, 2016.

——. *Shakespeare's Legal Ecologies: Law and Distributed Selfhood.* Chicago: Northwestern University Press, 2017.

Curtis, Mary and Puck. 'From the Page to the Practice,' *In the Service of Mars*, vol 2. ed. Gregory Mele. Wheaton: Freelance Academy Press, 2013.

Dall'Agocchie, Giovanni. *Dell'Arte di Scrima Libri Tre.* Venice, 1572.

Dickson, Vernon Guy. '"A pattern, precedent, and lively warrant": Emulation, Rhetoric, and Cruel Propriety in *Titus Andronicus*', *Renaissance Quarterly* 62 (2009): 376–409.

Di Grassi, Giacomo. *Ragione di Adoprar Sicuramente l'Arme Si Da Offesa, Come Da Difesa, Con un Trattato dell'inganno, & con un modo di esercitarsi da se stesso, per acquistare forza, giudicio, & prestezza.* Venice, 1570.

——. *Di Grassi his true Arte of Defence, plainlie teaching by infallible Demonstrations, apt Figures and perfect Rules the manner and forme how a man without other Teacher or Master may safelie handle all sortes of Weapons well offensive and defensive: With a Treatise of Diceit or Falsinge: And with a waie or meane by private Industrie to obtaine Strength, Judgement and Activitie*, trans. I. G. London, 1594.

Dinshaw, Carolyn. *How Soon is Now?* Durham, NC: Duke University Press, 2012.

——. 'All Kinds of Time', *Studies in the Age of Chaucer* 35 (2013): 3–25.

Docciolino, Marco. *Treatise on the Subject of Fencing*, Florence, 1601 trans. Steven Reich and Piermarco Terminello. Vulpes, 2017.

Donaldson, Ian. *Ben Jonson: A Life.* Oxford: Oxford University Press, 2011.

Dutton, Richard. *Ben Jonson: Authority, Criticism.* Houndmills, Hamps: Macmillan Press; New York: St. Martin' s Press, 1996.

Eisenstein, Elizabeth. *The Printing Press as an Agent of Change: Communications and Cultural Transformations in Early-Modern Europe.* Cambridge: Cambridge University Press, 1979.

Eliot, T. S. 'Ben Jonson', *Times Literary Supplement*, 13 November 1919.

Engel, William. 'Slips of Thought from Alciato's *Emblematum liber* to Holbein's *Imagines Mortis, Icones Historiarum Veteris Testamenti* and *Allegory of the Old and New Testaments*', Mellon Foundation Sawyer Seminars. Emory University, Atlanta, GA. 31 March 2014.

Enterline, Lynn. *Shakespeare's Schoolroom: Rhetoric, Discipline, Emotion.* Philadelphia: University of Pennsylvania Press, 2011.

Fabian, Johannes. *Time and the Other: How Anthropology Makes its Object*. Columbia: Columbia University Press, 2002 [1983].

Fabris, Salvator. *Lo Schermo, overo Scienza d'Arme*. Copenhagen, 1606.

Fawcett, Mary. 'Arms/Words/Tears: Language and the Body in *Titus Andronicus*', *ELH* 50.2 (1983): 261–77.

Feather, Jennifer. *Writing Combat and the Self in Early Modern English Literature: The Pen and the Sword*. New York: Palgrave Macmillan, 2010.

Finkelstein, Richard. '*The Comedy of Errors* and the Theology of Things', *Studies in English Literature* 52.2 (2012): 325–44.

Fiore dei Liberi. *Il Fior di battaglia*. Ludwig M.S. XV 13. J. Paul Getty Museum, Los Angeles.

Florio, John. *A World of Wordes, or Most copius and exact* dictionarie *in Italian and* English *edited by John Florio*. London, 1598.

——. *Queen Anna's New World of Words or Dictionarie of the* Italian *and* English *tongues, collected and newly much augmented by John Florio*. London, 1611.

Forgeng, Jeffrey. *Pietro Monte's Collectanea: The Arms, Armour and Fighting Techniques of a Fifteenth-Century Soldier*. Suffolk: Boydell Press, 2018.

Foucault, Michel. *The Use of Pleasure: Volume 2 of the History of Sexuality*. New York: Vintage Books, 1986.

——. *Discipline and Punish: The Birth of the Prison*, trans. Alan Sheridan. New York: Vintage Books, 1995.

Frevert, Ute. *Men of Honour: A Social and Cultural History of the Duel*. Cambridge: Polity, 1995.

G. A. *Pallas Armata: The Gentlemens Armorie; Wherein the right and genuine use of the Rapier and of the Sword, as well against the right handed as against the left handed man is displayed; And so set forth and first published for the common good by the Author*. London, 1639.

Garber, Marjorie. *Shakespeare after All*. New York: Anchor Books, 2005.

Garrett. '"Arden lay murdered in that plot of ground"': Surveying, Land and *Arden of Faversham*', *English Literary History* 61.2 (1994): 231–52.

Gaugler, William. *The History of Fencing: Foundations of Modern European Swordplay*. Bangor: Laureate Press, 1998.

——. *The Science of Fencing*. Egg Harbor City: Laureate Press, 2004.

Giganti, Nicoletto. *Scola, overo, teatro: nel qual sono rappresentate diverse maniere, e modi di parare et di ferire di spada sola, e di spada e pugnale*. Venice, 1606.

——. *Libro Secondo di Niccoletto Giganti Venetiano, Mastro d'Arme dell'Illustrissimi Signori Cavalieri della Sacra Religione di Santo Stefano. Dove sono rappresentate diverse maniere e modi di parare e di ferire. Di spada e Pugnale. Di spada sola. Di spada e Rotella. Di spada e Targa. Di spada e Brocchiero. Di Spada e Cappa e' di Pugnale solo. Dove ogni studioso potrà esercitarsi, e farsi prattico nella profession dell'Arme*. Pisa, 1608.

Goldberg, Jonathan. *Writing Matter: From the Hands of the English Renaissance*. Stanford: Stanford University Press, 1990.

Grasseni, Christina, ed. *Skilled Visions: Between Apprenticeship and Standards*. New York: Berghahn Books, 2009.

Greenblatt, Stephen. *Renaissance Self-Fashioning from More to Shakespeare*. Chicago: University of Chicago Press, 1980.

Greene, Thomas M. '*Il Cortegiano* and the Choice of a Game', *Renaissance Quarterly* 32.2 (Summer 1979): 173–86.

Guidi, José. 'Thyrsis ou la cour transfigure', in *Centre de recherches sur la renaissance italienne* 6. Paris, 1977. 141–78.

Gurr, Andrew. *Playgoing in Shakespeare's London*. Cambridge: Cambridge University Press, 2004.

Hale, George. *The Private Schoole of Defence: Or, the Defects of Publique Teachers, exactly discovered, by way of objection and Resolution Together with the True Practice of the Science, set down in Judicious Rules and Observances; in a Method never before explained*. London, 1614.

Hale, John Rigbey. 'Castiglione's Military Career', in *Castiglione: The Ideal and Real in Renaissance Culture*, ed. Robert W. Hanning and David Rosand. New Haven, CT, and London: Yale University Press, 1983.

Halio, Jay. '"No Clock in the Forest"': Time in *As You Like It*', *SEL* 2.2 (1962): 197–217.

Halpern, Richard, 'Eclipse of Action: *Hamlet* and the Political Economy of Playing', *Shakespeare Quarterly* 59.4 (2008): 450–82.

Hamel, Guy. 'Order and Judgement in *Bartholomew Fair*', *University of Toronto Quarterly* 43 (1973–4): 48–67.

Happe, Peter. *English Drama Before Shakespeare*. London: Longman, 1999.

Harris, Jonathan Gil. *Untimely Matter in the Time of Shakespeare*. Philadelphia: University of Pennsylvania Press, 2009.

Harvey, Elizabeth D. *On Touch in Early Modern Culture*. Philadelphia: University of Pennsylvania Press, 2002.

Helgerson, Richard. *Forms of Nationhood: The Elizabethan Writing of England*. Chicago: University of Chicago Press, 1992.

——. *Adulterous Alliances: Home, State, and History in Early Modern European Drama and Painting*. Chicago and London: The University of Chicago Press, 2000.

Heller-Roazen, Daniel. *The Inner Touch: Archaeology of a Sensation*. Princeton: Princeton University Press, 2007.

Herzfeld, Michael. 'Rhythm, Tempo, and Historical Time: Experiencing Temporality in the Neoliberal Age', *Public Archaeology* 8.2 (2009): 108–23.

Hobgood, Allison. *Passionate Playgoing in Early Modern England*. Cambridge: Cambridge University Press, 2014.

Holinshed, Raphael et al. *Holinshed's Chronicles of England Scotland, and Ireland*, 865 (1808) 'Edward the Sixt, Sonne and Successor to Henrie the Eight'. 1024–30.

Hughes, Steven. *Politics of the Sword: Dueling, Honor, and Masculinity in Modern Italy.* Columbus: Ohio State University Press, 2007.

Huizinga, Johan. *Homo Ludens: A Study of the Play Element in Culture*, trans. R. F. C. Hull. London: Routledge, 1949.

Hunt, Maurice. '*Kairos* and the Ripeness of Time in *As You Like It*', *Modern Language Quarterly* 52.2 (1991): 113–35.

Hurley, Matthew, Daniel Dennett and Reginald Adams. *Inside Jokes: Using Humor to Reverse-Engineer the Mind.* Cambridge, MA: MIT Press, 2011.

Hutson, Lorna. 'Fortunate Travelers: Reading for the Plot in Sixteenth-Century England', *Representations* 41 (Winter 1993): 83–103.

——. *The Invention of Suspicion: Law and Mimesis in Shakespeare and Renaissance Drama.* Oxford: Oxford University Press, 2007.

Ioppolo, Grace. *Dramatists and Their Manuscripts in the Age of Shakespeare, Jonson, Middleton and Heywood: Authorship, Authority and the Playhouse.* Oxford: Routledge, 2006.

Jackson, MacDonald P. 'Shakespearean Features of the Poetic Style of *Arden of Faversham*', *Archiv für das Studium der neueren Sprachen und Literaturen* 230 (1993): 279–304.

——. 'Shakespeare and the Quarrel Scene in *Arden of Faversham*', *Shakespeare Quarterly* 57.3 (2006): 249–90.

James, Heather. 'Cultural Disintegration in *Titus Andronicus:* Mutilating Titus, Vergil, and Rome', in *Themes in Drama*, ed. James Redmond. Cambridge: Cambridge University Press, 1991. 123–40.

——. *Shakespeare's Troy: Drama, Politics, and the Translation of Empire.* Cambridge: Cambridge University Press, 1997.

Johns, Adrian. *The Nature of the Book.* Chicago: University of Chicago Press, 1998.

Jones, Eldred. 'Aaron', in *Titus Andronicus: Critical Essays*, ed. Philip C. Kolin. New York and London: Garland, 1995. 147–56.

Jonson, Benjamin. *Bartholomew Fair*, ed. David Bevington et al. Cambridge: Cambridge University Press, 2012.

——. *Every Man in His Humour*, ed. David Bevington et al. Cambridge: Cambridge University Press, 2012.

——. *Cambridge Edition of the Works of Ben Jonson Online*, ed. Martin Butler. Cambridge: Cambridge University Press.

——. *Timber, or Discoveries*, ed. Lorna Hutson, in *The Cambridge Edition of the Works of Ben Jonson Online*, ed. Martin Butler. Cambridge: Cambridge University Press.

Judovitz, Dalia. *The Culture of the Body: Genealogies of Modernity.* Ann Arbor: University of Michigan Press, 2001.

Kant, Immanuel. *Critique of Judgment*, trans. J. H. Bernard. Mineola: Dover Publications, 2012.

Kaplan, Joel. 'Dramatic and Moral Energy in Ben Jonson's *Bartholomew Fair*', *Renaissance Drama*, n.s., 3 (1970): 137–56.

Kelso, Ruth, 'Saviolo and His Practice', *Modern Language Notes* 39.1 (1924): 33–5.

Kiernan, V. G. *The Duel in European History: Honour and the Reign of the Aristocracy.* Oxford: Oxford University Press, 1988.

Kinneavy, James L. and Catherine R. Eskin. 'Kairos in Aristotle's Rhetoric', *Written Communication* 17.3 (2000). 432–44.

Kinney, Arthur F. 'Shakespeare's *Comedy of Errors* and the Nature of Kinds', *Studies in Philology* 85.1 (1988): 29–52.

——. 'Authoring *Arden of Faversham*', in *Shakespeare, Computers, and the Mystery of Authorship*, ed. Hugh Craig and Arthur F. Kinney. Cambridge: Cambridge University Press, 2009. 78–99.

Klotz, Lisa. 'Ben Jonson's Legal Imagination in *Volpone*', *SEL* 51.2 (2011): 385–408.

Knecht, Ross. *The Grammar Rules of Affection.* Cambridge: Cambridge University Press, 2021.

Kolsky, Stephen. 'Graceful Performances: The Social and Political Context of Music and Dance in the *Cortegiano*', *Italian Studies* 53.1 (1998): 1–19.

——. *Courts and Courtiers in Renaissance Northern Italy.* London: Routledge, 2003.

Korda, Natasha. 'How to Do Things with Shoes', *Shakespeare and Costume.* New York: Bloomsbury, 2015.

Koslow, Julian. 'Humanist Schooling and Ben Jonson's *Poetaster*', *ELH* 72.1 (2006): 119–59.

Kuhn, Maura. 'Much Virtue in *If*', *Shakespeare Quarterly* 28 (1977): 40–50.

Lanham, Richard. *The Motives of Eloquence: Literary Rhetoric in the Renaissance.* New Haven: Yale University Press, 1976.

Lanier, Douglas. '"Stigmatical in Making": The Material Character of *The Comedy of Errors*', *English Literary Renaissance* 23.1 (1993): 81–112.

Langley, Eric III. *Shakespeare's Contagious Sympathies.* Oxford: Oxford University Press, 2018.

LaPerle, Carol. 'Rhetorical Situationality: Alice Arden's Kairotic Effect in *The Tragedy of Master Arden of Faversham*', *Women's Studies* 39.175 (2010): 175–93.

Leoni, Tommaso. *The Art of Duelling: Salvator Fabris' Rapier Fencing Treatise of 1606.* Highland Village: Chivalry Bookshelf, 2005.

Levine, Caroline. *Forms: Whole, Rhythm, Hierarchy, Network.* Princeton: Princeton University Press, 2017.

Lim, Paul. 'Adiaphora, Ecclesiology and Reformation: John Owen's Theology of Religious Toleration in Context', in *Persecution and Pluralism: Calvinists and Religious Minorities in Early Modern Europe, 1550–1700*, ed. Richard Bonney and D. J. B. Trim. Bern: Peter Lang, 2006. 243–72.

Linden, David. *Touch: The Science of Hand, Heart and Mind.* New York: Penguin Books, 2015.

Low, Jennifer. *Manhood and the Duel: Masculinity in Early Modern Drama.* New York: Palgrave Macmillan, 2003.

Lyne, Raphael. 'The Shakespearean Grasp', *The Cambridge Quarterly* 42.1 (2013): 38–61.

McCarthy, Penny. *Pseudonymous Shakespeare.* Burlington: Ashgate, 2006.

Manning, Roger. *Swordsmen: The Martial Ethos in the Three Kingdoms.* Oxford: Oxford University Press, 2003.

Manciolino, Antonio. *Opera Nova, dove li sono tutti li documenti et vantaggi che si ponno havere nel mestier de l'armi d'ogni sorte novamente corretta et stampata.* Venice, 1531.

Matthey, Cyril, ed. *The Works of George Silver.* London, 1898.

Marshall, Cynthia. 'Wrestling as Play and Game in *As You Like It*', *Studies in English Literature* 33.2 (1993): 265–87.

Maus, Katherine Eisaman. *Inwardness and Theater in the English Renaissance.* Chicago: University of Chicago Press, 1995.

Mazzio, Carla. 'Acting with Tact: Touch and Theater in the Renaissance', in *Sensible Flesh: On Touch in Early Modern Culture*, ed. Elizabeth Harvey. Philadelphia: University of Pennsylvania Press, 2003. 159–86.

Meyer, Joachim. *Gründtliche Beschreibung der Kunst des Fechtens.* Strasbourg, 1570.

——. *The Art of Combat: A German Martial Arts Treatise of 1570*, trans. Jeffrey Forgang, New York: Palgrave Macmillan, 2006.

Milton, John. 'Of Education', *John Milton: The Major Works*, ed. Jonathan Goldberg and Stephen Orgel. Oxford: Oxford University Press, 2003.

Mondschein, Ken. *Fencing: A Renaissance Treatise by Camillo Agrippa.* New York: Italica Press, 2009.

Montaigne, Michel de. 'Cowardice the Mother of Cruelty', *The Essays of Montaigne*, trans. Charles Cotton. London, 1877.

Monte, Pietro. *Exercitiorum Atque Artis Militaris Collectanea.* Milan, 1509.

Mulcaster, Richard. *Positions concerning the training up of children*, ed. William Barker. Toronto: University of Toronto Press, 1994.

Nancy, Jean-Luc. *Noli me tangere: On the Raising of the Body*, trans. Sarah Clift, Pascale-Anne Brault and Michael Naas. New York: Fordham University Press, 2008.

Nicholson, A. '"Rook," its Double Metaphorical Signification in Elizabethan English', *Notes and Queries* (1889) s7-VII (179): 423–4.

Orlin, Lena. 'Man's House as His Castle in *Arden of Faversham*', *Medieval and Renaissance Drama in England* 2 (1985): 57–89.

Pallavicini, Giuseppe. *La Scherma Illustrata.* Palermo, 1670.

Pascha, Johann Georg. *Short Though Clear Description Treating of Fencing on the Thrust and Cut*, trans. Reineir van Noort. Halle, 1661.

Paster, Gail Kern. *Humoring the Body: Emotions and the Shakespearean Stage.* Chicago: University of Chicago Press, 2004.

——. '*Bartholomew Fair* and the Humoral Body', in *Early Modern English Drama: A Critical Companion*, ed. Garrett Sullivan, Jr., Patrick Cheney and Andrew Hadfield. Oxford: Oxford University Press, 2005. 260–71

Paul, Joanne. '*Kairos* in Political Philosophy', *Renaissance Quarterly* 67.1 (2014): 43–78.

Peltonen, Markku. *The Duel in Early Modern England: Civility, Politeness, and Honour.* Cambridge: Cambridge University Press, 2003.

Price, Margaret. *Mad at School: Rhetorics of Mental Disability and Academic Life.* Ann Arbor: University of Michigan Press, 2011.

Quinones, Ricardo. 'View of Time in Shakespeare', *Journal of the History of Ideas* 26.3 (1965): 327–52.

——. *The Renaissance Discovery of Time.* Cambridge, MA: Harvard University Press, 1972.

Quint, David. 'Dueling and Civility in Sixteenth-Century Italy', in *Contextualizing the Renaissance: Returns to History*, ed. Albert H. Tricomi. Turnout: Brepols, 1999.

Raman, Shankar. 'Marking Time: Memory and Market in *The Comedy of Errors*', *Shakespeare Quarterly* 56.2 (2005): 176–205.

Rebecchini, Guido. 'Pietro Bembo e Baldassarre Castiglione: teorici dell'arte e collezionisti,' in *Pietro Bembo e le arti*, ed. Guido Beltramini, Howard Burns and Davide Gasparotto, Venice: Marsilio, 2013. 257–66

Robinson, James E. '*Bartholomew Fair*: Comedy of Vapors', *SEL* 1.2 (1961): 65–80.

Rossi, Sergio. '*Vincentio Saviolo, His Practise* (1595): A Problem of Authorship', in *England and the Continental Renaissance*, ed. Edward Chaney and Peter Mack. Woodbridge: Boydell Press, 1990. 191–202.

Rowe, G. E. *Distinguishing Jonson: Imitation, Rivalry, and the Direction of a Dramatic Career.* Lincoln: University of Nebraska Press, 1988.

Saccone, Eduardo. '*Grazia, Sprezzatura, Affettazione* in the *Courtier*', in *Castiglione: The Ideal and the Real in Renaissance Culture*, ed. Robert Hanning and David Rosand. New Haven: Yale University Press, 1983.

Sale, Carolyn. 'Black Aeneas: Race, English Literary History, and the "Barbarous" Poetics of *Titus Andronicus*', *Shakespeare Quarterly* 62.1 (2011): 25–52.

Saviolo, Vincentio. *Vincentio Saviolo, his practice, in two books, the first intreating of the use of the Rapier and Dagger, the second of Honor and honorable Quarrels*, 2 vols. London, 1595.

Sawday, Jonathan. *The Body Emblazoned: Dissection and the Human Body in Renaissance Culture.* New York: Routledge, 1995.

Schoenfeldt, Michael. *Bodies and Selves in Early Modern England: Physiology and Inwardness in Spenser, Shakespeare, Herbert, and Milton.* Cambridge: Cambridge University Press, 1999.

Schutzman, Julie. 'Alice Arden's Freedom and the Suspended Moment of *Arden of Faversham*', *Studies in English Literature, 1500–1900* 36.2 (1996): 289–314.

Semenza, Gregory. *Sport, Politics, and Literature in the English Renaissance.* Delaware: University of Delaware Press, 2003.

Serres, Michel. *Conversations on Science, Culture, and Time*, trans. Roxanne Lapidus. Michigan: University of Michigan Press, 1995.

Shakespeare, William. *As You Like It*, ed. Stephen Greenblatt et al. New York: W. W. Norton, 2008.

——. *The Comedy of Errors. The Norton Shakespeare*, 2nd edn, ed. Stephen Greenblatt, Walter Cohen, Jean E. Howard and Katherine Eisaman Maus. New York: W. W. Norton, 2008. 253–93.

——. *Hamlet*, ed. Stephen Greenblatt et al. New York: W. W. Norton, 2008.

——. *Romeo and Juliet*, ed. Stephen Greenblatt et. al. New York: W. W. Norton, 2008.

——. *Titus Andronicus*, ed. Jonathan Bate. The Arden Shakespeare Third Series. London: Thomson, 1995.

——. *Twelfth Night*, ed. Stephen Greenblatt et. al. New York: W. W. Norton, 2008.

Shannon, Laurie. 'Poor, Bare, Forked: Animal Sovereignty, Human Negative Exceptionalism, and the Natural History of King Lear', *Shakespeare Quarterly* 60.2 (2009): 168–96.

Shapiro, James. *A Year in the Life of William Shakespeare: 1599*. London: Faber & Faber, 2015.

Shershow, Scott. *Puppets and 'Popular' Culture*. Ithaca: Cornell University Press, 1995.

Silver, George. *Brief Instructions upon my Paradoxes of Defence* (c. 1605), ed. Cyril Matthew. London: 1898.

——. *Paradoxes of Defence: wherein is proued the true grounds of fight to be in the short auncient weapons, and that the short sword hath aduantage of the long sword or long rapier. And the weakenesse and imperfection of the rapier-fights displayed. Together with an admonition to the noble, ancient, victorious, valiant, and most braue nation of Englishmen, to beware of false teachers of defence, and how they forsake their owne naturall fights: with a briefe commendation of the noble science or exercising of armes*. London, 1599.

Sipiora, Philip and James Baumlin, eds. *Rhetoric and Kairos: Essays in History, Theory, and Praxis*. Albany: State University of New York Press, 2002.

Smith, Bruce. 'Pre-modern Sexualities', *PMLA* 115.3 (2000): 318–29.

Smith, Pamela. *The Body of the Artisan: Art and Experience in the Scientific Revolution*. Chicago: University of Chicago Press, 2004.

Soni, Vivasvan. 'Judgment and Indecision in *Hamlet*', *Shakespeare and Judgement*, ed. Kevin Curran. Edinburgh: Edinburgh University Press, 2017.

Spenser, Edmund. *The Faerie Queene*, ed. Hugh MacLean and Anne Lake Prescott. New York: W. W. Norton, 2013.

Spolsky, Ellen. 'Elaborated Knowledge: Reading Kinesis in Pictures', *Poetics Today* 17.2 (1996): 157–80.

Stern, Tiffany. 'Time for Shakespeare: Hourglasses, Sundials, Clocks, and Early Modern Theatre', *Journal of the British Academy* 3 (2015): 1–33.

Stewart, Douglas. 'Falstaff the Centaur', *Shakespeare Quarterly* 28.1 (1977): 5–21.

Sullivan, Garrett. '"Arden Lay Murdered in that Plot of Ground": Surveying, Land and *Arden of Faversham*', *English Literary History* 61.2 (1994): 231–52.

Sweeney, J. G. *Jonson and the Psychology of Public Theater: To Coin the Spirit, Spend the Soul*. Princeton: Princeton University Press, 1984.

Swetnam, Joseph. *The Schoole of the Noble and Worthy Science of Defence: Being the first of any English mans invention, which professed the sayd Science; So plainly described, that any man may quickly come to the true knowledge of their weapons with small paines and little practice Then reade it advisedly, and use the benefit thereof when occasion shall serve, so shalt thou be a good Common-wealth man, live happy to they selfe, and comfortable to thy friend, Also many other good and profitable Precepts and Counsels for the managing of Quarrels and ordering thy selfe in many other matters*. London, 1617.

Taylor, Donn. 'Try in Time in Despite of a Fall: Time and Occasion in *As You Like It*', *Texas Studies in Literature and Language* 24.2 (1982): 121–36.

Terminello, Piermarco. 'Giovanni Battista Gaiani (1619) – An Italian Perspective on Competitive Fencing', on the historical martial arts blog *HROARR*, at *hroarr.com*

Terminiello, Piermarco and Joshua Pendragon, *The 'Lost' Second Book of Nicoletto Giganti: A Rapier Treatise Rediscovered and Translated*. London, 2013.

Teske, J. A. 'From Embodied to Extended Cognition', *Zygon: Journal of Science and Religion* 48 (2013): 759–87.

Tribble, Evelyn. *Cognition in the Globe: Attention and Memory in Shakespeare's Theatre*. New York: Palgrave, 2011.

——. *Cognitive Ecologies and the History of Remembering*. New York: Palgrave, 2011.

——. 'Skill', in *Early Modern Theatricality*, ed. Henry Turner. Oxford: Oxford University Press, 2014. 173–88.

——. *Early Modern Actors in Shakespeare's Theatre: Thinking with the Body*. New York: Bloomsbury, 2017.

Tribble, Evelyn and John Sutton, 'Minds in and out of Time: Memory, Embodied Skill, Anachronism, and Performance', *Textual Practice* 26.4 (2012): 587–607.

Tricomi, Albert. 'The Aesthetics of Mutilation in *Titus Andronicus*', *Shakespeare Survey* 27 (1974): 11–19.

Turner, Craig and Tony Soper, *Methods and Practice of Elizabethan Swordplay*. Carbondale: Southern Illinois University Press, 1990.

Turner, Frederick. *Shakespeare and the Nature of Time: Moral and Philosophical Themes in Some Plays and Poems of William Shakespeare*. Oxford: Clarendon Press, 1971.

Turner, Henry. *The English Renaissance Stage: Geometry, Poetics, and the Practical Spatial Arts, 1580–1630*. Oxford: Oxford University Press, 2006.

Vadi, Philippo. *De Arte Gladiatoria Dimicandi*, c. 1482–7. Biblioteca Nazionale Centrale di Roma, MS Vitt.Em.1342.

van Orden, Kate. *Music, Discipline, and Arms in Early Modern France.* Chicago: University of Chicago Press, 2006.

Varela, Francisco J., Evan Thompson and Eleanor Rosch. *The Embodied Mind: Cognitive Science and Human Experience*, revised edn. Cambridge, MA: MIT Press, 2017.

Viggiani, Angelo. *Lo Schermo d'Angelo Viggiani Dal Montone Da Balogna: Nel quale per via di Dialogo si discorre intorno all'eccellenza dell'armi, & delle lettere: intorno all'offesa & alla difesa : & s'insegna uno schermo di spade sola da filo, co'l quale può l'huomo non pure difendersi da qual si voglia colpo del nimico ; ma anchora offender lui non poco.* Venice, 1575.

Wagner, Matthew. *Shakespeare, Theatre, and Time.* New York: Routledge, 2012.

Wagner, Paul. 'Hawks, Rabbits, and Tumbling Cats: An Analysis of English Longsword Terminology', in *In the Service of Mars: Proceedings from the Western Martial Arts Workshop, 1999–2009*, vol. 1, ed. Gregory Mele. Wheaton: Freelance Academy Press, 2010. 41–85.

Waller, G. F. *The Strong Necessity of Time: The Philosophy of Time in Shakespeare and Elizabethan Literature.* Paris: Mouton & Co., 1976.

Watson, Foster. *Tudor School-Boy Life, the Dialogues of Juan Luis Vives.* London: J. M. Dent, 1908.

White, Eric. *Kaironomia: On the Will-to-Invent.* Ithaca: Cornell University Press, 1987.

Wiles, David. *The Players' Advice to Hamlet: The Rhetorical Acting Method from the Renaissance to the Enlightenment.* Cambridge: Cambridge University Press, 2020.

Wilson, Luke. *Theaters of Intention: Drama and the Law in Early Modern England.* Stanford: Stanford University Press, 2000.

Wilson, Thomas. *The rule of reason, conteinyng the arte of logique, set forth in Englishe.* London, 1551.

Wittkower, Rudolf. 'Chance, Time, and Virtue', *Journal of the Warburg Institute* 1.4 (1938): 313–21.

Wolfe, Jessica. *Humanism, Machinery, and Renaissance Literature.* Cambridge: Cambridge University Press, 2009.

Woodbridge, Linda. *English Revenge Drama: Money, Resistance, Equality.* Cambridge: Cambridge University Press, 2010.

Wyatt, Michael. *The Italian Encounter with Tudor England: A Cultural Politics of Translation.* Cambridge: Cambridge University Press, 2005.

Young, Katharine. 'Aesthetic Ecologies: Reflections on What Makes Artifacts Art', *Journal of Folklore Research* 51.2 (2014): 177–98.

Index